THE
ACTIVIST'S
MEDIA
HANDBOOK

THE ACTIVIST'S MEDIA HANDBOOK

LESSONS FROM FIFTY YEARS AS A PROGRESSIVE AGITATOR

David Fenton

Foreword by **George Lakoff, PhD**

EARTH AWARE

SAN RAFAEL · LOS ANGELES · LONDON

"Public sentiment is everything. With public sentiment, nothing can fail. Without it, nothing can succeed."

—Abraham Lincoln

"People can only act on the information made available to them."

—Huey P. Newton, cofounder of the Black Panther Party

This book is dedicated to the visionary progressive activists and philanthropists who made my early work possible, including Cora Weiss, Leonard Boudin, David Lubell, Wade Greene, David Hunter, Stanley Sheinbaum, Jay Harris, Peggy Dulany, Carrie Cameron, Randall Robinson, Leni Sinclair, Allen Young, Robert Zevin, and many others.

A special tribute in memoriam to my inspiration and muse, Abbie Hoffman, and to friend, colleague, journalist, and environmentalist, the late Arlie Schardt.

CONTENTS

If progressives lose the future, it will not be due to a lack of good policy ideas. If we lose the future, ceding democracy to authoritarians or bad corporate actors, it will be due mostly to a stunning failure to communicate with people in simple language that connects with them on the level of their moral values. And it will be due to a stubborn rejection of tried-and-true scientific methods of mass communications—methods that conservatives have repeatedly deployed to winning effect.

David Fenton spent most of his life trying to convince Democrats and progressives to take the art of communication seriously. Long before others in the progressive movement understood public relations as a core function of social change, David grasped the power of unconscious thought, metaphor, symbolism, and media strategy to shape the public discourse. David understood the importance of presenting issues in a way that taps into the most deeply held values of an audience. All politics are moral politics, and people act in line with their moral identities, not because they agree with a list of policies. Sound bites and slogans mean nothing if they fail to resonate with a person's moral worldview.

With his deep understanding of how communication works, David pioneered the field of progressive PR, helping social change organizations adopt professional communications strategies and tactics to win major victories for truth, freedom, democracy, the people, and the planet. In 1982, he founded the first communications firm dedicated solely to progressive causes.

In this captivating memoir, David provides readers with a personal tour of his journey through recent US history. Starting as a seventeen-year-old photographer with the Liberation News Service (LNS), David had a front-row seat for some of the most tumultuous years of the 1960s. He covered protests against the Vietnam War, the trial of the Chicago Seven, the fight for People's Park in Berkeley, and the rise of the Black Panther movement. He documented the sea change in US culture, politics, and music.

Along the way, he learned from both the successes and mistakes of US activist movements. And he never wavered in his determination to tell the truth, challenge powerful interests, and stand up for people.

The lessons David draws from his life as a pioneer of progressive communications remain urgently relevant for activists today. As we confront the rising specter of authoritarianism and economic injustice—as well as the rapid destruction of our common home due to global warming driven by greedy fossil fuel corporations—we must not forget the lessons of the past.

This book is essential reading for anyone who wishes to grasp the lessons of history and understand the crucial role of communications in changing minds and winning progress.

—George Lakoff, PhD

GEORGE LAKOFF IS A PROFESSOR EMERITUS OF COGNITIVE SCIENCE AND LINGUISTICS AT THE UNIVERSITY OF CALIFORNIA AT BERKELEY. HE IS THE AUTHOR OF *DON'T THINK OF AN ELEPHANT!*, *MORAL POLITICS*, AND OTHER BOOKS. HE IS @GEORGELAKOFF ON TWITTER.

YOKO ONO BEATS NEW YORK GOVERNOR ANDREW CUOMO

It's the winter of 2012. Yoko Ono, her son, Sean Ono Lennon, and actress Susan Sarandon get off a chartered bus accompanied by fifteen reporters, several colleagues at Fenton Communications—the progressive public relations firm I founded—and me. Everyone piles into a modest home across the street from a loud gas fracking well that is belching fumes. The family who lives there shows everyone into the bathroom, where the Pennsylvania Department of Health has posted warning stickers. These say that the bathroom windows must be left open while taking a shower.

Why? The authorities fear the house might explode from the methane gas coming through the showerhead. The family explains that they had no problems with methane until fracking wells were drilled right next door. Yet gas industry stooges insist the family is lying. The gas endangering them is "naturally" in the water.

At another nearby home, the family hands Yoko and Sean a plastic bottle full of their disgustingly discolored, dirty-brown tap water. Their polluted water—also a direct result of fracking. The cameras whirl.

This made news all over the country.

Yoko and Sean had hired Fenton Communications to help pass a permanent moratorium on fracking in New York State. I had never met Yoko, although in 1971 in Ann Arbor, Michigan, she performed with John Lennon

Yoko Ono in Albany protesting fracking, January 11, 2013.

Yoko Ono, Sean Ono Lennon, and Susan Sarandon (far right) hold a bottle of this family's tap water. The home is near a fracking well in Pennsylvania.

at the John Sinclair Freedom Rally I helped organize. She and her son, Sean, arrived at the Fenton office bearing a ton of sushi, and together we developed a plan to pressure Governor Andrew Cuomo to ban fracking for methane gas in New York.

Notice I didn't say "natural gas." The word "natural" evokes a positive image in the brain—and in a world threatened by climate change, there's nothing natural about methane. This so-called natural gas is actually poison. It heats the planet and must be phased out rapidly. Research clearly shows that calling it, accurately, "methane gas" results in much more public concern.

Yoko and Sean became active after discovering that a planned new pipeline for fracked gas would run near their home in Upstate New York. Learning more about the many problems with fracking, they decided to act. They reached out to many other celebrities, including Paul McCartney, and formed Artists Against Fracking.

They weren't the only ones to oppose fracking. For some time, a grass-roots antifracking movement had been working hard to prevent the practice in New York. When the celebrity artists joined in, the effort attracted far more attention. In time, the combination of both won the day.

At a conference a few years before, I had watched Dr. Anthony Ingraffea of Cornell University demolish industry myths about fracking, the process by which rocks deep underground are fractured to release the methane gas trapped within. A former oil and gas industry engineer, he clearly showed that, over time, a large percentage of fracked wells leak. This releases toxic chemicals and methane gas into underground water supplies. It also sends methane directly into the atmosphere, where it is a highly potent greenhouse gas. Methane traps almost one hundred times more heat on Earth than carbon dioxide for the first twenty years, which is all we have to save our climate. Professor Ingraffea explained why—the thin layers of cement used to line the fracking wells deep under the earth inevitably crack from pressure and

FAMILIES SHOWED HOW THEIR TAP WATER COULD BE LIT ON FIRE.

temperature changes. And at those depths, nothing can be done to fix the inevitable leaks.

This is exactly the opposite of what the fracking industry claims in their advertising and other propaganda. According to them, fracking is perfectly safe. When people living near the drilling sites complain of contaminated water supplies, the gas industry claims it is "completely unrelated" to the drilling close to their homes. In Josh Fox's seminal HBO documentary *Gasland*, families showed how their tap water could literally be lit on fire, right in the sink. The industry accused Josh of staging a hoax and portrayed the families as victims of hysteria. The methane in their water supply was "natural," the industry claimed, even though methane had never previously made the families' water combustible. This was typical slimy, sleazy bullshit, courtesy of gas industry public relations firms. The very firms that Fenton was founded to counter.

Working with Yoko and Sean, we decided on a simple message: "Don't Frack New York." We showed journalists, and through them the public, that fracking wells frequently leak, poisoning water supplies. It was a simple message, easily understood. It spoke to the heart. It focused on something

Our billboard on the highway Governor Cuomo took to Albany, November, 2012.

everyone values: clean water, an iconic symbol of health and well-being. And everything we said was true.

Artists Against Fracking bought full-page newspaper ads that explained why fracking should be banned. Then, to get Governor Cuomo's attention, we bought a huge billboard on the highway Cuomo regularly took between Manhattan and the state capital, Albany. "Governor Cuomo," the giant sign read, "IMAGINE THERE'S NO FRACKING . . . Love, Yoko and Sean."

Cuomo's chief aide called immediately. "This sign is unfair. You should direct it at the state head of environmental conservation," he said.

"What? It's the governor's decision," I replied. "Meanwhile, why are you so mad? It only says 'imagine.' It's not an attack ad."

That billboard definitely got the governor's attention. Soon after, fracking opponents were invited to meet with Cuomo's aides. But despite repeated requests, Cuomo stubbornly refused to meet with Yoko. So, we made a TV ad with Yoko looking directly into the camera. "Governor Cuomo. You haven't been able to meet with me about fracking," she narrated. "So, I'm going to show you what it looks like here on TV."

The video rolled with horrific scenes of fracking wells that were right on top of people's homes and sinks being lit on fire. John Lennon's classic song "Gimme Some Truth" played in the background. At the end, Yoko came back on camera. "Nice to meet you, governor."

Cuomo met with her a few days later. Really, there's nothing like *guaranteed* visibility. Advertising works.

Artists Against Fracking joined with grassroots antifracking groups in a giant petition drive. Actor Mark Ruffalo played an important role in the coalition. They delivered more petitions with more signatures than the New York State Department of Environmental Conservation had ever previously received. Yoko and Sean personally helped deliver boxes of them, while cameras whirled. Yoko also recruited Lady Gaga, whose tweet to her seventy million followers asking people to call Cuomo's office melted down his phone system.

The result? Cuomo did the right thing. He banned fracking in New York State, one of only two states to do so—the other is progressive Vermont. Industry was surprised and furious.

So was Cuomo. He resented the pressure and personally blacklisted Fenton Communications from working for any New York State agency.

FOR MORE THAN FIFTY YEARS, I HAVE BEEN A PROGRESSIVE MEDIA ACTIVIST

This book combines the lessons I've learned with vignettes from my life, which largely parallels the story of the modern Left in the United States. I started as a teenage, high school dropout photojournalist shooting riots and rock stars for the underground press of the '60s. Then I became a hippie activist, living in a commune that took over the Ann Arbor, Michigan, city government in the early 1970s, when we legalized pot and opened free day care and medical centers. After working at *High Times* and *Rolling Stone* magazines, I coproduced the 1979 No Nukes concerts at Madison Square Garden in New York.

In 1982, I created the first public relations firm dedicated solely to progressive causes—Fenton Communications. We helped many activist groups reverse the nuclear arms race, free Nelson Mandela from prison, end apartheid, boost sales of organic foods, fight the death penalty and a racist criminal "justice" system, oppose America's imperial adventures abroad, and fight for clean energy and a livable climate. The firm is still at it, and so am I.

During my half century of activism, I've learned how to use the media for social change, starting in the late 1960s, an era when idealists, activists, and utopians did so brilliantly, even dominating popular culture. Alas, today that's all changed.

Me being shoved around by an angry Chicago plainclothes cop while trying to photograph the Weatherman Days of Rage, October 1969.

Reflecting back on a lifetime of media organizing, here is what I have learned, the precepts that can power progressives to success. Unfortunately, today's Republicans apply them much more effectively than Democrats and progressives. Please note: Good ideas do *not* sell themselves. Use the following principles to advance your cause.

I started thinking about all of this as a high school dropout in New York City. At that time, Martin Luther King was choreographing television to spread the moral imperatives of civil rights into every home. Anti-Vietnam War campaigners and draft resistors often achieved equal billing with the war itself, using brilliant tactics to get news coverage. The Black Panthers were on TV resisting police violence, spreading Black pride, and feeding breakfast to poor children. In 1970, millions turned out for the first Earth Day, leading

PEOPLE ON THE LEFT LOOK DOWN ON THE IDEA OF SELLING IDEAS.

to landmark environmental legislation. The Beatles, Jefferson Airplane, the Doors, and so many other musicians spread progressive values—and personal liberation—to huge audiences.

In the 1960s, political and cultural progressives often dominated popular culture and the news. But then, the Left started to lose its connections with the US public, while the Right eventually triumphed with think tanks, talk radio, FOX News, and a sophisticated online disinformation machine. We built no such infrastructure. So, we went from flower power to President Donald Trump.

The accomplishments of the '60s have been lasting and profound: greater personal freedoms, more rights for women and the LGBTQ+ population, the end of Jim Crow segregation, the election of the first Black president, almost the end of pot persecution, greater sexual freedom, freedom from stultifying religious and cultural norms, and the end of drafting hundreds of thousands of soldiers to fight against popular uprisings abroad. We still have a long way to go on these issues, but we have made so much amazing progress.

However, the failures of the '60s still haunt us. We totally failed when it comes to the most important political imperative of all, gaining *power*.

Reactionary, right-wing monopoly corporate forces are more in control of our country today than ever. They have brainwashed a large portion of the population. (As Jane Mayer concludes in her important book *Dark Money*, "What the Koch brothers really did was pay to change how Americans think.") And now they threaten our democracy and even the very survival of humanity by attacking science while profiting from heating the globe with fossil fuels. All for a few companies and billionaires, while systemic racism still dominates America.

Why have progressives and Democrats been so much less effective at public communications than the right? Partly because people on the left look down on the idea of "selling" ideas. People from the liberal arts (or law or the sciences) are inculcated with the false belief that the facts persuade by themselves. They are up against people on the Right who go to business school and who, to advance their careers, have mastered marketing, communications, and cognitive science to sell products and services. Ironically, they have triumphed by using communications principles we pioneered in the '60s, then largely abandoned.

Now, we are in a new era of activism, as young people rise up to conquer racism, protect science, ensure a livable planet, and fight for economic, racial, and gender justice. If we pay attention to the principles on the following pages, I'm convinced we can win again. To ensure civilization's very survival, we must.

The great free-form radio newscaster of the 1960s, Wes "Scoop" Nisker of KSAN in San Francisco, coined a slogan we could all try to live by: "If you don't like the news, go out and make your own!" So, I did.

DAVID FENTON BERKELEY, CALIFORNIA *JANUARY, 2022*

COMMUNICATION RULES FOR ACTIVISTS

CRAFT SIMPLE MESSAGES EVERYONE CAN UNDERSTAND. Use short, clear, unpretentious language already in common use. Avoid jargon and wonky technical terms, and above all, avoid rhetoric. Not: "We have to cut carbon emissions." Rather: "We have to stop pollution." We may not like "Make America Great Again," but it worked.

SPEAK TO THE HEART FIRST, THE MIND SECOND. Don't just recite facts—they only work inside stories that touch people's emotions through moral narratives. Whoever holds the moral high ground wins. Not: "We have to get to net zero by 2050." Rather: "Our children deserve a future, so we must act against polluters."

STORIES NEED GOOD AND BAD CHARACTERS. People learn from stories about people. Think climate activist Greta Thunberg against the "blah, blah" politicians doing nothing.

REPEAT, REPEAT, REPEAT YOUR MESSAGES. People learn from incessant repetition, which sticks in the brain, changing its very circuitry. Therefore, only repetition of simple messages changes public opinion. Only when you are sick to death of saying the same thing over and over do you have any chance of breaking through. Repetition also creates political pressure on leaders. They know one-time messages or actions, like a demonstration, go away. Repetition forces leaders to pay attention.

PRACTICE FRAMING ISSUES YOUR WAY. People think in what linguists call frames—existing circuitry in the brain formed by years of exposure to language. So, frame issues to activate people's existing neural wiring. For example, when you say "pollution," everyone thinks "bad." When you say "carbon," most people don't know what to think, as there is little existing circuitry attached to the word. Also, don't get suckered by responding to the other side's framing—you're only helping them if you repeat it. Not: "We aren't taking away anyone's jobs." Rather: "Those who block climate action are allowing extreme weather to destroy our economy and jobs."

USE SYMBOLISM. Incorporate familiar images and phrases with cultural resonance (another form of framing). An apple a day keeps the doctor away. Three strikes and you're out. Don't judge a book by its cover. Pick symbols that are *sticky*, hard to forget. For example: How much heat energy is climate change trapping on Earth? The same energy as exploding 600,000 atomic bombs a day.

TELL THE TRUTH. Spin is deceit. Expect your opponents to lie and mislead—don't do it yourself. The truth is more powerful, and it's the only ethical choice. You can simplify the truth, but do not distort it. If you make mistakes, quickly admit them and move on.

ENSURE YOU ARE REACHING PEOPLE BY USING ADVERTISING. Don't assume your message is reaching the public. People can only act on information that reaches them. While you may not like a world awash in advertising, that's the world we live in. If you're not buying attention, you risk getting none. Digital advertising usually costs far less than most progressives think. You can also drop advertising bombs to change narratives and make news.

RECRUIT CELEBRITIES, INFLUENCERS, AND CULTURAL FIGURES. They attract attention and have large followings. Recruit athletes, actors, rock stars, CEOs, and YouTube and Instagram influencers to promote your message. Think Lady Gaga on LGBTQ+ rights, Leonardo DiCaprio on climate, John Legend on criminal justice reform.

FIGHT FALSEHOOD AND DISINFORMATION IMMEDIATELY. If you don't, it can stick in people's minds, enabling a big lie to become "truth." To fight it, double down on all of the directives above. If a journalist is regurgitating disinformation, complain respectfully to them, and their bosses, too.

IT'S WHO YOU KNOW. And who you get to know. In the media, as elsewhere, relationships are crucial. Get to know journalists, editors, social media decision-makers, and broadcasters. Most are inclined toward progressive ideals, but need to trust activists. Take them to lunch. Throw parties. Go drinking with them. Unless they work for right-wing phony media like FOX, never treat journalists as the enemy. Understand the culture of news and news hooks. Use them to hook media coverage.

ORGANIZE TO WIN

Good communication is half the battle. You also have to run an organized campaign. Some points to remember:

- ◆ NOTHING IS BLACK AND WHITE—EVERYTHING CONTAINS CONTRADICTIONS. DON'T MAKE THE PERFECT THE ENEMY OF THE GOOD.

- ◆ AVOID SECTARIANISM, THE CANCER OF THE LEFT. IT USUALLY REFLECTS RIGID IDEOLOGY.

- ◆ SPEND MORE ENSURING YOU REACH PEOPLE, OR YOU WON'T. OFTEN THIS IS A BETTER USE OF FUNDS THAN HIRING MORE STAFF.

- ◆ PAY GOOD PEOPLE WELL. A FEW REALLY TALENTED PEOPLE CAN ACCOMPLISH MORE THAN A CROWD OF THOSE LESS TALENTED. USE BONUS AND INCENTIVE PAY SO PEOPLE DO THEIR BEST.

- BEWARE ENDLESS MEETINGS AND PROCESSES.

- BUREAUCRACY IS A BALL AND CHAIN. STOP IT AS SOON AS IT APPEARS, WHICH IT WILL.

- YOUR FEELINGS AND IDENTITY ARE IMPORTANT—BUT FOCUSING ON THEM MAY NOT BE THE BEST WAY TO GET YOUR MESSAGE ACROSS OR BUILD MAJORITIES.

- WE NEED GOOD LEADERS, SO FOLLOW THEM. WARS AREN'T WON WITHOUT GENERALS. BEWARE PARALYZING ULTRA-DEMOCRACY. WORK TOWARD CONSENSUS, BUT WAITING FOR IT BEFORE ACTION CAN MEAN LAME ACTION OR NO ACTION AT ALL.

CHAPTER 1

ADVERSITY MAKES AN ACTIVIST: OR, THE ORIGINS OF AN ACTIVIST

So, how did a nice Jewish boy from Manhattan decide to drop out of high school and wind up founding the nation's first politically progressive public relations firm?

It started when I was eleven, when my mother had a nervous breakdown.

"Will you please come help my mother?" I asked, knocking on the doors of at least ten psychiatrists on my street, East 74th Street, on New York's fancy Upper East Side. Of course, none would leave their patients for the eleven-year-old boy at their door.

It was 1963. I had come home from junior high school that afternoon to find my mother in the mail room off the lobby of our high-rise apartment building. She had a wild look in her eyes. Her clothes were torn, and there were smudge marks on her face.

"David, something wonderful has happened."

"What, Mom?"

"God has revealed something amazing to me."

Confused and frightened, I brought her upstairs to my grandmother in our twentieth-floor penthouse apartment. Nana was beside herself. She told me that Mom had suffered a mental breakdown in the aftermath of my stepfather's sudden death two weeks earlier. She didn't know how to help her.

Me at 17, the summer of 1969. **PREVIOUS SPREAD** *Mounted police chase a boy who burned an American flag in New York's Central Park. The boy was then badly beaten by the police and arrested. October 12, 1968.*

Scared to death, I took the elevator down, sailed past the doorman, and started knocking on all those psychiatrists' doors, to no avail.

Two weeks before, my brother and I had suddenly, without explanation, been sent to live with our aunt and uncle on Long Island. When we returned, we were told that my sweet, warm stepfather, Harry Markoff, had had a heart attack and died suddenly in bed, next to my mother. He was only forty-five. He and my mom had only been married a year and a half and were very much in love. When I heard the horrible news, I felt everything collapsing around me.

Thus began the disintegration of my family life and a lifetime of anxiety from, essentially, the disappearance of my parents. My mother and father had divorced four years earlier, when I was seven. My father was largely absent—especially emotionally. My stepfather was dead—he smoked three packs of Lucky Strikes a day and ate steak every night, frequently washed down with Dewar's on the rocks. Back then, people didn't know this could kill you. My mother went off to a mental institution, the first of many such hospitalizations for bipolar disorder over the next twenty years. And I set off on a long journey to find a substitute family in activist political collectives and hippie communes with the radicals, visionaries, and crazies of the '60s and '70s.

My mother's illness launched me on the unconventional path I took, dropping out of a prestigious high school in eleventh grade and never going to college. Instead, after my years as a radical photojournalist, I became the publisher of a hippie underground newspaper, then spent a lifetime living up to what the *National Journal* once called me: "the Robin Hood of public relations."

MY MANHATTAN ORIGINS

I was born in Manhattan in 1952 and first raised in Queens. My parents met at a Young Communist League meeting in the Bronx. They weren't particularly political, they once told me, but they were looking for dates. Mom was thin and beautiful, with high cheekbones and bleached blonde hair. She became a garment-industry runway fashion model. My handsome father graduated from the The Wharton School of Business at the University of Pennsylvania. on the GI Bill after the war and worked at an accounting firm. But he was seriously damaged emotionally. During the war, he navigated planes that bombed Germany. At age nineteen, he lost many friends in aerial combat, leaving lifelong trauma. That, and having been abandoned by his own father, led to his emotional shutdown.

While at Wharton, an accounting professor told my father that, due to anti-Semitism, it would be hard for him to get a job unless he changed his name. His name was Paul Fanaberia. Dad consulted the phone book, looked under *F*, and chose Fenton, a proper British name. Otherwise, I'd be David Fanaberia.

We were solidly middle-class Jews of Russian and Eastern European descent. My paternal grandfather, Yefime (Harold) Fanaberia, fled the czar's Sino-Soviet war draft in 1905 for the United States. My father's mother, Alice Sabloff, was born in the United States to Russian parents. She divorced my grandfather in the 1920s, which was almost unheard of at the time.

At Miami's Eden Roc Hotel, 1962. From left: my stepfather, Harry Markoff, my mother, Alexandra Markoff, cousin Sue-Ann Slavin, and me, age ten.

I went to public elementary schools, first in Queens, and after my mother married Harry, to PS6 at 81st Street and Madison Avenue in New York. While public, it was a fancy-schmancy school in a wealthy neighborhood. Some kids even arrived by limousine. With my stepfather, Harry, we rose in social class. He became a magnate in the garment industry, or as Jews called it, the schmata trade—the word "schmata" is Yiddish for "rags." I truly loved him. Harry was a "joie de vivre" kind of guy and remarkably positive and upbeat. Unlike my traumatized father, he loved life. Tragically, I knew him for less than two years.

Newly rich thanks to Harry, my mother designed our penthouse duplex with custom-made frilly Louis XIV furniture. Every Thursday night, when the maid was off, we went out to the Stork Club, the 21 Club, the Latin Quarter, or my favorite, the Copacabana, where we saw Tony Bennet and Sammy Davis Jr. Harry would take all of us—including my aunt, uncle, and cousins—on vacation to the Fontainebleau Hotel in Miami and give us carte blanche to sign for anything we wanted. I would take my dates in elementary school to the nearby Metropolitan Museum of Art for lunch, or to see Joel Grey in

Police dragging anti-Vietnam war protestors away. New York City, 1968.

Cabaret on Broadway. Fancy-schmancy and privileged, indeed.

We were culturally Jewish but not religious. Every Passover, we flew to Montreal, where my paternal grandfather had moved after his divorce. During these visits, my domineering, utterly patriarchal, old-school grandfather would drag me to temple. But he struck me as hypocritical. His religious piety contrasted with the cold-water tenements he rented to French-speaking tenants—and his quick evictions when they were late with the rent. I think my grandfather may have helped

public Wagner Junior High School on East 76th Street and 2nd Avenue. The 1964 Harlem riots had started there, when a cop shot a Black kid dead on the playground. The school was 75 percent Black and Puerto Rican. This turned out to be a blessing. I learned about the real world in a way that would not have been possible had I taken the Upper East Side rich white boy path.

My maternal grandparents were Democrats, but also racists, decrying the "schvartzes," the pejorative Yiddish term for Black. Even though my mother was progressive, she literally forbade

MY MOTHER'S MENTAL ILLNESS LAUNCHED MY UNCONVENTIONAL PATH.

fuel the Quebecois movement for independence against Montreal's English-speaking overlords. This turned me off to religion and probably contributed to my lifelong identification with the underdog.

At Passover dinners, my grandfather made a great show of giving the grandchildren Israeli bonds as presents for our college funds. Years after my grandfather's death, I asked my father where that money was. "Oh, that was one of your grandfather's tax evasion scams," he explained. "You were never going to get a dime."

So much for religion.

When my stepfather died, he left no will, causing a financial mess. I'd planned to attend a private school for seventh grade, with an indoor swimming pool and squash courts. Suddenly, we could no longer afford that. Instead, I attended

me to go to the more integrated West Side of Manhattan, which she deemed "more dangerous," despite the fancy buildings along Central Park West. (My father was devoted to John Coltrane and Black jazz musicians, but I didn't find out about his hidden emotional life until later.)

Before I set foot in Wagner, I'd never spent time with Black people. I was frankly and stupidly scared. So were my white friends from public elementary school. On the first day of junior high, we walked in a small group surrounded by our parents to "protect us." It's embarrassing to recall this now. Most of the white kids were placed in what were then called Special Progress classes, taught by some truly great teachers, who pampered us. Meanwhile, most of the Black and Hispanic students were neglected. Outrageously, this is still the case in many US public schools.

MY FIRST MENTOR, AND BEGINNING MY POLITICAL EDUCATION

Robert Greenhut, one of the Special Progress teachers, became my mentor and the first of a series of the substitute fathers I craved. To emulate him, I subscribed to the *New Republic, Commentary*, the *Nation*, and other intellectual left magazines, thus beginning my political education. I read *The New York Times* every day, cover to cover. Fifty-five years later, I still do. I also joined Mr. Greenhut's photography club, which included access to the tiny but well-equipped school darkroom, way down in a deep, dark subbasement. I took to the medium quickly, mostly teaching myself by reading *Popular Photography*. Photography was also useful as I roamed the halls taking photos. "Hey man, take my picture," someone would say, and I would. It made me popular and helped me feel comfortable being in the white minority.

The first time I photographed a demonstration against the war in Vietnam, on Fifth Avenue near Central Park, I was so concerned about being mistaken for an unpatriotic antiwar protestor that I wore a button that said "Bomb Hanoi." Fortunately for my political education, my best friend, Jamie Friar, had a stepfather named John Williams, who had been blacklisted after refusing to testify before the House Un-American Activities Committee. John explained that the United States had blocked planned elections to reunify North and South Vietnam, as called for in the Geneva Accords that ended the French war in Indochina. We were now intervening to prop up a corrupt dictatorship in South Vietnam while literally making war on the peasant population, who largely supported reunification with North Vietnam.

I visited the public library to search news articles on microfilm (no Google then) and discovered he was right. I felt shocked to discover my government was flat out lying. This wasn't what I'd learned in civics class. John turned me against the Vietnam War, which made me question my other beliefs about the United States being the land of the free.

Then, it was time to apply to public high school. The best in New York were Stuyvesant and Bronx Science. Both required the same entrance examination. I passed and could choose either school—but in those days Stuyvesant was boys only. So, despite my indifference to science or math, I opted for Bronx Science. What would high school be without girls? I was shy and inexperienced, but definitely interested.

The trip to Bronx Science took an hour on the subway each way from our now much smaller apartment on East 79th Street in Manhattan. Then

Student smoking in a Bronx High School of Science bathroom, 1968.

I had to move to my grandmother's place way out in Queens, as my mom was back in the mental hospital. That meant almost two hours each way, which was really tough. Then I moved again to join my younger brother, Jonathan, who was living at my father's apartment with his new wife, Carol, across the Hudson in Fort Lee, New Jersey. That didn't last. Carol, a beautiful former Broadway dancer and raging alcoholic, threw me out for being too argumentative. My father didn't try to stop her. So, I moved back in with Mom, now on East 56th Street and 1st Avenue, in a white brick apartment building with a doorman.

semester of tenth grade. Then I started cutting classes, smoking more pot, and demonstrating against the war with a group of radical students. My average dropped through the floor.

I was an insecure, scared, thin, tall, and nerdy kid. Until high school, I mostly listened to classical music, which I also played on the piano. I made out with my girlfriend to Beethoven piano concertos. One day, she came out from the bathroom into the living room of my mom's apartment stark naked. I got so freaked out I asked her to put clothes on! Later, at her parent's apartment in a Bronx housing project, we kissed and she put her hand in my

I WATCHED JIMI HENDRIX PLAY THE GUITAR WITH HIS MOUTH.

Living with my mom was literally crazy. In her manic phases, she attracted all kinds of bizarre people—which New York is full of. Crazy people attract each other. I mostly stayed away, using my bathroom as a darkroom, careful to put a blanket under the door so she wouldn't smell the marijuana I had started using at fifteen. (Later, she told me she knew all along.) When she crashed into the depressive phase of her illness, she stayed in bed, often catatonic for weeks at a time, so Jonathan and I largely had to fend for ourselves. At other times, she disappeared for months at a time, leaving me no home to speak of.

I arrived at Bronx Science to start tenth grade in the fall of 1966. It was a huge school of more than three thousand students with a science mural depicting the atom in the lobby. Initially, I excelled, achieving an A average during that first

pants. Suddenly, I was all warm and wet down there—I had no idea what it was. I had to ask her. That was how sexually educated most of us were in the early '60s. No wonder she broke up with me soon after. I was no fun. Sorry, Karen!

But hanging out with the radical kids—and marijuana and rock and roll—started to change me inside and out. Pot soothed my anxiety, arousing my senses, sexuality, and creativity in new ways. I was an instant convert and later an advocate. I largely dropped classical music, stopped piano lessons (the dumbest thing I ever did), and stood in line to buy *Sgt. Pepper's Lonely Hearts Club Band* the day it came out. I saw the Doors and Jefferson Airplane, which changed me even more. Jimi Hendrix blew my mind in the very small Hunter College auditorium

Issue #2 of the New York High School Free Press, *October 1968.*

new york
HIGH SCHOOL
FREE PRESS

Issue 2

Special Halloweelection Edition

FIVE CENTS CHEAP

"Of, by, and for liberated High School Students"

Strike Against The Death Elections Nov. 5

in Manhattan. Sitting in the second row, my body was vibrated by something like twenty guitar amps on the stage right in front of me. I watched Jimi play the guitar with his mouth, then pour lighter fluid out of his crotch and light it on fire. I don't think I've been the same since. The late-night Bob Fass show on WBAI-FM introduced me to Bob Dylan's longer songs on *Blonde on Blonde*, Ed Sander's group The Fugs (their hit was "Kill for Peace"), and yippie radical crazy Abbie Hoffman, a frequent guest.

CIVIL DISOBEDIENCE AT THE PRINCIPAL'S OFFICE

At Bronx Science, a group started an unauthorized underground student newspaper called *Sans Culottes*, inspired by the French Revolution. Distributing the paper at school brought immediate suspension. I nervously visited Paul Steiner and Meredith Maran, the student couple who founded it, at their pad on the Lower East Side. They were the coolest kids in the school, glamorous, artsy activists who were living together full-time at the home of Paul's father, an ex-Communist. I sheepishly offered Paul and Merry photographs of police who had beaten up students at an antiwar demonstration. They were thrilled and accepted me into the cool kids' corner! They also gave me my first photo byline.

Bronx Science's strict dress code prohibited pants for girls and blue jeans for boys. At the time, we were all reading Black Panther Eldridge Cleaver's *Soul on Ice*, his prison memoir. It inspired us. One day, all three thousand students showed up at school in blue jeans, boys and girls alike. That was the end of the dress code. What could the principal do in the face of that? It was my first

lesson in grassroots organizing. We did it by word of mouth—there was no internet, no Instagram, *nada*. We did distribute leaflets, which we printed on a rudimentary home mimeograph machine. That was the cutting-edge technology of the time.

Next, we demanded the school begin a Black studies program. In high school, no less. The principal refused, so we staged a sit-in and took over his office. The police were called, and several students were arrested. But we got the Black studies program. Bronx Science was almost entirely white and largely Jewish at the time (today, it's mostly Asian). Two of my closest friends were Black, including Reggie Lucas, who later played guitar for Miles Davis, produced Madonna's first album, and wrote "The Closer I Get to You" for Roberta Flack. Reggie— short, thin, and with a goatee—wrote the music column for our underground school newspaper and turned me on to all kinds of great Black music.

In the summer of 1967, when I was fifteen, my parents sent me to Europe on a thirty-day teen tour. The trip ended in Amsterdam, where I volunteered to procure hashish for our group of fifteen. Right after buying red Afghani hash at a bar, I got back on my rented motorbike and was seized by two plainclothes cops who pushed me into their police car while pushing their hands into my pockets. They took me to jail, where I spent five days in solitary confinement. I know, I know. I thought it was legal in Amsterdam, too.

The prosecuting attorney threatened me with six months of "hard labor" unless I identified who had sold me the hash. Hard labor? I had never done *any* labor. So, I sheepishly identified the guy

A Bronx Science High School student pleads with police not to arrest him during an antiwar demonstration, New York City, 1968.

from mug shots. Next thing I knew, I was in a police paddy wagon with the dealer I had ratted out. I was sure I was going to die.

But white New York privilege got me out, as the head of my father's family accounting firm knew the US senator from New York, Jacob Javits, who arranged for my deportation back to New York. I hadn't showered, shaved, or changed my clothes in five days, and must have been quite a sight (and smell), being brought onto the KLM airliner in handcuffs. I spent the whole trip convinced the FBI would arrest me when I landed. But my father met me without incident, and all was well. I still have an Interpol record from the arrest.

Soon after, I joined a group of high school students who started the High School Mobilization Against the War in Vietnam and the New York High School Student Union. We were all terrified of the draft, which sent many of us to Vietnam. "Hell no, we won't go" was our slogan at many protests under the watchful eyes of the police. Next, we started the

New York High School Free Press, the newspaper of the radical New York High School Student Union. I took the cover photo for the inaugural issue—a Black baby waving a Black anarchist flag.

The *High School Free Press* was assembled under the tutelage and at the offices of an adult antiwar underground paper, the *New York Free Press*, on West 72nd Street. The editors of the grown-up paper started publishing my photographs of riots and demonstrations around New York. (They also started the first major pornographic newspaper, *Screw*, in a major city in their dank, dark, messy offices above a grocery store.) This, in turn, led to calls from *The New York Times, Newsweek, Time, Life*, and other magazines, asking to publish my photos. It was heady stuff, and my mother was finally happy, as she could show her friends my bylines in the *Times*. The best part was that I started making serious money from photography. I was delighted to realize I could support myself on my own.

CHAPTER 2

MY PROFESSOR, ABBIE HOFFMAN

My first professor in the rules of media activism was Abbie Hoffman, the most creative activist of his generation, and certainly the funniest.

In the '60s, he was already approaching thirty, but with his long hair and impish style personified youth rebellion. He founded the Youth International Party (also known as the yippies) largely as a joke. It was far more myth than reality. Yet amazingly, he seduced the mainstream media into covering yippie actions and pronouncements as if they were much more than just Abbie and a few fellow activists. On the CBS *Evening News*, Walter Cronkite, "the most trusted man in America," would report "today, the Youth International Party announced." Abbie was a genius at mythmaking and appealing to the culture of the media.

In 1967, New York's WBAI-FM radio introduced me to Abbie when I was fifteen years old. When he asked his radio listeners to turn out at New York's Grand Central Terminal to protest the Vietnam War, thousands of us did and were roundly beaten by the police. They pushed a number of us through plate-glass windows, causing severe injury.

When Abbie asked us to turn out on East 7th Street on the Lower East Side for a sweep-in to clean up the block, hundreds of us did. Truly, he was the pied piper of youth activism. In August 1968, Abbie called on young people to protest the war at a "Festival of Life" at the Democratic National Convention

Abbie Hoffman speaking against the Vietnam War at New York's Central Park bandshell, 1968.

The Chicago 7 hold a press conference right after being charged with contempt of court, April 8, 1969. From left: Abbie Hoffman, John Froines, Lee Weiner, David Dellinger, Rennie Davis, Tom Hayden. Seated: Jerry Rubin and girlfriend, Nancy Kurshan.

in Chicago—where the police rioted against the demonstrators on national TV while protestors chanted "the whole world is watching." I watched it live, crying in outrage. For his trouble, Abbie was one of the activists charged by the Richard Nixon administration with "crossing state lines to incite a riot." Their indictments led to the Chicago Seven conspiracy trial.

MEETING ABBIE, AND COVERING THE CHICAGO SEVEN TRIAL

I first met Abbie in 1969 while working as a photographer for Liberation News Service (LNS), the AP/UPI for what at the time were hundreds of hippie, countercultural, antiwar underground newspapers across the country. We became friends and stayed that way until his tragic suicide at the age of fifty-three in 1989. He'd been bipolar most of his life. It fueled his creativity but also killed him. Abbie was my professor of media arts, and I

was his eager student. In fifty years of media activism, I've never seen anyone gain media attention for causes the way Abbie did.

The LNS assigned me to cover the Chicago Seven trial. I watched Abbie and his yippie partner, Jerry Rubin, turn it into agitprop theater the TV news media brought into millions of homes almost nightly. Abbie and Jerry had an unwitting theatrical partner in the judge, whose name was also, amazingly, Hoffman. At times, Abbie would come to trial dressed in American Revolutionary War attire or guerilla war outfits or a Chicago police uniform. Abbie took great delight in mocking the judge, saying he, Abbie, was Judge Hoffman's illegitimate child. The judge responded by citing him for contempt of court many times.

Who else would throw a kiss to the jury during the trial? Judge Hoffman responded by admonishing the jurors, "The jury will ignore the kiss from defendant Hoffman." It was hysterical.

The defendants turned the trial on its head. Instead of mounting a traditional defense, they put the war in Vietnam on trial. Every evening after the day's courtroom escapades, I accompanied Abbie and the other defendants (Tom Hayden, Jerry Rubin, Rennie Davis, John Froines, Dave Dellinger, and Lee Weiner) and their attorneys, Bill Kunstler and Leonard Weinglass, back to defense headquarters. We watched the day's "reviews" on the CBS *Evening News* and other programs. I was astonished how creatively the defendants used the media to educate the public about the war. And the strategy worked—ultimately, all charges were dropped and, except for a few days' imprisonment for contempt of court, nobody went to jail.

Abbie's media imagination was second to none. Who else would launch a nightly radio program in New York simultaneously with Walter Cronkite's CBS *Evening News*, during which Abbie commented on the very news reports Uncle Walter delivered? I marveled at Abbie's genius and outrageousness.

THE TRIAL OF THE CHICAGO 7

If you want to know what Abbie was like, watch the Netflix film *The Trial of the Chicago 7*. Sacha Baron Cohen plays him to absolute, uncanny perfection. Cohen is Abbie reincarnated, right down to his Boston accent, quirky mannerisms, and impish twinkle.

ABBIE AND THE WIT AND THEATER OF POLITICS

Abbie was a trip. He threw dollar bills down onto the trading floor of the New York Stock Exchange, knowing traders would scramble to scoop up the bills. They obliged. He insisted the most popular word in the English language was "free." He painted it on his forehead before going on TV. (Later, in his more militant phase, he painted the word "fuck" on his forehead instead.) He opened the short-lived Free Store in the East Village where, literally, everything was free. He titled his first book *Revolution for the Hell of It*. This greatly upset doctrinaire leftists, who retorted, "What? Revolution is serious!" Of course it is, but Abbie made it fun. His next book was famously called *Steal This Book*, which the bookstores were none too happy about.

Abbie and the yippies ran a pig for president—an actual pig named Pigasus, which they carried around at many demonstrations.

The first time Abbie wore an American flag shirt in public, he was instantly arrested for desecrating the flag, a crime at the time. When Abbie appeared in his flag shirt on the popular Merv Griffin talk show, producer Roger Ailes (later the founder of Fox "News") blocked out the image of his shirt. Like one of his mentors, the great comedian Lenny Bruce, Abbie understood humor as a key ingredient in social change campaigning. He also proved that your image, the myth you create about yourself or your organization, is as important to communicating your message as what you actually do. It's a nonliteral approach to projecting activist power. I wish today's progressive activists appreciated it. Trump certainly does.

Perhaps the most creative antiwar protest of the '60s took place in 1967, when Abbie and others called on demonstrators to attend a March Against Death at the Pentagon. "We're going to levitate the Pentagon," Abbie told the TV cameras. The claim was so outrageous that the media covered the demonstration extensively. The Pentagon was surrounded by protestors who held hands, closed their eyes, and "levitated" the building in front of thousands of heavily armed troops.

Abbie was close to some of my radical friends from high school, who were living in a youth commune on West 85th Street. One day, he asked them to guard two brown-glass vials containing a half liter of pure Owsley LSD in their refrigerator. "Don't get any on your fingers," he warned them. "You'll get too high real fast." Of course, my friends consumed one of the vials and tripped for days. Abbie said he planned to use the other to spike the punch bowl at a White House event. Everyone scoffed—there goes Abbie, spreading myths again.

Years later, we learned from Jefferson Airplane lead singer Grace Slick's autobiography that it was indeed his plan for that vial. Grace had been a college classmate of one of Richard Nixon's daughters, who invited her class to the White House. Slick wrote that she had taken Abbie to the Nixon White House as her date. They planned to "raise the consciousness" of those in attendance. The plot was thwarted at the last minute by the Secret Service, who recognized Abbie, refusing to admit him. Phew. In retrospect, I'm glad. That was one of Abbie's craziest bad ideas.

Abbie Hoffman at a rally in support of the Black Panther Party. New Haven, Connecticut, April 30, 1970.

FROM "OFF THE PIGS" TO "DEFUND THE POLICE"

Fueled perhaps by what we later learned was his bipolar disorder, Abbie sometimes made big mistakes that turned the public against the movement. Puerto Ricans and Black people in Harlem started chanting "off the pigs" at public demonstrations—an understandable sentiment from the victims of so much police brutality, but as a way to create sympathy and support across the United States, it was a loser. Abbie picked it up and chanted "off the pigs" at demonstrations and press conferences. Now, this may have made sense coming from Black and brown people being victimized by violent cops, but it enabled Nixon to portray Abbie and the movement as crazy and violent. It was stupid, just like the recent use of the slogan "defund the police," which people hear as "you don't want any police to protect me." That slogan almost certainly lost the Democrats several House seats in 2020. Language matters, folks!

Once at a press conference for the campaign to release a movement leader from prison, Abbie took a switchblade from his pocket, opened it, and rammed it violently into the table in front of him, in full view of television cameras, saying, "This is what we're going to do to the police." Not smart. Most famously, he kept threatening to "put LSD in the water supply" to turn on the public. I'm sure he meant it as a joke, but the media took it seriously, spreading fear. Scaring the public is not the way to build a movement. Of course, it wouldn't have even worked, becoming far too dilute in the drinking water.

But, despite his mistakes, I loved Abbie and learned so much from him. He was so charismatic and truly dedicated to the cause of peace and justice.

SHOTS: MY BOOK IS BANNED

I'll always feel grateful to Abbie for naming my first book. After two years of activist photojournalism, at the ripe old age of seventeen, I decided to collect the most compelling photographs from underground newspapers across the country and turn them into a book with pithy quotes from movement leaders. Macmillan agreed to publish the book and paid LNS an advance. I asked Abbie what to call it.

"Call it *Shots of War*," he said. That was a bit too militaristic for me, so I named the book simply *Shots*. I flew around the country collecting photos. During the trip, I witnessed the Bank of America building in Santa Barbara burned down by antiwar protestors and photographed the impressive first Chicano Moratorium march in Los Angeles. Macmillan hired the design director of the popular *Look* magazine to worka with me to choose the photos and layout. But when the chairman of Macmillan saw the finished product, he refused to publish the book. It was "too radical." Maybe he felt turned off by the dedication page, which featured a poem by Mao Zedong (this was before we knew what a criminal Mao had become). It took two years, but eventually Alan Douglas published *Shots*. (He also published Lenny Bruce and spent a lifetime issuing Jimi Hendrix reissues.)

In the early '60s, he had risked his life repeatedly while helping register Black voters in the South. While his fame affected his ego, the movement was always his focus. He even gave movement groups most of the money his books earned, dying without any money, even for his kids. Before he died, I was one of many people who helped him while he was a fugitive on the FBI's Ten Most Wanted Fugitives list, living underground under a different identity for many years. More on that later.

OPPOSITE *Abbie was frequently arrested for wearing this American flag shirt—it was illegal at the time.* **TOP** *Abbie speaking in support of the Black Panther Party. New Haven, Connecticut, May 1, 1970.* **BOTTOM** *Abbie (center) with coconspirator Jerry Rubin (left) on New York's Lower East Side, at a "Vote Pig" demonstration.*

CHAPTER 3

THE HIGH SCHOOL DROPOUT RADICAL PHOTOJOURNALIST

IN WHICH I LEARN...

- **THE POWER OF IMAGES FOR SOCIAL CHANGE.**

- **HOW PSYCHEDELICS HELPED FUEL THE ENVIRONMENTAL MOVEMENT.**

With a camera always in hand and a Liberation News Service press pass in my wallet, I started to meet many radical, antiwar journalists and activists in New York. Back then, there was an underground newspaper in every major city—the *Chicago Seed*, the *Great Speckled Bird* in Atlanta, the *Berkeley Barb*, the *San Francisco Express Times*, the *Rat Subterranean News* in New York, the *Rag* in Austin, and dozens of others. Underground newspapers were the only publications that revealed the truth about the Vietnam War, drugs, racism, sex, and rock and roll. These tabloid, graphics-heavy, quirkily written newspapers changed a generation—and they all subscribed to LNS.

LNS published hundreds of my photographs, which appeared in underground papers from coast to coast and around the world. I shot one influential photo just outside the military jail at Fort Dix, New Jersey, where soldiers who refused to go to Vietnam were incarcerated in tiny cells. The sign at the entrance to the jail—or, in military parlance, "stockade"—was truly Orwellian: "Obedience to the Law Is Freedom." My photo of this sign, with two armed guards and barbed wire below it, was an instant hit, published around the world. Within a month, the army removed the sign. My first media victory.

Seventeen years old, at a D.C. anti-war demonstration with camera, helmet, gas mask, and my lawyer's phone number written on my wrist, just in case.

SHOOTING FOR *LIFE*

Then I hit the jackpot. *Life* magazine assigned me to photograph "alienation and rebellion" at my high school, Bronx Science, for three weeks. They paid me the professional day rate of $150 a day in 1968 dollars. This was a lot of money and a staggering fortune to me. I roamed the school's halls, photographing students on drugs, peace symbols on bathroom walls, and demonstrations both spontaneous and planned against the school and the war. The photos were supposed to be part of a feature spread about rebellious high school kids. But the editors found it too radical and killed it. Instead, on the cover of *Life* and without my permission, they published a photo I had taken, implicating it in a story that claimed high school students were happy with school and the war. Incensed, I threatened to sue *Life* and received a significant settlement thanks to my terrific lawyer, David Lubell.

How did a pot-smoking, sixteen-year-old radical hippie activist like me find a lawyer? He found me. At a demonstration protesting Vice President Hubert Humphrey's support of the war, I'd photographed the police beating the crap out of demonstrators. Soon after, I received a call from a man with a nasal voice. He identified himself as the lawyer for the arrested, police-assaulted demonstrators. David Lubell used my photos to get everyone released with all charges dropped because of the police violence. David became my lifelong attorney, mentor, and my next substitute father figure. He was another former member of the Communist Party USA, who had almost been thrown out of Harvard Law School for taking the Fifth Amendment at a congressional hearing. David also represented

James Baldwin, Martin Luther King, and the Black Panther Party. He had three daughters, so I became his surrogate son. Very short, unassuming, and mustached, David was the epitome of the progressive Jewish tradition. I felt very lucky to find him.

With the money I'd earned from *Life*, I suddenly became financially independent (thank you, Time Inc.!). Meanwhile, that fall, the beginning of my junior year, New York teachers launched the longest teacher strike in the city's history. It revolved around community control of schools, especially in Black neighborhoods. There was no school from September into November. So, a group of us forced the school to open for our own "liberation classes," featuring well-known authors, activists, and radicals like philosopher Paul Goodman, Abbie Hoffman, and others. At last, I thought, I'm finally getting a real, stimulating, relevant education.

LEAVING SCHOOL, AND GETTING A BETTER EDUCATION

When regular classes resumed in November, I couldn't believe the stark contrast. The first day of chemistry class was the last straw for me. The nerdy teacher divided the room in two, one side for the boys, the other for the girls. That class was a sure cure for insomnia, and homework was just as dull—answering the rote questions at the end of each rote chapter. I was finished. I never went back to high school, not even for a day. I never attended college, either. Of course, my mother

The entrance to the Fort Dix stockade, New Jersey, October 12, 1969.

seize the time!

LIBERATION NEWS SERVICE

No. 243

March 28, 1970

flipped. Her overachieving Jewish son was supposed to go to Harvard Law School. For years, until my midtwenties, she sent me books of matches that proclaimed on the cover, "You can earn a high school equivalency diploma and get a good job." I never did.

Instead, I dropped out of school and joined LNS full-time as a staff photographer and graphics editor. LNS was located in the seedy basement of an apartment building on Claremont Avenue, on Manhattan's Upper West Side near Columbia University. My father, feeling guilty that I had no safe place to live, guaranteed the lease for my first apartment, a one bedroom also on Claremont, on the fifth floor with big bars on the windows to deter burglaries, then rampant in New York. But, except for rent, even though I was not yet seventeen, I supported myself quite well with my photography.

My salary at LNS was $25 a week plus free communal lunches and dinners. Now I had a whole new family—twenty photographers, reporters, editors, and printers. LNS became my university: I learned about Marxism, the Palestinian cause, the terrible oppression of Black Americans, and the liberation movements in Africa and Latin America to overthrow colonialism. Many of that era's major activists and thinkers of the day visited our offices. It was perhaps the best education I could have received anywhere, in real life, no less. Unlike today, back then it wasn't easy to find the point of view of the oppressed. It was very powerful to me, consolidating and deepening my desire to help change the world.

By 1969, my photographs were frequently on the cover of LNS news packets: a picture I took of Nixon next to a quote by him saying, "I understand that there has been and continues to be opposition to the war in Vietnam … however, under no circumstances, will I be affected whatsoever by it." My photo of guitarist Jeff Beck at the Fillmore East. A single dispatch would cover everything from torture in Brazil to the trials of protestors at San Francisco State University. And we did this twice a week, necessitating twelve-hour days, six days a week or more.

My main professor was LNS writer and editor Allen Young, a former *Washington Post* reporter who'd quit the paper to protest its dreadful, servile Vietnam War coverage. He was another red diaper baby, the child of former Communist Party USA members. Allen was patient, teaching me a different perspective on the world. But while he was influenced by the "old left," Allen was no stick in the mud. When US soldiers in Vietnam thanked us for our antiwar coverage by anonymously sending potent Thai marijuana to our office via the US Army mail, Allen and I were among the very few LNSers to partake.

When I turned seventeen, I was still a virgin. But not for long, thanks to Barbara Rothkrug. She was a member of the LNS Collective, as we called ourselves, who had recently graduated from Barnard College. She had been part of the Columbia/Barnard uprising, where students had occupied campus buildings to protest the war and Columbia's mistreatment of its Harlem neighbors. The cops beat the hell out of the demonstrators while removing them from the buildings in a "police riot." Barbara was Jewish, with dark hair and complexion. At her request, I taught her photography, which involved long

Cover of the twice-weekly Liberation News Service "packet" of graphics and news for underground papers. March 28, 1970.

stints together in the darkroom. We started flirting, which got really intense as we drove from New York to Austin, Texas, to attend a national meeting of Students for a Democratic Society (SDS). When we returned, she moved into my apartment.

A MIND-ALTERING EDUCATION

Soon after joining LNS, I had my first psychedelic drug experience. It is not a cliché to say it changed me forever, in a miraculous instant, like so many of my generation. Some folks at LNS invited me to come strawberry picking with them at a friend's

and I spent the summer of 1969 on a cross-country camping and hiking trip through a half dozen national parks out West. Hard to believe, but this naturephobe spent seven weeks mostly sleeping outdoors at Zion National Park, Yellowstone, the Black Hills National Forest, and Olympic National Park. Barbara and I took psychedelics again on that trip, during a visit to Jewel Cave National Monument in South Dakota. Stalagmites never looked so glowing. As we started coming down, we went to the National Park Lodge for dinner, looked up at the TV screen, and saw Richard Nixon

PSYCHEDELICS CHANGED ME FOREVER, IN A MIRACULOUS INSTANT.

farm in Connecticut. This was not my idea of a good time—I was a nerdy New York City kid who literally hated going to the country. Plus, I was allergic to the outdoors and frightened of insects. Manhattan was nature to me; I preferred to stay there. But they convinced me to go, and I was a mess.

Then they fed me a tablet of synthetic mescaline, the active ingredient in peyote.

After about twenty minutes, I became a different person, as if someone had turned on a brilliant light. Experiencing myself to be one with nature, profoundly connected to the ecosystem, I got down on my knees and fell in love with the crawling insects, seeing them as the coolest things ever. I started hugging people, took off my clothes, and went swimming naked in the pond with the others. It was a classic instant hippie freak-out. And suddenly my allergies disappeared.

Newly at one with the natural world, Barbara

speaking to the astronauts on the moon. For a minute, I thought it was an LSD hallucination.

Psychedelic drugs changed many of my generation in ways not sufficiently appreciated, even now. Tripping increased one's sensory input and awareness of nature, spirit, and the body. It boosted the environmental and human potential movements, a yearning for clean, natural food, the adoption of Eastern religions like Buddhism, and even the physical fitness movement. It fueled new directions in art, music, and design. As Steve Jobs, the writer John Markoff, and others have shown, psychedelics also had a profound effect on Silicon Valley and the ability of engineers to imagine new approaches to silicon chip and product design. Psychedelics definitely made me a lifelong environmentalist. When the boundaries between you and the rest of creation disappear, it is a profoundly moving spiritual experience.

THE DARK SIDE OF PSYCHEDELICS

Like everything else in our contradictory universe, psychedelics can sometimes have a dark side. In those with a predisposition to mental illness, they can induce temporary and, rarely, permanent psychosis. I experienced several bad trips. Once, at Tom's Restaurant in Manhattan, made famous in Seinfeld, I came on to a large dose of LSD as I watched the room spin and seem to dissolve. Somehow, I made my way home and hid under the blankets until the drug wore off.

In 1971, at a demonstration in Washington, D.C., against the war, Abbie Hoffman gave me a tab of LSD to take among the bayoneted army troops surrounding the demonstration, with military helicopters overhead. Not exactly a great "set and setting"! I was an idiot to take that pill there—but it was the great Abbie Hoffman, my mentor, so I threw caution to the wind like a nut. At first, it was wonderful listening to the great jazz musician Charles Mingus play with his full band from the outdoor stage while coming onto acid. But as I started peaking on the drug, I completely freaked out on the tension and implied violence—and guns—all around me.

I went to the medical tent on the National Mall for a tranquilizer to come down, helped by my friend and fellow photographer Ken Light. Abbie was an idiot to take LSD in that situation, and even more so to give it to a punk kid like me. Talk about taking your ideology to extremes! Meanwhile, the next day he was arrested along with ten thousand other demonstrators—the largest roundup of protesters in US history to this day. Before his arrest, a cop punched Abbie in the face, smashing his nose. I hope he wasn't high when that happened.

Later, living in Ann Arbor, I had several bad experiences. When my younger brother, Jonathan, was thirteen, I was called to rescue him from a particularly bad LSD trip. Arriving at his friend's apartment, I found Jonathan stark naked and practically climbing the walls in manic anxiety. It took hours to talk him down and convince him to get dressed and come home with me. That was scary.

Psychedelics are not casual party drugs. Someday, I predict, they will become legal in therapeutic settings with trained guides—and that is how people should take them. I've never regretted taking psychedelics. In fact, I'm glad I took them. The experience lives with me to this day. Recently, nearing age seventy, with the help of a guide, I have had several profound, spiritual experiences with psilocybin mushrooms and LSD.

SHOOTING RIOTS, ROCK STARS, AND TEAR GAS

Meanwhile, as an LNS photographer, I traveled around the country, photographing demonstrations, riots, tear gas, police violence, the Black Panthers, hippies, Abbie's yippies, the Weathermen faction of SDS, and the emerging rock and roll stars of the '60s. While photographing huge antiwar demonstrations in New York and Washington, or the battle over People's Park in Berkeley, I always carried several items with me: a helmet, gas mask, two Leica M4s, and my trusty Nikon F. In case the police busted me, I always wrote my lawyer's phone number on my wrist.

It was exhilarating—and frightening at times—when the police attacked the demonstrators. It was exhausting, too, running back and forth to photograph as many as a half million people marching. Luckily, I was issued a prized New York City official police press pass (not just a press ID), which entitled me to cross police barricades and venture just about anywhere.

For a photographer, tear gas was particularly tricky. Demonstrators would pick up the tear gas canisters and throw them back at the police. I didn't want the police to think I was doing it. After one day of heavy tear gassing at a demonstration in Washington, I removed my gas mask and went to a party at a Georgetown townhouse. After a short while, we were all coughing, gagging, and crying. It was our clothes—they were saturated with tear gas, and we were regassing ourselves again in the close proximity of the party.

Sometimes the police were particularly nasty. They would allow demonstrators onto a street, then block all exits and fire tear gas into the middle of the totally nonviolent, peaceful crowd. (Recently I saw the same thing happen during the demonstrations against George Floyd's murder and ongoing police violence.) The cops once did this to us in front of the US Department of Justice's headquarters, with Attorney General John Mitchell clearly visible, watching from his office window. The only way out was to run a gauntlet of cops hitting everybody with their nightsticks. Fortunately, my police press pass protected me.

My LNS credentials and police pass also got lucky me free weekend entry to the legendary Fillmore East, where I photographed the great musicians of the day, including Howlin' Wolf, B. B. and Albert King, Jefferson Airplane, the Grateful Dead, Creedence Clearwater Revival, Country Joe and the Fish, Jeff Beck with Rod Stewart at their US debut together, Sly and the Family Stone, the Doors, Miles Davis, Bob Marley, and, most memorably, Janis Joplin with Big Brother and the Holding Company. Janis's voice was full of raw pain and great love at the same time. It was truly haunting, as was watching her singing while constantly swigging a bottle of Wild Turkey. I also took pictures of the Rolling Stones in concert in New York. Heady stuff for a seventeen-year-old.

A mock crucifixion during an antiwar rally, Washington, D.C., May 9, 1970.

SHOOTING THE REVOLUTION
'60s PROTEST PHOTOGRAPHY

TOP *Women demonstrate outside Fort Dix, New Jersey, where soldiers who refused to go to Vietnam were kept jailed in the stockade, October 12, 1969.* **BOTTOM** *Protestors overturn an army jeep in the Reflecting Pool during the "Honor America Day Smoke-In," Washington, D. C., July 4, 1970.* **OPPOSITE TOP** *Early gay liberation protest, New York City, April 15, 1970.* **OPPOSITE BOTTOM** *Yippies march with "Pigasus," their candidate for president, New York City, September 1968.*

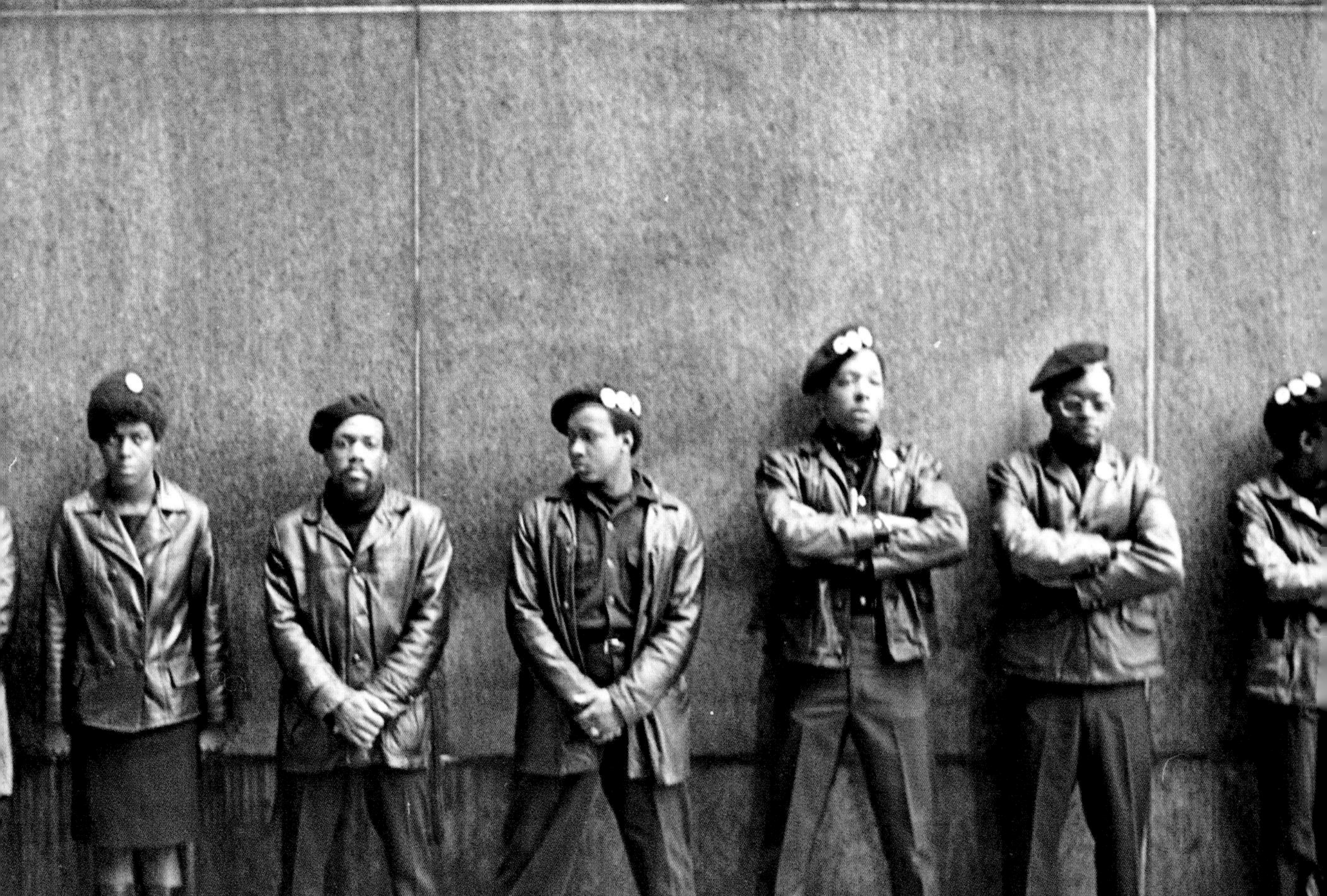
THE ULTIMATE JUSTICE OF THE PEOPLE

CHAPTER 4

CHAOS, RAGE, BOMBS, AND NIXON

IN WHICH I LEARN...

- **THE DANGERS OF SECTARIANISM, RAGE, AND VIOLENCE.**

- **HOW TO APPEAL ACROSS A WIDE RACIAL RAINBOW COALITION.**

- **HOW TO CHANNEL RAGE INTO POSITIVE ACTIVISM.**

- **HOW RIGHTEOUS EMOTIONS CAN TURN INTO NARCISSISM AND DERAIL EFFECTIVE TACTICS.**

My introduction to the racism of American jurisprudence came during the Chicago Seven trial. Defendant and Black Panther leader Bobby Seale had insisted on delaying the trial until his lawyer, Charles Garry, could get to Chicago. The judge refused. Seale, who then defended himself, objected. Loudly. The judge ordered something I thought unimaginable in US courts: Big, burly federal marshals grabbed Seale, bound him to his chair, and put a gag in his mouth. Pandemonium erupted as spectators screamed and flung themselves on the cops, knocking them to the floor as they attempted to protect Seale. "Wow," I thought, watching the melee, "so this is what the law does to Black people." As a privileged white kid, I had only learned of Black oppression from books—now I was seeing it played out dramatically in front of me and the whole nation. (You can see it re-created in Aaron Sorkin's Netflix film *The Trial of the Chicago 7*).

I also spent time photographing other Black Panther leaders at their Oakland, California, headquarters, including Huey P. Newton, David Hilliard, and others. On one assignment in Harlem, I photographed the Black Panther Party's youngest member, seventeen-year-old Jamal Joseph. Subsequently, he was arrested as one of the Panther 21. The case involved twenty-one New York Panthers who were rounded up on charges of plotting mayhem and violence, allegedly including a plan to plant bombs

OPPOSITE *Black Panthers demonstrate at the New York City courthouse in support of the "Panther 21" defendants, April 11, 1969.*
PREVIOUS PAGE *Protestors trying to down the flag at an anti-Vietnam war demonstration in Washington D.C., April 24, 1971.*

Chicago Black Panther head Fred Hampton, October 11, 1969.

Black Panther leader Fred Hampton was murdered by the FBI and the Chicago police in a fusillade of machine gun bullets through the wall of his bedroom while he slept. This is hard for people to believe, but it's a well-documented fact. Fred's bodyguard was an FBI informant, who fed him sleeping pills that night. The next day, the Panthers showed the media his bloody bed. Hampton's family sued and eventually the cops paid a large settlement to the family for this intentional, planned, deliberate murder of a Black leader. You can learn more from the recent Hollywood film *Judas and the Black Messiah*. It's based on the story of the FBI informant who helped arrange Fred's murder.

Black Panthers supporting the "Panther 21" defendants at the New York City courthouse, April 11, 1969.

at the New York Botanical Garden. Jamal spent months in prison. So did another of the Panther 21, Afeni Shakur, Tupac Shakur's mom. All twenty-one Panthers were eventually acquitted on all charges. It turned out that police informers had fabricated the whole thing to destroy the Panthers and their programs, like free breakfasts for school kids. It was pure police harassment.

I also photographed Black Panther leader Fred Hampton, the amazing twenty-year-old who headed the Chicago chapter. The police were particularly worried about Fred because he was forging alliances with white workers and Chicano gang members against their common oppressors. Watching his speeches today, you'll see a modern-day guide to how to appeal across the racial spectrum. He called it the Rainbow Coalition.

THE WEATHERMEN'S BOMBS HELP NIXON

LNS was a chapter of Students for a Democratic Society (SDS), the main organizing vehicle for students opposing the Vietnam War. Founded by University of Michigan student Tom Hayden and others involved in the free speech movement at Berkeley in 1964, it had chapters on hundreds of college campuses. SDS's founding document, "The Port Huron Statement," is making a comeback today. I'm not surprised. It's still remarkably relevant and prescient.

But SDS was imploding. Ideological differences rocked the organization, in particular a conflict between the doctrinaire Progressive Labor Party and the more adaptable, more countercultural faction. The latter became known as the Weathermen, after the Bob Dylan lyrics "you don't need a weatherman to know which way the wind blows." A group

SDS Weathermen members (left to right) Jim Mellen, Peter Clapp, John Jacobs, Bill Ayers, and Terry Robbins march during the "Days of Rage," Chicago, October 11, 1969.

of us LNSers attended the annual SDS convention in Chicago in June 1969 where this conflict came to a head. As I entered the hall, I saw hundreds of Progressive Labor Party activists chanting and waving Mao's *Little Red Book* in unison, like it was some kind of Chinese Communist Party meeting. I'd wager not a few police agents were among them to intentionally divide the movement.

The leaders of the Weathermen, among them the charismatic Bernardine Dohrn, Mark Rudd, and others, succeeded in expelling Progressive Labor, who filed out in protest, never to return to SDS, thank goodness. I photographed the whole thing.

But soon, the Weathermen went berserk. They were mostly a bunch of white, upper-middle-class Ivy League-educated kids, extremely privileged. One of them, Bill Ayers, was the son of the CEO of the main utility in Chicago, Commonwealth Edison. Their understandable anger at the war and the oppression and murder of the Black Panthers soon morphed, however, into craziness and violence.

I saw the Weathermen craziness up close and personal. My live-in girlfriend, Barbara, joined them. She came home to our apartment very late one day, with torn clothes and bruises on her face and body. She said, "The most wonderful thing just happened when I joined the Weathermen to break into a Pittsburgh high school to liberate the oppressed students. We fought the police." Yikes, it immediately reminded me of finding my mother in the lobby of our apartment building when she went mad.

In October 1969, the Weatherman called for a series of actions in Chicago. They called it the Days of Rage. I photographed a large group of them marching into Chicago's Gold Coast neighborhood when, suddenly, they all pulled police nightsticks from under their clothes and

Rudd tried to recruit me to move to Chicago and help run the paper. Luckily, I had the good sense to turn them down.

Had I gone with them, who knows what might have happened to me. They all soon went underground, hiding from the police as they planted bombs at the Pentagon, in the US Capitol, and at police headquarters in New York and other cities. And one small group of them, some of whom I knew, made a big mistake. They blew themselves up while making bombs at a townhouse on West 11th Street in Manhattan. Apparently, the bombs

THE WEATHERMEN WENT CRAZY. THEY BECAME A CULT.

started smashing every window in the luxury buildings along Lake Michigan. I thought, "Gee, this is completely stupid." It will turn the public against the antiwar demonstrators—which it did. The police actually opened fire on them—the only time I saw cops shooting demonstrators.

The next day, the Weatherwomen marched waving North Vietnamese flags. This time, the police acted preemptively, arresting all of them and twisting their arms violently behind their backs. I felt bad for the women, but I couldn't really blame the police for stopping them before things got out of hand.

Around this time, the Weathermen took over the SDS newspaper, a normally staid publication called *New Left Notes*. To show you the mentality, they immediately changed the name to *FIRE!*, including the exclamation point. Their thinking was apocalyptic. Bernardine Dohrn and Mark

were intended to be exploded at Fort Dix, the New Jersey army base where soldiers stopped before going to Vietnam.

The Weathermen went crazy, no question about it. They became a cult centered around the beautiful and commanding Dohrn, who was soon on the FBI's Ten Most Wanted Fugitive list. While I didn't participate, I heard about multiple LSD sessions the group used to "raise their consciousness" and potentially expose any police agents in their midst (on the theory undercover agents would refuse the drug). I believe the Weathermen's profligate use of LSD contributed to their feelings of grandiosity, a classic psychotic symptom the drug can induce, as in "We are going to overthrow the US government by force." Sure. At one point, they even celebrated Charles Manson's attack on rich LA celebrities. The Weatherman devolved into madness. (For the best account, read Mark Rudd's remarkably revealing and self-critical memoir *Underground: My Life with SDS and the Weatherman*.)

Another crazy cultlike group I came across at the time came from an anarchist commune on New York's Lower East Side. For some unfathomable reason, they called themselves the Motherfuckers. They embraced a greasy biker aesthetic and were omnipresent at demonstrations and meetings. The group joined a bunch of us alternative press and LNS types in chartered buses from New York to an underground press convention in Madison, Wisconsin. We stopped at a restaurant on the New Jersey Turnpike, where the Motherfuckers passed word that all fifty of us should leave the restaurant without paying, as our "revolutionary" act. We all filed out without leaving a dime, even for the waitresses I'm afraid, and got back on the bus. I was terrified, convinced the New Jersey state troopers would pull us over and take us off to jail at any moment. But nothing happened.

There was a lesson in all this. Activists sometimes fall into acting on their emotions and rage, rather than employing smart tactics to win majority opinion and thereby gain power. Ideological rigidity and sectarianism are constant problems— and always will be. I've seen it again and again. Another wave of this is sweeping parts of the progressive movement right now. The violence of the Weathermen and, later, the Black Liberation Army, sectarianism on the left, the use of violent rhetoric, the failure to put forward a clear program and language that appeals to most working Americans—these all contributed to the Left's failure to gain power, which continues to this day. The lesson: Channel your anger in ways that win

the hearts of suburban soccer moms, the swing voters in our country.

Despite many foolish errors, '60s activism did win some big victories: an end to the Vietnam War and the draft, a decrease in institutional racism (although nowhere near enough), the end of legal segregation, increases in personal freedom, and greater acceptance of LGBTQ+ rights (though again, much remains to be done). Barack Obama would never have become president without the '60s.

THE WOMEN'S AND GAY RIGHTS MOVEMENTS EMERGE

I witnessed the women's and gay rights movements emerge in the late '60s. It played out at LNS. Like all movements of oppressed people, as they first gather steam, they can channel pent-up rage and act emotionally charged and difficult. I witnessed the women of the LNS collective wake up to their subjugation, often at the hands of their male partners. Through a painful but necessary cathartic process, many couples broke up and families were destroyed. It was intense.

I photographed the first gay liberation demonstrations in New York, impressed by their passion and creativity. LNS had a reporter at the rebellion at the now iconic Stonewall Inn in New York, where for the first time, gay people fought back against the police.

My mentor at LNS, Allen Young, came out as gay. It was very difficult for him. Just a couple of years before, doing so would have cost him his job and many friends. But things were

Women protest during President Richard Nixon's inauguration, Washington, D.C., January 21, 1969.

changing fast. During a psychedelic experience shared with other LNSers, Allen confessed he was in love with me. "David, you'll never know what life is really like till you hold another man in your arms," he said. This was startling enough for a seventeen-year-old, but on psychedelics it hit me even harder. I did respect and love Allen, and told him so, but also stressed I was 100 percent straight. We remain friends to this day.

CONSENSUS OR CHAOS? LEAVING LNS

Before my book *Shots* was canceled, I signed another contract with Macmillan for a book of photographs I planned to take in North Vietnam and Cuba. I wanted to show Americans what was really happening in those countries. But this set me up for a huge confrontation with the women on the LNS Collective, contributing to my decision to leave in 1970.

I was brash, insensitive, insecure, and certainly arrogant and sexist. I was striving to be open to new ways of seeing the world, but was only seventeen. As my girlfriend at that time, Barbara, told me recently, "David, you had trouble listening to other people and acting collectively." Yes, I did, and I made many other mistakes, to my lasting regret.

As the LNS women exercised their new-found power, they decided I had become too big for my britches. They accused me of becoming "too famous" as a photographer. It was time, they decided, to put others forward. They pulled me off the Vietnam/Cuba photo book, selecting instead a woman who had some talent but was brand new to photography. Not only did this seem unfair, but I was also sure Macmillan would cancel the project if someone unknown, untested, and essentially unpublished was sent in my place. Which is exactly what happened. Macmillan pulled out completely, and the opportunity evaporated.

At the same time, the LNS women objected to a photograph I had selected for *Shots*. It showed a young girl of about twelve smoking a joint. "She looks like a cocktease," they said and ordered me to delete it. I could understand questioning a twelve-year-old getting high, but I thought the "cocktease" business was mistaken—and ridiculous.

OUR RHETORIC AND SECTARIANISM TURNED THE PUBLIC AGAINST US.

I decided on my own to keep that photo. When the book was finally published in 1971, there it was.

Meanwhile, I felt conflicted. The women almost had me convinced I was becoming "too famous" and should give up photography. Instead, I quit LNS. I made plans to move to California to join Jane Fonda's efforts to organize American GIs who opposed the war.

In retrospect, I realize I was an arrogant kid, but I have seen the Left turn on its own time and time again. Unless people are really careful, righteous emotions can turn into narcissism and an excessive focus on feelings to the detriment of smart strategy and effective tactics. Today, the problem manifests as an excessive focus on identity politics. Identity is important for sure. But when it displaces all other issues, it limits our appeal to a mass audience. It allows the Right to win.

I questioned the ultra-democratic, faux equality excesses of the LNS collective. And I still do, as I see the Left reject leaders in favor of consensus. Sure, when you can achieve it, consensus is great. But throughout history, leaders have always been essential. You can't win a war without generals. Refusing to appoint and follow leaders is another kind of individualism. You don't find this questioning of social and political leadership in poor countries—only in those that are wealthy. It's a luxury I don't think we can afford.

In the '60s, the Left used media and popular culture to communicate brilliantly with the public, changing the values of a generation. The civil rights and antiwar movements were largely won on television. But our excesses, rhetoric, utopianism, sectarianism, ideological rigidity, and even violence soon turned important parts of the public against us. As did our sliding into left-wing rhetoric, identity politics, and political correctness, which plagues the Left again today.

Then Nixon and corporate America mounted a counterattack. It began with Lewis Powell, who became a Supreme Court justice. Before joining the Court, he wrote a detailed memo urging business and the Right to set up a network of think tanks—the Heritage Foundation, the American Enterprise Institute, the Federalist Society, the American Legislative Exchange Council, and others. These institutions allowed the Right to define the Left as un-American and crazy—and defeat us. They succeeded and continue to dominate the conversation today.

Disillusioned, confused, and burned out on New York, I left for California. Along the way, I stopped to visit some people I had met who lived in a hippie political commune in Ann Arbor, Michigan. I ended up staying there for six years. For me, those years marked another major period of learning how to be a progressive media activist.

CHAPTER 5

THE POLITICAL POWER OF ROCK AND ROLL

IN WHICH I LEARN...

- SIMPLE SLOGANS ARE POWERFUL.

- DON'T BE BLINDED BY IDEOLOGY.

- MUSIC IS THE GREAT UNIFIER.

- LISTENING TO CRITICISM IS HELPFUL— AND CRUCIAL.

- THE IMPORTANCE OF EVENTS HAVING NEWS HOOKS TO APPEAL TO THE MEDIA.

Entertainment has tremendous power to influence politics— and even the courts. I learned this in 1971 when a small group of us harnessed rock and roll to free Michigan political prisoner John Sinclair. We organized John Lennon and Yoko Ono, Stevie Wonder, and many other rock stars to play a benefit concert before an audience of fifteen thousand in Ann Arbor. Abbie Hoffman and Jerry Rubin had been spending time with John and Yoko in New York—they recruited them to come to Ann Arbor and perform. Three days later, Sinclair was released from prison.

The John Sinclair Freedom Rally was the biggest thing that had happened in Michigan in decades—imagine! A Beatle in Ann Arbor! The Beatles had just broken up, but John and Yoko's mythological power to command media attention continued. Their coming to town got huge attention throughout Michigan and the entire Midwest. They were "bigger than Jesus," as Lennon once quipped—and quickly regretted saying.

But Beatles magic worked.

Sinclair had been convicted for giving two free joints of marijuana to an undercover narcotics agent. He appealed, filing a constitutional challenge to the state for classifying the herb as a dangerous narcotic like heroin—as our antiquated federal laws still do to this day. In cases like Sinclair's, Michigan courts had a long history of routinely granting bond, pending appeals. But a horrid judge denied bond and sent Sinclair to prison. Just before the concert, the Michigan Supreme Court also refused Sinclair's motion for bail.

Me working the phones for the John Sinclair Freedom Rally. December, 1971, age 19.

Sinclair had already served several years of a ten-year sentence in a maximum-security prison for the sale of two marijuana joints, often in solitary confinement. Actually, they weren't joints—they were just roaches that he gave to an undercover agent for free.

Then came the December 10 concert at the huge University of Michigan arena. Acts included Lennon, Ono, Stevie Wonder, Bob Seger, Commander Cody, folk singer Phil Ochs, jazz great Archie Shepp, and a host of speakers, including Black Panther Chairman Bobby Seale, poet Allen Ginsberg, and Chicago Seven defendants Rennie Davis, Jerry Rubin, and David Dellinger.

It was a twelve-hour extravaganza, broadcast live on TV and radio all over the state. There were pounds of marijuana displayed openly in the aisles of Crisler Center that night—the smell alone was enough to get you high. The police couldn't do a thing, although they certainly wanted to bust everyone there.

The concert took place on a Friday night, and media coverage of the event dominated the news all week. The Michigan Supreme Court and the state's politicians were stunned. Then, magically, on Monday morning, the court reversed itself, granting appeal bond and releasing Sinclair immediately. Not long after, they also threw out the state's marijuana laws as unconstitutional—as Sinclair had asked throughout his years in prison.

I thought, "Man, rock and roll is powerful!" The sustained media attention changed Michigan's political and judicial dynamics over a weekend. This lesson on the impact culture and celebrity can

Official poster for the John Sinclair Freedom Rally, Ann Arbor, Michigan, December 10, 1971.

THE SONG

John Lennon even wrote a song, "John Sinclair," a few weeks before the concert, which Michigan rock radio stations played constantly.

It ain't fair, John Sinclair
In the stir for breathing air
Won't you care for
John Sinclair?
In the stir for breathing air
Let him be, set him free
Let him be like you and me
They gave him ten for two
What else can
the judges do?
Gotta, gotta, gotta, gotta,
Gotta, gotta, gotta
set him free
If he'd been a soldier man
Shooting gooks in Vietnam
If he was the CIA
Selling dope and making hay
He'd be free, they'd
let him be
Breathing air, like
you and me
They gave him ten for two
What else can
the judges do?
Gotta, gotta, gotta, gotta,

Gotta, gotta, gotta
set him free
They gave him ten for two
They got Pun
Plamondon too.
Gotta, gotta, gotta, gotta,
Gotta, gotta, gotta
set him free
Was he jailed for
what he done?
Or representing everyone
Free John now, if we can
From the clutches
of the man
Let him be, lift the lid
Bring him to his
wife and kids
They gave him ten for two
What else can the
bastards do?
Gotta, gotta, gotta, gotta,
Gotta, gotta, gotta, gotta,
Gotta, gotta, gotta
set him free

FREE JOHN SINCLAIR AND ALL POLITICAL PRISONERS!

JOHN SINCLAIR FREEDOM RALLY

FRIDAY
DEC
10
1971

FRIDAY
DEC
10
1971

JOHN LENNON & YOKO ONO
STEVIE WONDER · BOB SEGER · COMMANDER CODY
ED SANDERS · BOBBY SEALE · TEAGARDEN & VANWINKLE · ALLEN GINSBERG
PHIL OCHS · ARCHIE SHEPP & ROSWELL RUDD WITH CJQ · JERRY RUBIN · THE UP
RENNIE DAVIS · DAVE DELLINGER · DAVID PEEL · FR. JAMES GROPPI
MC's BOB RUDNICK & ANNE LAVASSEUR

CRISLER ARENA
ANN ARBOR

Gary Grimshaw

Gary Grimshaw

have on events, cognition, and political power has stayed with me throughout my career. Politicians respond to the pressures of repeated news coverage and public opinion. Celebrity participation helps get coverage and attention, which adds to the pressure.

With the release order in hand, Sinclair's wife, Leni, along with their two toddlers, drove to Michigan's Jackson State Prison. As Sinclair strode out of prison, suddenly free, a small army of reporters converged on him, microphones and television lights everywhere. Asked what he would do when he got home that day, Sinclair told the cameras, "I'm going to smoke a joint!"

Lennon's appearance at the John Sinclair Freedom Rally scared President Richard Nixon. The FBI was watching, letting the president know that Lennon, Ono, Hoffman, Sinclair, and Rubin were now plotting a series of anti-Nixon, antiwar concerts across the country, which were to culminate in 1972 at a giant rally at the Republican National Convention in Miami. In response, Nixon moved to deport Lennon to England, using the pretext of Lennon's earlier arrest for the possession of marijuana. Sadly, but perhaps understandably, this led Lennon and Ono to cease all their political activity. Lennon and Ono had also financed a feature-length documentary

"It ain't fair, John Sinclair..." Yoko Ono and John Lennon performing at the John Sinclair Freedom Rally, December 10, 1971, in Ann Arbor, Michigan. That's yippie Jerry Rubin on congas.

Openly smoking pot at a press conference after the Michigan Supreme Court struck down the state marijuana laws. Ann Arbor, Michigan, March 1972. From left: Genie Plamondon, John Sinclair, Leni Sinclair, and me.

of the Sinclair Freedom Rally, *Ten for Two*, but with Nixon breathing down Lennon's neck, they refused to release it. The film has still never been seen. What a shame. It's amazing! (You can learn more about this whole episode in the excellent documentary *The U.S. vs. John Lennon*.)

Meanwhile, the Michigan Supreme Court's action meant there was temporarily no law against marijuana on the books in the state of Michigan. How did we respond at Sinclair's commune, where I now lived? We called a press conference, of course, and smoked pot openly in front of the many TV cameras. "It's legal!" we proclaimed. This, of course, prodded the Michigan Legislature to act quickly and pass a new constitutional marijuana law. So, we turned to legalizing pot in Ann Arbor. In 1972, we succeeded, essentially getting the police off our backs once and for all. More on that in a bit.

Okay, so how did I get involved in freeing John Sinclair at the age of nineteen? Here's the story.

SEX, DRUGS, AND JOHN COLTRANE

As I mentioned, after leaving Liberation News Service in New York, I was headed for California, but I stopped off at Sinclair's hippie commune in Ann Arbor. He was in prison, but I had met his wife, Leni, during one of her trips to New York to raise funds for the campaign to free him.

The commune was housed in a big yellow former fraternity house in the middle of a wealthy Ann Arbor neighborhood, close to the university campus. Indian tapestries hung from the ceilings. Lava lamps shimmered. The walls were covered with bright multicolored psychedelic rock and roll and marijuana posters. The smell of marijuana was everywhere, and a bottle of liquid LSD sat in the refrigerator. Thirty long-hair activist hippies lived there—most were runaways from working class families and wore patched clothes, bell-bottoms, and boots. They frequently took LSD while pursuing a "political education" by reading Mao's *Little Red Book*. The commune was supported by an in-house rock and roll band called the Up, by dealing large quantities of marijuana, and by charitable contributions from some sympathetic rich people. It was a true commune—there was no private property. You had to ask permission to buy a pair of blue jeans, which was often denied. One summer night in 1970, at age eighteen, I arrived at the Ann Arbor commune house after a long bus trip from Ohio with a photographer friend, Ken Light. I felt depressed and disoriented, having just abandoned my promising career as a radical photojournalist in the hope of becoming a political organizer instead.

I was still smarting about the way the women at LNS had put me down. They were right about my brashness and big ego. I was an arrogant punk kid, regularly getting my photos and credits into *The New York Times*, *Life* magazine, and *Newsweek*, among other publications. I had signed a contract for a photo book with a major publisher. And for a teenager, I was remarkably good at capturing iconic images. But success had gone to my head. In retrospect, it's clear that I compensated for my childhood difficulties with false-confident swaggering. Insecurity is the mother of many people's personalities. Ego boosting was my way of compensating for feeling unworthy deep inside.

When I arrived at the commune, after greetings and several large cannabis spliffs, I was assigned to share one of the waterbeds for the night with the commune's only Black member, Hiawatha Bailey, a tall, lanky, creative artist. I didn't know he was gay but soon learned. As he pushed his legs against me, I politely demurred. He was very cool, and we became friends.

SEDUCED FOR THE CAUSE BY LENI SINCLAIR

My plan was to spend a few days there and continue to California. But I felt curious about the organization behind the commune, at that time also known as the White Panther Party. Its charismatic leader, hippie jazz and blues fanatic John Sinclair, was in prison, sentenced to ten years for two joints, as I've described. The commune was focused on the campaign to free him, which became a national cause célèbre. I'd heard quite a bit about it in New York, and it was widely covered in the underground press.

Sinclair had been one of the early beat poets of Detroit, where he organized an artists' collective called Trans-Love Energies. The police didn't take too kindly to these flamboyant long-hairs and harassed them constantly, mostly with arrests for marijuana possession. Inspired by the Black Panther Party, whose members had taken up guns and declared their right of self-defense, Sinclair and his acolytes did the same. They bought guns to protect themselves from the police. Bad move.

When I arrived in Ann Arbor, Sinclair was in solitary confinement. And the campaign to free him wasn't making much progress. Leni, originally from Communist East Germany, was in her thirties. She was petite, with long, straight blonde hair. Her accent was so thick it was sometimes difficult to understand her recitations from

jazz musician Sun Ra) and Cecilia (named after Fidel Castro's girlfriend Celia Sánchez). Leni became my sexual-political-music professor—and introduced me to the great Black American music that has sustained me emotionally ever since. Still, it was weird. I wasn't in love and neither was she. I knew she was mainly using me to help Sinclair.

MY FIRST CAMPAIGN: SINCLAIR'S RELEASE

I was feeling more than a little guilty about sleeping with Sinclair's wife when she asked me to accompany her to visit Sinclair in prison. I had

SINCLAIR'S SLOGAN WAS "ROCK AND ROLL, DOPE, AND FUCKING IN THE STREETS."

Marx, Lenin, and Mao. Like Sinclair, she was a jazz fanatic, always playing John Coltrane and the avant-garde jazz musician Sun Ra on the record player. She and Sinclair had two young children living in the commune.

Leni fed me psychedelics, and after a marathon trip in the commune's center of gravity— the music room lined with hundreds of LPs— she seduced me to the sounds of Coltrane and Monk. She was only the second woman I had ever slept with. It was all heady and exotic. Why did Leni want me? Because she saw potential in this skinny, high school dropout to help run a campaign to get her husband out of prison. Who knows how she saw this, but she did. I moved into the commune. I thought I'd stay only a little while—which turned into six years.

Leni had me sleep in her room, next door to her daughters, Sunny (named for the avant garde

never set foot in a prison, and certainly not under these circumstances. Jackson State Prison in Michigan is a dark, foreboding place in the middle of nowhere. After going through multiple searches and checkpoints, we were brought to a towering, broad-shouldered hippie in prison garb. The guy was clearly charismatic, and, after more than two years inside, he was desperate to get out.

I had never met Sinclair but had followed his case and read many of his writings and interviews. In New York radical circles, he was viewed as something of a culture hero and booster of the peculiar notion that long-haired freaks would make a revolution. His slogan was "rock and roll, dope, and fucking in the streets." That was Sinclair—always a bit over the top. At first, I felt wowed by his charisma, but it didn't take long to feel turned off by his overbearing personality and willingness to use people.

During that prison visit, Sinclair asked if I would help lead the campaign for his release. Who, me? Nineteen, a high school dropout, and new in town? His request signaled how desperate he was. But Leni saw leadership potential in me that I didn't see and touted me to Sinclair. Not to mention that they didn't have a dime to pay anyone more experienced and I was willing to work for free.

I said I would try—under Sinclair's direction. What followed was an extended correspondence course in activist public relations. Sinclair handwrote me long, detailed, letters on yellow legal pad paper, instructing me about how to run the campaign for his release. I was to call this reporter and that columnist, stage all kinds of theatrical actions to attract television cameras, and solicit help from radical celebrities, especially the two I already knew: Abbie Hoffman and Jerry Rubin in New York. Sinclair provided talking points and a step-by-step action plan. Meanwhile, I continued to share a bed with Leni, not knowing if Sinclair knew. We never discussed it and haven't to this day.

I had to learn fast—but having been a faithful reader of the *New Republic*, *Commentary*, and the *Nation* from age fourteen, even without high school or college, I had a decent understanding of our political possibilities. Sinclair had designed his case as a constitutional challenge to Michigan's marijuana laws. The courts repeatedly refused to let him out on bail, pending the constitutional challenge, which was unusual and clearly politically motivated. He was frequently locked in solitary confinement for trying to organize other prisoners.

John Sinclair at home soon after his release from prison in late 1971.

KICK OUT THE JAMS

Why were the Michigan authorities so determined to keep Sinclair locked up? You might think they took his rhetoric seriously—as he called for "rock and roll, dope, and fucking in the streets." You might think it was the guns Sinclair and his White Panther Party embraced to defend themselves against police harassment. Or his exhortations to young people to smoke marijuana openly. All these played a role. But to my way of thinking, the government wanted Sinclair muzzled mainly because of Sinclair's secret weapon. He managed the popular Michigan rock and roll band the Motor City Five (MC5). This gave him a direct connection to the state's young people, and the establishment was very concerned that Sinclair was turning their children against them. He was.

I'd seen the MC5 at the Hotel Diplomat in New York and hated them. Their music was a deafening wall of noise to me then. It's a measure of my own cultural and sensual transformation that I later came to view them as moving musical innovators. Sinclair signed the band to Elektra Records. Their first album included the hit song "Kick Out the Jams," which originally rallied listeners to "kick out the jams, motherfuckers."

It was a minor hit nationally but a major force in the industrial Midwest. In the heartland, the song engendered enormous pushback from Christian preachers and politicians—so Elektra ordered the band to record a sanitized version that went "kick out the jams, brothers and sisters." They also removed Sinclair's liner notes, which were a call to hippie revolution.

One of the first punk bands, the MC5 urged followers to break with their parents, smoke pot, make love, and rebel. The band and Sinclair created a huge mythology around them—and the state of Michigan believed it. (Sinclair also managed the Ann Arbor band Iggy and the Stooges. Iggy later transformed himself into Iggy Pop.)

Like Abbie Hoffman, Sinclair thought the countercultural movement of young people in the '60s was a potentially potent political force. Music was the great unifier, spreading higher political and cultural awareness. Sinclair called it the Guitar Army of young people in his book of the same name. Abbie wrote a book with a similar thesis that he called *Woodstock Nation*. At that time, music was, indeed, spreading utopian ideals: "Smile on your brother, everybody get together." But they overstated their case. At Woodstock, Abbie got up on the main stage during a set by the Who to preach his concept of hippies composing

know if Pun planted that explosive, but he was arrested. I visited him in federal prison in Indiana and worked with his lawyers to publicize his case. Nixon's attorney general at the time, John Mitchell, said he had authorized warrantless electronic surveillance of the White Panther Party because, the administration claimed, it was attempting to subvert the government. Pun, John Sinclair, and John Forrest—who were both tried with him—won ruling after ruling against the government for wiretapping without a warrant. The wiretap, we later learned, included our phone at the commune. They had transcripts of everything we said—every love

NIXON'S ATTORNEY GENERAL HAD OUR COMMUNE PHONE WIRETAPPED.

a "nation." Pete Townshend hit Abbie over the head and pushed him off the stage. I guess he found the rap overstated. Still, many, if not most, young people at the time shared a common ideal of more peace and love, less racism, and an end to the Vietnam War. It's hard to imagine now, but those feelings were definitely intensified by the music of the time.

Meanwhile, another leader of the commune was also in trouble with the law. Lawrence "Pun" Plamondon held the grandiose title of Minister of Defense of the White Panther Party. As I settled into Michigan, he was on the FBI's Ten Most Wanted Fugitives list, charged with planting a bomb at the CIA's Ann Arbor recruiting office. What also blew up was the revelation that the CIA maintained an office in town. By law, the CIA could not have domestic offices. To this day, I don't

affair, dope deal, everything.

The government appealed every verdict until the case reached the US Supreme Court, which ruled—8 to 0—that the government could not spy on its citizens domestically simply by declaring them "terrorists." This was a landmark decision, whose Fourth Amendment protections would be challenged again some thirty years later when President Bush started warrantless wiretapping after 9/11.

I first met Pun at an alternative media conference in Ann Arbor before moving there—he was guarding the entrance with rifles. Pun hailed from Michigan's remote Upper Peninsula. He was a macho guy to say the least. The guns served no purpose other than to bring the police down on us. While lounging on the grass with underground press editors from around the country, we were

In Ann Arbor, I had no idea the FBI was following me. But they were, starting with my Liberation News Service days in New York and continuing for years. I discovered all this a decade later, thanks to a Freedom of Information Act request.

The FBI and the Detroit Police's so-called Red Squad released my voluminous files. They were so detailed, they clearly had informers all over the Left. The names of the informers were blacked out, supposedly to protect them from reprisals.

The FBI claimed that "all individuals involved in New Left extremist activity should be considered dangerous because of their known advocacy and use of explosives, reported acquisition of firearms and incendiary devices, and known propensity for violence." Hey—none of that applied to me whatsoever. Ironically, the accusation

that I advocated violence occurs on the very pages where the FBI files refer to my efforts in 1972 to elect progressive candidates to the Ann Arbor City Council. Apparently, the FBI can't tell the difference between terrorism and voting.

Why did the FBI spy on our electoral activities? Perhaps because, as it noted, we advocated "community control of the police and a change in local narcotic enforcement priorities." Hell, yes. But hey, the FBI also said I "displayed a great deal of political know-how" and that "according to [redacted], Fenton is probably the most articulate and best received public spokesman for this group." I'd sure like to know who [redacted] was!

By 1976, the files show the FBI recommended removing me from the list of potentially violent leftists. From the memorandum to the Acting Director of the FBI, July 17, 1972:

[REDACTED] advised that subject, whose specialty is the press and propaganda, serves essentially as the press agent and PR man for the WPP.

[REDACTED] advised additionally that subject has displayed a great deal of political know how … also that subject has been principally involved in something called the "Michigan Marijuana Initiative," which is an attempt to force the question of legalization of marijuana on the Michigan ballot for 11/72.

In a large "freedom rally" … held at the University of Michigan in December, 1971 … subject was prominent as a key organizer of this event. Subject handled all of the press releases, press conferences, and publicity for this event and demonstrated himself to the satisfaction of WPP leadership as an outstanding public relations man.

suddenly surrounded by uniformed Michigan state troopers. Suddenly, everyone emptied the reefer from their pockets, throwing plastic bags on the ground. I felt terrified! So much for armed self-defense.

WE VOTE TO END MONOGAMY—THAT NIGHT

While involved in the campaign to free Sinclair, I came under the influence of his hippie ideology and culture. My hair grew down past my shoulders—a curly Jewfro tangle. I stopped shaving—not even a trim for me. Every day started and ended with cannabis—but I was no lazy stoner. Leni insisted that the goal of getting high was to increase awareness, not disappear into a smoke haze on the couch. Believe me, that took discipline. So, while high, I wrote press releases, plotted strategy, published the commune's *Ann Arbor Sun* alternative newspaper, started a local radio show, and organized, organized, day and night. Looking back, I certainly wish

I had done more of that sober—it would have been easier. But we celebrated marijuana as a "sacrament" that was key to higher consciousness. There is some truth to that, but we took it to extremes. Ideology can be blinding.

The commune used a chart system to assign tasks: shopping, cooking dinner, answering the phone and front door, doing the laundry, and caring for the three children we were raising communally. I had never cooked more than eggs—suddenly once a week I was cooking macrobiotic vegetarian meals for thirty hippies. We did it from scratch. We hand ground our own organic flour for bread and pasta. I learned to make brown rice pies—which I don't recommend. At first, vegetarianism was weird for this hamburger and meat loaf teenager, but my body started changing for the better with the new diet. I was *feeling* more alert and energized. This was the early days of the sustainable food movement—unquestionably fueled in part by LSD, which by increasing sensual input, helped people realize that the junk-food American diet was, as we called it at the time, "skonk." Our slogan was "You are what you eat." We soon helped start the People's Food Co-op to ensure a steady supply of organic fruits and vegetables. Remember, this was early—1971.

Two of the three children we raised were the Sinclairs' Sunny and Cecilia, and the other, Uma, was the child of the UP's lead singer, Frank Bach, whose estranged wife did not live with us. Back then, Frank was a somewhat rigid, spartan, macrobiotic vegan, and Uma was allowed no animal

products whatsoever, not even milk, cheese, or ice cream. I worried this might be too extreme for a child. Being a strict vegetarian should be an adult choice—but in your twenties, ideological inflexibility comes easily.

Once a week I was assigned to put the kids to bed and sleep next to them. Of course, looking back, having a different person sleeping with them every night of the week didn't exactly help the kids with stability or emotional growth. I believe we took the important idea of shared child-rearing too far. But we took everything to extremes! The isolated nuclear family model isn't right for kids,

LEFT *My communal family. I'm at the top right. Leni Sinclair at the bottom left. Ann Arbor, 1971.* RIGHT *Una Bach, daughter of the band The UP's singer Frank Bach, at the commune, 1971.*

either. A few generations ago, most kids grew up in large, multigenerational homes.

We were out to prove, as opposed to what we called the "death culture," that there was a better, more utopian, collective way to live. We even adopted a somewhat drug-addled version of Maoist and Marxist-Leninist "criticism self-criticism" sessions. Imagine thirty long-hairs sitting around one big dining-room table. The task: Tell everyone what you didn't like about them and how they were falling down at the task of serving the people and organizing. Even though we gave lip service to Mao's admonishment to start and end by praising people—he called it "unity, criticism, unity"—it was *brutal*. People were cruel, taking out all kinds of emotions on others. It was scary. You never knew who might turn on you next. At the same time, these sessions taught me much about myself—it was helpful to listen to criticisms. I learned that no one can see themselves completely—the feedback of others can be crucial. I had first experienced a milder version of this at Liberation News Service, where I was forced to confront my male chauvinism. Years later, at my PR company, I made a point of asking employees to be sure to tell me when I was mistaken or insensitive. I got quite an earful.

At times, our communal drug-crazed life got completely out of hand. Most of us were all barely out of adolescence and had no idea what we were doing. We had broken with the culture of our parents, with religion, with the American diet, and with sexual and social norms of all kinds. Of course, there was a lot of sexual tension at the commune. While this was the early '70s, it was still the free-love '60s at our house. There was no HIV, and sex was very casual and frequent.

At a series of commune meetings, we discussed whether monogamy was the best form of social organization. At one of our meetings, we decided it was not and banned it. Just like that. Thirty hippies sitting around a huge wooden dining-room table took a vote. I don't think it was unanimous, but the majority ruled. So, sure enough, that night, all the couples were instructed to sleep with other people. I mean, it was fine for me—I was single and had a deep crush on one of the married women. What the hell, I thought. Of course, that didn't last more than a week—with people in tears and moving out, we thought better of the edict and went back to "allowing" monogamy. Imagine, that's how crazy we were. And we weren't alone—things like that were happening at hippie and radical enclaves across the country.

We crazily saw ourselves as Maoists leading an American cultural revolution. So, just like in China, we "sentenced" intellectuals to physical labor. I was an intellectual. I was sentenced to scraping and painting the outside of our house for weeks on end in the cold. I hated every minute of it. But whenever I complained, the leadership extended my sentence. There I was, a New Yorker among the children of Michigan's auto workers. I was picked on constantly. It wasn't fair, but without realizing it, I also helped provoke it. I believed in the ideals of the commune, but was a nonconformist at heart. I was also often tone-deaf to the reactions of others. My mother, in her rare lucid moments, used to say to me, "David, you lack tact." That was an understatement. My emotional antennas had not yet developed—that would take years of therapy, and I regret it's still not my strong suit.

WHY I STAYED

I was such an easy target that as a joke, one day our in-house rock band's ace guitarist squirted ten doses of LSD into my mouth. Some joke! It took me two days to come down from the temporary psychosis. During that trip, I strolled among the beautiful, towering trees of Ann Arbor's arboretum and swore I heard people talking about me behind my back. At our house, I thought the kids were laughing at me. But it wasn't true. But that's what an overdose of LSD can do. While there appears to be no lethal dose of LSD, you sure can take too much.

So, with all the abuse, why did I stay at the commune? First, it was educational. I learned so much about politics, organizing, jazz, blues, food, sex, drugs, public relations, the media, rhythm and blues, and rock and roll. The nexus of media and social change made sense, beginning my PR activist career. As a high school dropout, my crazy Ann Arbor life became my University of the Streets—I published a newspaper, hosted a local radio show, created radio ads, called press conferences, and appeared as a spokesperson on radio and TV.

But there was a deeper reason I stayed. The commune became the family I never had. My mother was crazy and gone much of the time. My father was emotionally absent before my parents' divorce and even more after. Sinclair became another father figure, with other commune members becoming my surrogate aunts, uncles, and cousins.

The commune was a dysfunctional family but the best I had. John Sinclair's brother, David, was the strong uncle, running our finances, overseeing the sale of tons of pot to support us, and soliciting donations from wealthy supporters. Leni Sinclair was my lover/teacher and head of ideology. Pun Plamondon's wife, Genie, served as our resident headband-wearing, beaded hippie therapist, astrologer, and tarot card reader. She did my chart and announced I was a double Taurus with Gemini rising. If you believe this stuff, you understand why I'm so stubborn: double Taurus, the bull! And on the flip side, often dependable. We threw the I Ching together, seeking celestial wisdom to figure out our next moves. Frank Bach was our macrobiotic food cop. Shy, introverted, genius artist Gary Grimshaw quietly drew our psychedelic posters, museum pieces to this day.

To put it mildly, I was not the best communard. I loved the ideals in principle, but completely sublimating myself to the group just wasn't who I was at nineteen and twenty. I stood accused of "individualism," and I was guilty.

The slogan of our campaign was "Free John now." And now he was. It was my first public relations campaign. It became clear that by building relationships with prominent journalists we could directly affect public knowledge, influence the narrative, and pressure people in power. Watching Abbie Hoffman manipulate the media to help the antiwar and civil rights movements was another lesson. The key was to create events with news hooks likely to appeal to the media.

I didn't know it at the time, but activist PR would become my life's work. My next project: using hippie and student power to take over the Ann Arbor city government.

ROCK PHOTOGRAPHY

TOP *Sympathy for the Devil: The Rolling Stones at Madison Square Garden, 1969..* **BOTTOM** *B. B. King at the Central Park bandshell, October 1969.* **OPPOSITE** *Janis Joplin, bottle of Wild Turkey in hand, as usual, at the Fillmore East, 1968.*

CHAPTER 6

A $5 FINE FOR MARIJUANA, FREE MEDICAL AND DAY CARE

Now that Sinclair and Plamondon were both out of prison and living with us, we thought, at last, we could make the revolution. Internally, our Ann Arbor hippie commune now became far less communal. The problem, in a word, was Sinclair. We made fewer decisions collectively. Sinclair, the big cheese celebrity returning from prison, became the boss. At first, this wasn't so bad.

We all shared similar goals. But as the month passed, Sinclair became more of a dictator. Sinclair was a classic example of flawed leadership. He used ideology as a smoke screen for his narcissism. Unfortunately, it took me several years to realize this.

HIPPIES TAKE OVER LOCAL GOVERNMENT

In July of 1971, we got lucky. The United States lowered the voting age to eighteen, and the Supreme Court ruled that, instead of voting in their hometowns, students could vote where they attended college. There we were, in a college town of a hundred thousand, almost half of whom were students, at a time when, at least in Ann Arbor, a majority of young people opposed the war, supported civil rights, and smoked pot.

So, we decided to take over the city government. The Ann Arbor City Council had been controlled by Republicans for one hundred years. We assembled a group of progressive candidates to replace them—but had no idea if we'd get any traction in a town with a long history of liberalism at the university and conservatism everywhere else.

The Ann Arbor Sun *staff. I'm in the back on the right; my first wife, Barbara Weinberg, is in front.*

Our first big question was how to fund the campaign. That turned out to be easy. We just went next door. Adjacent to the large ex-fraternity house where we lived was another big old ex-frat house full of communally living marijuana dealers. They were always generous, supported our social and political goals, and provided us with our marijuana "sacrament" gratis in times of need. (One memorable '60s slogan was "Dope will get you through times of no money better than money will get you through times of no dope.")

At the time, Ann Arbor's Democratic party was lame and pretty powerless. So, we helped start a third party, the Human Rights Party, and ran a slate of candidates for city council. Our agenda included decriminalizing marijuana, rent control, free day care, free medical care for city residents, and free summer rock and roll concerts in a city park.

The underground community newspaper we published, the *Ann Arbor Sun*, became the official organ for the Human Rights Party. My media learning curve accelerated as I organized press conferences with the candidates and wrote their radio ads. I had never done this before, but people told me I had a knack, and no one else wanted to do it. In retrospect, the experience was on-the-job training. As it turned out, the rock radio stations and local bands played an important role in spreading excitement about voting.

It was quite a change for a bunch of long-haired hippies to canvass voters, knock on doors, hand out leaflets, and jump into "straight" electoral politics. But we took to it with gusto. While the form—elections—was traditional, the content was radical.

PUBLIC SERVANTS OF POT

To enter the house of pot dealers next door was to be overwhelmed with the smell of cannabis. The house was decorated like ours, with Indian mandala tapestries on the walls and ceilings and large hookah pipes everywhere. I spent many contemplative hours there sampling their wares while doing what hippies do—chatting and listening to music on big speakers. Our neighbors dealt very large quantities of pot—hundreds of pounds—taking enormous personal risks to keep the community supplied. They drove to Mexico in small trucks fitted with camper shells, hid the weed as best they could, and on the return trip, braved vicious police, especially through Arizona and Texas. Someday, I hope we erect a monument to thank the public servants who took enormous risks to keep the creative juices of the '60s and '70s flowing. The dealers agreed to help finance the campaign with the understanding that, if we won, we would get the local police off their—and everyone's—backs.

To our enormous surprise, we won two seats. Our council people—Nancy Wechsler and Jerry DeGrieck—became the crucial swing votes on the city council. Neither the Republicans nor the Democrats could pass anything without them.

Our very first act was to pay back the dope dealers by engineering passage of a local ordinance that made both the possession and sale of cannabis an infraction on the order of a parking ticket, punishable with a maximum $5 fine. The law covered not just possession but also *sales*. This

The cover of the Ann Arbor Sun *touting $5 weed and bomb craters on the diag, May 1972.*

Issue 32   Published by the RAINBOW PEOPLE'S PARTY   May 26-June 9, 1972

WIN A POUND OF COLOMBIAN!

Grand Prize
(Anyone can win--)
1 LB OF COLOMBIAN MARIJUANA

2nd Prize
(4 people win--) 1 WINTER TERM PASS TO THE NEW WORLD FILM COOP FILM SERIES (free admission to over 50 films-- worth $75)

3rd Prize
(10 people win--) 1 HARDBOUND COPY OF GUITAR ARMY (Autographed by John Sinclair) AND 1 YEAR OF THE ANN ARBOR SUN, FREE

4th Prize
(15 people win--) 1 ANN ARBOR SUN T-SHIRT (any size) AND 1 YEAR OF THE ANN ARBOR SUN, FREE

Yes--your eyes do not deceive you! As part of the new SUN Pound-of-Colombian Contest the Ann Arbor SUN will GIVE AWAY, FREE OF CHARGE, one pound of high grade Colombian marijuana for the smoking pleasure of our lucky Grand Prize winner. Other prizes include season passes to the New World Film Co-op Film series (worth $75 each), hardbound copies of Guitar Army autographed by author John Sinclair, Ann Arbor SUN T-shirts, and free 1-year subscriptions to the Ann Arbor SUN.

ANYONE CAN ENTER the SUN Pound-of-Colombian Contest just by filling out an official entry blank and sending it to: Ann Arbor SUN, 603 E.William, Ann Arbor, Mich.,48108. Entries will be accepted and kept in humungous zip-lock bags until our contest closes on January 1,1975.

On January 3, 1975 Michigan Representative Perry Bullard (53 District)

will randomly select entry blanks from the zip-locks. The first name picked gets the pound of Colombian, other names picked get second, third, and fourth prizes, in that order.

Winners will be announced January 24 and Representative Bullard will certify that the Grand Prize Columbian is, indeed, delivered. (The name of the Grand Prize winner will be kept strictly confidential unless the winner authorizes us to do otherwise.)

So send your entry now--anyone can enter, as many times as you like-- but you must use official entry blanks (printed in the Ann Arbor SUN) and include your address and phone number (if any) for your entry to be accepted. And, in these times of inflation, don't forget Freewheelin' Franklin who said:

"Dope will get you through times of no money better than money will get you through times of no dope."

Offical Entry Blank And Home Delivery Subscription Form

This Entry Blank good for residents of ANN ARBOR AND YPSILANTI ONLY

___ I already subscribe. Enter my name in the SUN Pound-of-Colombian Contest.

___ Enter my name in the SUN Pound-of-Colombian Contest and start my subscription to the SUN.

___ I don't want to subscribe right now, but enter my name in the SUN Pound-of-Colombian Contest anyway.

Name _____

Address/Street _____ Apt. No. _____

City/State _____ Zip _____

Phone _____

___ Deliver 4 months (16 issues of the SUN. Cost: $4.00 (25¢ an issue)

___ Deliver 8 months (32 issues of the SUN. Cost: $7.70 (24¢ an issue)

___ Deliver 1 year (48 issues) of the SUN and give me a free book, record, or t-shirt. Cost: $11.00 (23¢ an issue)

___ Payment Enclosed ___ Bill me later

1st Choice Bonus: _____ 2nd Choice: _____

T-Shirt Size: ___ S ___ M ___ L ___ X-L

(Make all checks payable to Rainbow Agency, Inc.)

Offical Entry Blank And Mail Delivery Subscription Form

This Entry Blank good for people OUTSIDE OF AA AND YPSI ONLY

___ I already subscribe. Enter my name in the SUN Pound-of-Colombian Contest.

___ Enter my name in the SUN Pound-of-Colombian Contest and start my subscription to the SUN.

___ I don't want to subscribe right now, but enter my name in the SUN Pound-of-Colombian Contest anyway.

Name _____

Address/Street _____ Apt. No. _____

City/State _____ Zip _____

Phone _____

___ Mail 6 months (24 issues) of the SUN. Cost: $5.50 (23¢ an issue)

___ Mail 1 year (48 issues) of the SUN and a free book, record, or t-shirt. Cost: $10.00 (21¢ an issue) SAVE $2.00

___ Mail 2 years (96 issues) of the SUN and a free book, record, or t-shirt. Cost: $18.00 (19¢ an issue) SAVE $6.00

___ Mail 3 years (144 issues) of the SUN and a free book, record, or t-shirt. Cost: $24.00 (17¢ an issue) SAVE $12.00

___ Payment Enclosed ___ Bill me later

1st Choice Bonus: _____ 2nd Choice: _____

T-Shirt Size: ___ S ___ M ___ L ___ X-L

(Make all checks payable to Rainbow Agency, Inc.)

Don't Forget
If you subscribe to the SUN for 1 year or more we automatically give you your choice of one of these FREE BONUSES: *A beautiful red-on-yellow Ann Arbor SUN t-shirt (s,m,l,or x-l) *GUITAR ARMY by John Sinclair (paperback) *Marion Brown's tasty new jazz album SWEET EARTH FLYING (ABC/Impulse) AND--no matter how long you subscribe -- if you live in Ann Arbor or Ypsilanti we'll HOME DELIVER every copy of your subscription the day we hit the streets, EVERY FRIDAY!

was truly radical in 1973—and at least forty years ahead of its time. The Ann Arbor police could no longer arrest anyone for getting high on pot.

We horse-traded some highway construction funds the Republicans wanted in exchange for their votes to pass city funding of a free medical clinic, located in a medically underserved part of town. Next, we opened a free day care center for working mothers. Finally, we funded free summer rock and roll "tribal gatherings," concerts in the park patrolled by our very own Psychedelic Rangers, so the police—who hated long-hairs

WIN A POUND OF COLOMBIAN POT CONTEST

Unfortunately, sales of the *Ann Arbor Sun* didn't grow as planned. So, we started trying to dream up a promotion that might increase circulation—maybe a contest. While getting high one night, we came up with the obvious choice. We decided on a raffle with a grand prize of a pound of Colombian gold marijuana. Our lawyers advised against it—too risky. When we announced we would proceed anyway, they insisted that we couldn't require purchase of the newspaper to enter—it had to be "no purchase necessary." But we said fuck that: The

THE COURT UPHELD OUR RIGHT TO PUBLISH PHOTOS OF UNDERCOVER NARCS.

anyway—wouldn't be the ones dealing with overdoses or bad trips. This, too, was far ahead of its time. The police should focus on real crimes, not mental health issues.

For the most part, I stopped taking photographs. I was too busy publishing the paper and doing other political work. I still loved photography, but my identity had changed. I was an activist first, so I went where I thought I could have the biggest impact. Plus, I was so busy; working fifteen-hour days, there was no time to think about my own evolution. But now that the Ann Arbor police couldn't do anything about it but write a $5 ticket, I did enjoy photographing local rock bands in front of the enormous marijuana plants we grew in our backyard.

An ad for the Sun's *edgy Win a Pound of Colombian pot contest, 1974.*

whole thing was so illegal anyway that we would require people to buy the *Sun* and then fill out a coupon to enter.

When we held a press conference announcing the Win a Pound of Colombian Pot contest, the media went crazy. The *Sun* featured a back cover photo of the actual pound of Colombian pot we promised to give the winner. The state police threatened us, which was just what we wanted. With so much media coverage of their threat, sales of the paper boomed.

We arranged for the winning entry to be selected by our Democratic Party county commissioner—a sign of how our activism had changed local politics. The drawing took place in front of the Ann Arbor police station, with dozens of journalists on hand and many TV cameras. The commissioner pulled the winning entry from a big brown burlap bag and said, "The winner is—I can't tell you."

THE DARK SIDE OF DRUGS

Marijuana is about as dangerous as drinking a beer, only less so. The celebration of other drugs had a dark side, however. Some hippies were way too casual with stronger drugs. At a party to celebrate an anniversary of the paper, I drank from the proverbial punch bowl. After twenty minutes, I started to feel very strange. I soon realized the punch bowl had been spiked with LSD (by our head of advertising sales, no less). If you've ever taken psychedelics, you know it changes your experience of time. I had a hard time relating to my watch, a bar mitzvah gift, so removed it—and never saw it again. Not long after, our exuberant and creative head of ad sales, Tom Pomaski, died in a car accident while driving stoned. Driving intoxicated on anything is never a good idea.

The winner was a University of Michigan freshman who lived in a dormitory and had smoked weed only once in her life.

Have you ever seen a pound of marijuana? It's *big*. It fills a shopping bag. Boy, was the winner surprised. We covered her head with a brown paper bag with slits for her eyes, nose, and mouth, then snapped her photo holding the pound. The cover headline read "The Winner" and ran with the photo in the next issue of the *Sun*. Truth in advertising was very important to us, but we weren't about to identify her for obvious reasons.

Our next public service project was a regular column in the paper called "Know Your Enemies." We published photographs of undercover narcotics agents arresting innocent and peaceful marijuana users in order to protect our community. We staked out the local courthouse when narcs testified against their victims. We followed them out of the building, photographed them, and published the photos.

As you might imagine, the narcs were furious. We started getting threatening calls. As one big, burly, bearded narc emerged from the courthouse, our petite photographer snapped his photo. Startled, the cop rushed her, knocked her to the ground, and tried unsuccessfully to get her camera.

We published the photo of him running toward the photographer, then sued him for assault. He countersued us for "intentional infliction of emotional harm." The totally straight jury found for him and against us. They awarded big damages that threatened to bankrupt the paper. But I was from New York. I knew to call the ACLU's main office in Manhattan. Placing a cold call, I explained the situation and asked, "Don't we have a First Amendment right to publish the narcs' photographs?" They agreed and took the case *pro bono*. Ultimately, the federal court of appeals upheld our right to publish those photos, and the paper was saved. Thank you, ACLU!

As a community service, the Sun *publishes the photos of undercover cops busting people for weed, 1973.*

a photo gallery of the
Michigan State Police

KNOW YOUR ENEMIES

State Police Invade Dorms

"One more picture and you'll drop your camera," said William L. Burns of W.A.N.T. (Washtenaw Area Narcotics Team).

The place was 15th District Court on the sixth floor of City Hall and the event was a hearing for three U-M students charged with delivery of LSD, hash and marijuana.

The charges were brought by undercover narcs who infiltrated U-M dorms to promote paranoia and distrust in the university community. The SUN attended the hearing to try to photograph the narcs.

But the narcs didn't have to take the stand as the prosecution backed down and let the three students plead guilty to reduced charges of possession. So the narcs hid in a back room and ducked the two SUN photographers.

But out in a hallway the SUN photographers later found William L. Burns, who appears to be a W.A.N.T. co-ordinator more than an undercover agent, and also a young long-haired state undercover narc known as Sandy Burns or just as Dave (who apparently was not connected with the dorm busts).

The three U-M students are John Foster of South Quad, Richard Wood of West Quad, and Lanson Carrothers of Bursley. All three students were reportedly busted for small amounts.

The well co-ordinated busts of these people were the first invasion of the dorms by the police in almost three years.

"We knew nothing about the raids until they happened," said Col. Frederick Davids, head of U-M security. But Davids, former chief of the Michigan State Police, proved to be lying when Police Chief Walter Krasny admitted, "We had a number of people working closely" with Davids right before the raids.

"I think they're trying to scare people," theorized one student.

Name: **William L. Burns**
Description: This picture was taken during the preliminary examination of the three students set up by undercover narcs who infiltrated the dorms. He works with W.A.N.T. doing undercover narcotics work and was in on the dorm busts.

Name: **Sandy Burns, sometimes known as Dave**
Description: Wears blue jeans and drives a late model red Firebird or Camero or sometimes a blue Chevelle. The SUN took this picture as Burns turned up in court to testify against a friend of ours for sale of LSD. He has set up three other people on charges of sale of LSD. One of them in now in Ypsilanti State Hospital because of flipping out after 6 weeks in Washtenaw County Jail.

Name: **Unknown**
Description: This picture was taken in Cadillac, Michigan, outside the courtroom hearing on Pun Plamondon and Craig Blazier's motion for bond reduction. He was with two other state police at the time and has been identified as the state policeman who worked with Sandy Burns in busting three brothers for LSD.

Name: **Unknown**
Description: This undercover state policeman participated in the raid on the Rainbow House on March 1 when the State Police arrested Craig Blazier. He was stationed at the end of the front walk and kept trying to dodge the photographer.

Name: **Unknown**
Description: This dude was present at Pun Plamondon and Craig Blazier's bond hearing in Cadillac, Michigan. He said he was on special assignment to assist the prosecutor. He also added that he is usually stationed right across the street from Michigan State University.

WHO DUG THE BOMB CRATERS ON CAMPUS?

In a special *Sun* investigation, we discovered that a University of Michigan laboratory was working to perfect the electronic battlefield technology President Richard Nixon hoped could fight the Vietnam War using fewer US soldiers. Soon after our publication, large replica bomb craters appeared around campus. The university quickly filled them, but overnight, others mysteriously appeared. This stealthy protest culminated in a large public demonstration. Hundreds of shovel-wielding protesters gathered in the center of campus to dig a giant bomb crater—with TV cameras recording everything. The police went nuts, beat the demonstrators, and dragged them away for arrest. I was there as a photographer, but toward the end, I put my cameras down, jumped into the crater, and started digging with my bare hands. Arrested and hauled off to jail, I used my one phone call not to reach my lawyer but instead to call in live to the biggest radio station in Detroit to report on the violence and castigate the police. Use the media—or your protest has far less impact.

The *Sun*'s investigations were guided by our secret agent reporter, Howard Kohn. By day, he was an investigative reporter for the *Detroit Free Press*. Kohn was Clark Kent, the seemingly mild-mannered reporter, so quiet and ingratiating that people felt comfortable spilling their secrets. Kohn went undercover, posing as a heroin dealer in the Detroit underworld. Not long after, in an exposé that ran daily for several weeks, he exposed a rat's nest of Detroit policemen who took bribes to protect heroin dealers. Kohn's reporting eventually sent twenty-three Detroit cops to prison. Not long after, the Mafia retaliated and ran Kohn out of town, never to return.

We were just a bunch of young hippies—what did we know about journalism? Kohn was the real deal. He guided us, teaching us how to report, write, and edit. Everyone needs a mentor, and Kohn was ours. Had the *Detroit Free Press* ever found out he was helping us, they would have fired him. Thank you, Howard Kohn.

BEWARE YOUTHFUL FANATICISM

One day, a talented artist named Barbara Weinberg volunteered to help with the paper's design. Short, freckled, with deep blue eyes and brown hair, Barbara wore the hippie clothes of the era. She had a flare for graphic design and enhanced the *Sun*'s appearance, giving it a unique but readable psychedelic style. A few days after we first met, Barbara and I took a walk, and I felt that proverbial ground shaking beneath me. Uh-oh, this was dangerous. She worked for me. But resistance proved futile. Within a few months, we moved in together and married. For the wedding in Great Neck, Long Island, I cut half my hair off, all the way back to shoulder length. Traumatic!

I was deeply in love with Barbara—but that isn't the only reason we married so young, at twenty-one. There I was, living in a commune and rebelling against traditions of all sorts. So why get married? The answer troubles me to this day. I married Barbara for love, but I also wanted to use her inheritance to support our political work. It was part of the "we will make the revolution" grandiosity/delusion of the commune (and the time). I'm ashamed of this fanaticism now. It brought both of us all kinds of grief.

Barbara's father had made a small fortune selling jeweled dog collars, of all things, and had left her a $300,000 stock portfolio—back then, that was a lot of money, close to $2 million in today's dollars. We sold some of her stocks to finance the *Sun*. We agreed, however, that we would spend no more than one-third of her money to support the paper until it could finance itself. We figured with the two-thirds left—$200,000—we could recoup what we had spent.

I also sold advertising to local merchants to finance the paper. But with long, frizzy hair and a beard, and clothed in tie-dye and bell-bottoms, I didn't look like a trustworthy salesman. I was nervous, and it showed. I had a few successes. I sold an ad contract to a local stereo store—the headline said "Get High: Fidelity." But mostly I got turned down. The almost constant rejection got me down—until I read the classic self-help book *How to Win Friends and Influence People* by Dale Carnegie. I really recommend this book even now. Carnegie taught me to *love* rejection—because each one gets you closer to the next sale. He said that you had to hear at least ten noes to get to one yes. So, I learned to love the noes. With my change in attitude, ad sales increased. This life lesson came in handy years later when I founded my PR firm. Public relations is sales, to both potential clients and journalists when soliciting them to cover your client's story. Mostly, you get turned down. But if you let it affect your mood, you will succeed less often.

Running the paper's finances as publisher while selling advertising was my first business experience. Most activism relies on philanthropic or membership support. I chose a different path later on in forming a progressive for-profit PR and advertising firm, a business supported by client fees. I never found it difficult to reconcile being in business while being an activist, but I was often attacked for it. In fact, I often found that having

the measurement and built-in accountability of profitability increased the efficiency of our activism. More on that later.

With Barbara's money, we started promoting the paper and bought automated coin boxes that we placed around town. But sales didn't increase. Why? I felt the responsibility lay with our editor, John Sinclair. He filled the paper with far too much obscure, long-winded ideology rather than content our readers would find useful.

EVEN HIPPIES CAN BE IDEOLOGUES

After his release from prison, John Sinclair renamed the White Panther Party the Rainbow People's Party, complete with a "central committee" of long-hairs and a Maoist-like ideology. I was the "minister of information." John insisted that the *Sun* publish long ideological diatribes from the central committee, which looking back, was downright weird. No wonder readership declined, despite publication of several groundbreaking exposés about the Rockefeller family,

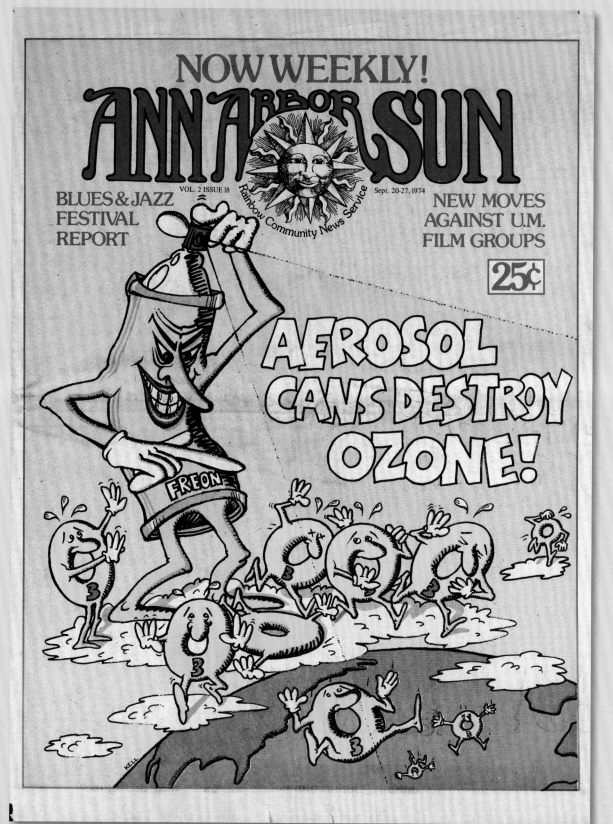

US companies' profiting from Nazi slave labor during World War II, newly discovered (and still relevant) fallacies in the official version of JFK's assassination, and our biggest coup, studies at the University of Michigan that showed chemicals in aerosol sprays were destroying the ozone layer. We broke this story on the cover of the *Sun*. Then media around the world picked it up, pressuring governments and ultimately spurring passage of the Montreal Protocol, in which the world agreed to phase out hydrofluorocarbons. The ozone hole is much smaller now.

Trotskyite organization called the International Socialists. While running for second terms, they promoted weird agendas completely irrelevant to Ann Arbor and guaranteed to turn the public against them—for example, they rooted for the North Vietnamese to win the war and kick out the Americans. I agreed with them, but it was beyond stupid to campaign for this while underemphasizing locally important issues. So, two years after our big victory in the city council, the Human Rights Party lost everything and never returned. (It did, however, help push Michigan Democrats to the left.)

FOR DECADES, I HAVE WATCHED CRAZY DOGMATISM HURT THE LEFT.

One day I received an irate but thoughtful letter from a reader who complained about the paper's domination by the "party," its long ideological rants, and Sinclair's self-indulgent writing. I called the writer, and we talked over coffee. Listening closely, I knew he was right. Michael Castleman became a lifelong friend (and the editor of this book!).

Sinclair wasn't the only one who had veered into rigid out-of-touch ideological dogmatism. Nancy Wechsler and Jerry DeGrieck, the two Human Rights Party candidates we had helped elect to the city council, secretly belonged to a far-left sectarian

For decades, I have watched this kind of crazy dogmatism hurt the Left. Beware: It keeps rearing its ugly head. The very first principle of communications is to start by reaching people *where they are now*. To present all one's beliefs at once, regardless of their impact on winning or losing, is to put emotions ahead of smart tactics. Activists' job is to *pass* progressive policies by winning mass support. It's a step-by-step process. *Never* let your feelings, however legitimate, get in the way of that.

Sinclair never learned this lesson. He insisted the *Sun* should be an organ of our allegedly Maoist political organization (of stoned hippies, no less), not a community newspaper. Readership kept declining.

The *Sun* breaks the ozone hole story, based on University of Michigan research, September 1974.

COMMUNE OR CULT?

Mysteriously, and out of the blue, a new competitive underground newspaper appeared, *New Morning*. It had almost no sales or advertising and no apparent source of funding. Its primary purpose seemed to be to attack Sinclair, the *Sun*, and the Rainbow People's Party, falsely charging us with misuse of public funds and other crimes. Its founder, George DePew, had been involved in obscure far-left sectarian organizations, which had been infiltrated by police counterintelligence agents. We suspected the FBI supported *New Morning* as part of a counterinsurgency effort against us, which was not uncommon at that time. Years later, I tried to research this using the Freedom of Information Act. This provided no proof, as all mentions of police and government agents were redacted files the government released.

The FBI had launched its infamous COINTELPRO counterintelligence program in an effort to smear, disrupt, and discredit movement groups in the late '60s and early '70s. COINTELPRO tactics included anonymous letters to members of leftist organizations, claiming the group's leader was embezzling funds or sleeping with staff. This divide-and-conquer tactic was frequently effective. Activists always need to be on the lookout for police agents and provocateurs. I strongly suspect that some of the violence at the 2020 Black Lives Matter protests of George Floyd's murder was instigated by police provocateurs.

Unfortunately, we offered *New Morning* an easy target. We kept publishing communiqués from the central committee that veered into navel-gazing masquerading as ideology. Support for Sinclair and the *Sun* kept declining.

SEX SELLS

I was still desperate to boost the *Sun*'s circulation. I thought, as is well known, sex sells. Michael Castleman worked at the free medical clinic that Ann Arbor taxpayers had funded with city money. He had also become our health and medical writer. "Michael, we need you to write a cover story about sex," I said. "Not on your life," he insisted. "I'm twenty-three. What do I know?" So, I called his girlfriend, Anne, and asked for help, which she graciously offered. Anne explained later that she "thought it might help our sex lives for Michael to learn more." Michael had no choice, and he wrote a great cover story that did, indeed, help circulation. It helped Michael, too. He became *Playboy*'s Advisor columnist and wrote dozens of magazine articles and several books about sexuality. His sex blog for *Psychology Today* online has attracted more than fifty-five million views. And Michael and his now wife, Anne, are still together today, fifty years later. Salute!

In response, Sinclair decided to move the paper from Ann Arbor to Detroit and focus on that city's Black community as our readership base. I told him this was politically dumb and economically crazy. We were white long-hairs—how were we supposed to speak to and for the Black community? It was preposterous and arrogant. What this was really about was Sinclair's emotional need for acceptance—the Black community appreciated his commitment to Black music and empowerment, but the hippies were turning against him. I also knew that even if we could get Black Detroit to buy copies of the *Sun*, a doubtful proposition, there was no advertising base in that community to support the paper. I argued that moving to Detroit might possibly work if we targeted white countercultural young people in the suburbs as our audience. This was the community we knew how to serve, and its hi-fi stereo stores, record shops, record companies, head shops, and related businesses could serve as our advertising base.

Sinclair decided otherwise, and the *Sun* attempted to become a Black newspaper. Predictably, despite an enormous investment of Barbara's money, it didn't work. The paper started losing more money than ever.

I witnessed the darkest side of John Sinclair as the date approached when Barbara would stop underwriting the paper—and Sinclair's salary. He finally avenged my sleeping with his wife, Leni, while he was in jail by sleeping with mine. Sinclair convinced Barbara that the paper would be fine if she got rid of me. And she did. He destroyed our marriage to keep the money flowing to him. In a six months' spending frenzy in 1976, Barbara's money disappeared and the paper closed for good.

Looking back, our commune was too much of a cult, with Sinclair the abusive leader. Friends saw it at the time and tried to warn me, but I was deaf and blind. We were saving the world. The revolution was coming.

The cover of the Ann Arbor Sun *showing the winner of the Win a Pound of Colombian contest, with a bag over her head to protect her identity.*

CHAPTER 7

NO NUKES, *HIGH TIMES,* AND *ROLLING STONE*

Disillusioned, down, and broke, I left Detroit and returned to New York. It was the spring of 1976, the nation's bicentennial and a presidential election year. On the way, I composed my very first résumé, attempting to fashion my story as a high school dropout and crazy hippie activist into something appealing to an employer. One version was straightforward for straight employers. The other, for the more adventurous, started with a quote from my FBI files: "Subject David Fenton demonstrated himself an outstanding public relations man."

I had no idea what I would do to make a living. For the first two weeks, I slept on the floor of my mother's tiny third-floor walk-up studio at 51st Street and 1st Avenue. She was out of the mental hospital for now, one of the first bipolar patients successfully treated with lithium. Unfortunately, lithium doses were much higher back then and caused enormous fluid retention, swelling, and weight gain. This was really tough on Mom, who had been a fashion model. Still, at least she was no longer raving crazy.

GOING TO *HIGH TIMES*

I called Tom Forcade, an old acquaintance from my Liberation News Service days. He had formerly run the Underground Press Syndicate, the trade organization for alternative newspapers. He had also helped a bit on the campaign to free John Sinclair. Forcade was the founder and publisher of *High Times*, the magazine of cannabis. Forcade was super shy and very withdrawn, always shrouded in weirdness and mystery. I felt quite wary around him. Some people on

The official program guide to the five No Nukes Concerts at Madison Square Garden, New York, 1979.

the hippie left thought he might have been a police agent. In the early '70s, he'd founded a strange group, the Zeitgeist International Party (the zippies), to attack Abbie Hoffman, Jerry Rubin, and the yippies. Forcade claimed he was the real author of Abbie's classic *Steal This Book*. It wasn't true.

Still, I needed a job, and Forcade was now a big-time publisher—*High Times* sold several hundred thousand copies a month. I didn't know it at the time, but he had founded *High Times* with the money he made smuggling pot into the United States in planes he personally piloted from Colombia and Mexico. Forcade's ability to get away with this, despite all the border and air surveillance and his involvement in a major crash, raised further concerns that he had government connections, or had been allowed to operate in return for information. Recently, Leni Sinclair told me she had found evidence in Detroit police files that Forcade was likely a police informant. Somebody really should make a movie about this guy's life.

Forcade invited me to the *High Times* offices in what was then completely desolate, depressing East 27th Street in Manhattan, where a bunch of stoners put out the monthly magazine. Right away, he offered me a job as an editor. The job description involved broadening the magazine's content beyond just marijuana coverage. He envisioned *High Times* as the stoner's *Playboy*, with celebrity interviews, music coverage, and investigative reporting. I was thrilled—here was a dream job, even if it only paid a pittance. It paid so little that, to make ends meet, I used my Ann Arbor reefer connections and dealt small bags of pot to the staff.

As a workplace, *High Times* was challenging, to put it mildly. It was always in chaos, but what made it really difficult was the constant competition among pot dealers and smugglers to get "their" marijuana buds featured in the centerfold that celebrated the "most beautiful flower" of the month. They visited the office every day, getting us so stoned that work took extra effort. A truly tough assignment.

At first, Forcade was true to his word, and I injected non-pot articles into the magazine. But it soon became clear that wouldn't last—Forcade changed his mind a lot. He was another manic depressive, alternately high energy and creative and dark and extremely paranoid. The staff was constantly confused, wondering which Forcade would show up each day. So, I started looking for another job. In 1978, a year after I left, Forcade committed suicide.

MY FIRST REAL JOB: ROLLING STONE MAGAZINE

Meanwhile, my Ann Arbor friend and writing mentor, Howard Kohn, had become an investigative reporter for *Rolling Stone* magazine in San Francisco. Kohn introduced me to its editor and publisher, Jann Wenner, who offered me a job in the magazine's public relations department. I jumped at the chance to join a real magazine. It was now 1977, and I was twenty-five.

At that time, *Rolling Stone* was flying high. It had diversified from a music-only magazine and had become a youth-culture force. In addition to the interview Howard Kohn and David Weird did with Patty Hearst, the magazine also featured artful celebrity photos by Annie Leibovitz and pioneering new journalism by Tom Wolfe and Hunter S.

"Special Harvest Issue" of High Times, *1976.*

SPECIAL! HARVEST ISSUE

Brotherhood of Eternal Love: The Senate Report

High Times

Collectors' Issue

$1.50

America's Top Narc Talks

Hash in the U.S.S.R.

'I Was Kennedy's Dealer'

Worldwide Crop Reports

Call Me Brick:
A Colombian Centerfold

'Cocaine Fiends'
Sneak Preview of
Reefer Madness Sequel

Book Bonus:
Underground Bestseller
'Laughing Gas'

N 230

TRANS-MARIJUANA
CARGOLINES

Thompson. Frequently, I had to resist Thompson's attempts to get me to take all kinds of mysterious pills. This guy fetishized taking uppers, downers, acid, and who knows what else, yet somehow still managed to write amazing pieces.

When I joined the staff, the director of public relations came from the British music scene and had difficulty transitioning to the new, more serious *Rolling Stone*. One day she assigned me to publicize a story about the first journalist to investigate the swarms of so-called African killer bees that were moving toward the United States from Latin America. Everyone was terrified of these bees, which were said to be particularly vicious to humans. Our reporter was among the first to see them in action.

After working with journalists since I was seventeen, I knew the major media would see killer bees as a sensational story about a new phenomenon people feared but knew little about. So, I issued a press release headlined "*Rolling Stone* Reporter Attacked by Killer Bees." He hadn't really been attacked, but in the PR biz, a little tongue in cheek goes a long way. In those days, to entice rock and news radio stations to cover a story, you couldn't email them audio files. Email and digital audio files were years away. All we had was tape. You had to feed them audio content by unscrewing your telephone mouthpiece and attaching alligator clips to the wires inside to connect your push-button tape recorder. I called the country's biggest radio stations asking if they wanted a prerecorded interview with the reporter that revealed what it was like to be "attacked by killer bees." They all did—I convinced at least a hundred stations to cover the story, laboriously unscrewing the phone mouthpiece and feeding them from the tape recorder,

My Rolling Stone *business card, 1977.*

one at a time. It took days but brought *Rolling Stone* a great deal of attention.

Wenner was impressed and soon promoted me to director of public relations, right as the magazine was moving from San Francisco to swank offices in New York. My new office overlooked Central Park from 59th Street and Fifth Avenue. Wenner was now hanging out with Jackie Onassis and the New York celebrity scene, far from the magazine's acid-rock San Francisco Summer of Love origins.

THE CIA INFILTRATES THE NEW YORK TIMES

One of my first assignments as director of public relations was publicizing a story by Carl Bernstein of Watergate fame. He was the first journalist to document how reporters and columnists at major US newspapers had for decades simultaneously worked for the Central Intelligence Agency. Even *The New York Times* used to have CIA agents on its payroll. At one point, their foreign affairs columnist, C. L. Sulzberger, had even published a column under his byline that was actually written by the CIA's E. Howard Hunt, who was later involved in the Watergate break-in.

I was nervous as hell when I visited the national editor of *The New York Times*. How could I tell him his paper was about to be embarrassed by the revelation that some of its journalists had long been CIA agents? I mean, I'd hoped my first big pitch to the mighty *New York Times* wouldn't be quite so difficult for them. But to *The Times'* credit, the paper covered Bernstein's revelation with a story headlined "400 U.S. Journalists Seen Linked to C.I.A." But the report left out that C. L. Sulzberger, a member of the family that owned the *Times*, had printed E. Howard Hunt's column verbatim. All the news fit to print? Apparently not in this case.

Years later, *Wall Street Journal* reporter Jonathan Kwitny accused a former *New York Times* Teheran bureau chief, Kenneth Love, of having helped lead the CIA's 1954 overthrow of Iranian President Mohammad Mosaddegh. Kwitny presented the evidence in his seminal book on US foreign policy, *Endless Enemies: The Making of an Unfriendly World*. When Love sued, the publisher responded by reprinting the book with those pages blanked out.

One of my rules for activists is to get to know journalists personally. *Rolling Stone* proved invaluable in helping me develop mutually respectful working relationships with print and broadcast journalists, columnists, editorial writers, and producers at major TV news shows, such as *Today, Good Morning America, 60 Minutes,* and the three network evening news programs. Back in the '60s and '70s, before the internet and cable, if you got a story on one or two of the network evening news programs, most of the country saw it. They had huge audiences, unlike today, when their audience is mostly the older generations.

I quickly noticed that, when I had a personal relationship with a top producer at, for example, CBS *Evening News,* I placed more stories on that broadcast. When that producer moved to one of the other networks, so did my *Rolling Stone* stories. In public relations, and really in sales and human commerce of all kinds, personal relationships are key. As the saying goes, it's not who you know—it's who you get to know.

HOW ISRAEL GOT THE BOMB

Soon I was promoting Howard Kohn's groundbreaking *Rolling Stone* investigation that showed how Israel obtained enriched uranium for its nuclear arsenal. They stole it from a Pennsylvania nuclear plant with the CIA's tacit approval. That story and others got my calls returned, allowing me to form even closer relationships with media decision-makers in New York and Washington.

Kohn also broke new ground investigating the death of Karen Silkwood, who died in a suspicious car accident. She was on her way to meet with a *New York Times* reporter who was investigating unsafe conditions at the Oklahoma plutonium processing plant where Silkwood worked. Silkwood risked her job, and ultimately her life, revealing numerous safety violations that exposed workers to dangerous levels of radiation. I publicized his stories, but I wanted to get more involved. It appeared obvious to us that Silkwood had been murdered by the owners of the plutonium plant to keep her from spilling secrets.

Even though Silkwood was dead, her family wanted to discover and punish who had murdered her. Silkwood's death became a cause célèbre for the anti–nuclear power movement. Lawyers for the family needed money to take depositions and investigate the murder. I had learned a good deal about producing benefit concerts under Sinclair's tutelage in Ann Arbor. At the *Ann Arbor Sun*, we'd published several articles on the dangers of nuclear power by Ralph Nader and scientists in the field. Kohn and I started producing small benefit concerts for the Silkwood legal defense fund, featuring rock artists we'd met at *Rolling Stone*: Bonnie Raitt, Jackson Browne, James Taylor, Carly Simon, John Hall, and others. (Meryl Streep, along with Cher, later starred in the powerful movie *Silkwood* about Karen's case.)

NO NUKES AT MADISON SQUARE GARDEN

I started thinking the rock artists could do much more to help fund the anti–nuclear power movement. They could educate the public about the folly of generating electricity by boiling water with nuclear chain reactions that produced poisonous plutonium and other highly toxic waste.

Then, after only a year at *Rolling Stone*, I needed a new job. My immediate boss fired me when I protested his refusal to grant promised raises to my staff. Wenner wasn't involved, but he refused to intervene.

John Hall of the then-popular rock band Orleans (and later a congressman from Upstate New York) suggested we produce consecutive nights of benefit concerts against nuclear power at New York's Madison Square Garden, featuring the top rock artists of the day. Some of the artists were game, but it was little more than a crazy idea. Then, at a 1978 conference for grassroots antinuclear organizers in St. Louis, I met Chuck Savitt and Steven Haft, who represented philanthropists funding the anti–nuclear power movement. Impressed with the concert idea, they took

me to meet philanthropic legend David Hunter at his New York office on East 42nd Street. Hunter worked for the Stern Family Foundation, whose money came from the founders of Sears, Roebuck & Co. He had helped fund the civil rights and antiwar movements.

An old-school, quiet, courtly, white-haired gentleman, Hunter listened intently as I shared our vision for a concert series with top rock acts at Madison Square Garden. The plan was to use the money it raised to fund grassroots antinuclear organizations, while using the media attention to brand nuclear power as dangerous. He asked if I had signed contracts from any of the artists. I didn't. Did I have a contract with Madison Square Garden? I didn't. "So, what do you need to make this happen?" he asked.

"Some money to fly to Los Angeles a few times and meet with the artists to get them to sign on the dotted line," I explained. He gave me $3,000 for this on the spot. Talk about venture philanthropy! He had just met me. I was all of twenty-five. And I'd never undertaken anything even close to this scale.

We eventually turned that $3,000 into the No Nukes concerts at Madison Square Garden in October 1979. They featured Bruce Springsteen, Carly Simon, James Taylor, the Doobie Brothers, Bonnie Raitt, Gil Scott-Heron, Chaka Khan, Jackson Browne, Crosby, Stills & Nash, Tom Petty, Peter Tosh, Sweet Honey in the Rock, and John Hall. The official name was the MUSE Concerts for a Non-Nuclear Future. MUSE stood for Musicians United for Safe Energy, the organization of musicians we created to own and run the concerts. (I'd like to see MUSE return where "safe energy" refers to avoiding the worst effects

No Nukes! (from left) John Hall, James Taylor, Carly Simon, and Graham Nash at the 1979 concerts in New York.

of climate change.) Our logo was the sun, which even then we promoted as the very best form of power. Under the tutelage of my longtime friend and attorney David Lubell, we set up a nonprofit organization and a sister foundation, whose job would be to give away the money from the concerts and an anticipated record album.

With signed commitment letters from the artists and a contract with Madison Square Garden, I raised $500,000 from foundations and philanthropists in the form of loans to produce the concerts. That was a lot of money in 1979, and I was nervous as hell about paying it back. Luckily, I paid back every penny from ticket proceeds. Thus began decades of recruiting philanthropic support for work promoting social and environmental justice.

MUSE: MUSICIANS UNITED FOR SAFE ENERGY

To produce the No-Nukes Concerts, MUSE opened a production office at Fifth Avenue and 13th Street in a big, open-air loft space that had only one private office. I took the office for myself, rationalizing that I needed privacy for meetings and the like. What an idiot! That move offended the grassroots, countercultural, communally minded antinuclear activists who came to work on the concerts. I should have made the office a conference room. Ah, hindsight. I lost considerable support because of this dumb move, which became a big problem later, as you will soon see. The private office issue also caused conflicts with my concert coproducer, Tom Campbell, a highly dedicated if irascible longtime producer of smaller antinuclear concerts who was close to the musicians and the movement—and resented my involvement.

I knew that one of the first big cause-related fundraising concerts, George Harrison's 1971 Concert for Bangladesh, had failed to raise much money for the cause. Much of the money got burned in expensive union overtime at Madison Square Garden, lavish backstage spreads for the musicians, first-class airfares, and the like. At the 1979 No-Nukes Concerts, I was determined to do things differently.

How naive. I booked discounted nonchangeable airfares for the musicians and insisted on not much more than catered sandwiches backstage, nothing fancy. I banned limousines and asked everyone to use taxis and cheaper car services. And I insisted that the MUSE concerts had to end on time, no matter how many musicians showed up to jam, to avoid huge union overtime charges at the Garden. This led to a giant blowup with singer-songwriter Jackson Browne, who after Springsteen, was the top musician and celebrity on the bill. I've always respected Browne as a committed activist, but his popularity gave him enormous power over the proceedings.

My MUSE business card, 1979.

THE EGO DRUG

One challenge of organizing the concerts involved the prodigious amounts of cocaine many of the musicians were using at the time. The musicians had to be in charge of the concerts, or they wouldn't play for free. But their frequent bathroom trips to snort coke in the middle of important meetings created special challenges. Cocaine is an ego-boosting drug. Rock stars have big egos to begin with, and cocaine fueled them even more. Personally, I never liked cocaine—it made me speedy, and I was already speedy enough. After using coke, I'd feel burned out for days. I prefer ego-reducing drugs. It felt disappointing watching the recreational drug culture change from grass and psychedelics, which usually promote positive group interactions, to cocaine, which makes it all about *me, me, me.*

(Unlike Browne, Springsteen wasn't involved in any decision-making.) Browne rebelled at my efforts to control expenses, leading to all kinds of conflict. He enlisted the grassroots activists against me, which was easy because I had alienated them by taking that sole private office. Just as the concerts began, I was pushed out. It was humiliating. So was being left off the album credits.

I also fought Browne about having a diverse roster of musicians. He thought the performers should mostly be rock groups with the mellow California sound, resisting my efforts at first. But with help from Bonnie Raitt, one of the warmest, most down-to-earth celebrities I've known, whose music is heavily influenced by the blues, we eventually booked Peter Tosh, Gil Scott-Heron, Chaka Khan, and Sweet Honey in the Rock.

I hoped we could make a documentary concert movie to both entertain and educate the public about the dangers of nuclear power. But movies cost a fortune, so I made sure the MUSE bylaws stated that no film financing could come from sales of concert tickets or a record album. Any film had to be financed independently by a film studio or investor. I recruited the great director John Avildsen to make the film—he made *Rocky, Save the Tiger,* and *The Karate Kid.* Avildsen was bankable and enthusiastic. I then naively recruited the great documentarian Barbara Kopple, who won an Oscar for a documentary about coal country, *Harlan County, USA.* I thought Avildsen would benefit from having a documentary filmmaker at his side. This turned out to be a big, and in hindsight, obvious mistake. Two brilliant filmmakers were one too many. Next thing I knew, Kopple had pushed Avildsen out. Next, she was out, as Browne ignored the bylaws and used the large advance for the record album to hire other filmmakers, some of whom had no real film experience.

As fate would have it, the Three Mile Island partial nuclear meltdown happened just before the concerts, which focused the media even more on the concerts and the issue. The concerts were a great success artistically and politically—their impact on the public's awareness of nuclear power continues to this day. As the film shows, there were many memorable, moving, artistic, and passionate moments on stage. I had never seen Springsteen perform live before. He was truly astonishing.

But, despite my best efforts, the musicians pushed the concerts late into expensive union overtime, booked limousines and first-class airline tickets, and insisted on lavish, expensive food and drink spreads backstage. As a result, despite selling out the Garden for five nights and charging high ticket prices—a whopping $18.50 instead of the going rate of $10—the concerts hardly made a dime. Then, much of the album proceeds went to make a disappointing movie. *No Nukes*, the film, bombed at the box office. Not nearly as much money as planned was left to be distributed to the grassroots antinuclear groups, as I had feared from the beginning could happen.

On the last day of the concerts, we held a free outdoor concert and rally with some of the musicians and speakers, including Jane Fonda, Tom Hayden, and Ralph Nader. There was a huge crowd at the event on the landfill in lower Manhattan that later became Battery Park City.

Ticket for the No Nukes concert Madison Square Garden. At the time, $18.50 was an unprecedented price for a rock concert ticket.

THE ISSUES OF NUCLEAR POWER

Nuclear power remains a contentious issue to this day. Some truly concerned about climate change are boosting it. But the problems with nuclear power plants we highlighted in the '70s remain. They are subject to horrendous accidents in the event of earthquakes (consider Fukushima), which spread radioactivity around the Pacific. They can lose power, which can cause loss of the coolant water for the hot reactors. This can cause full or partial meltdowns, like what happened at Three Mile Island in Pennsylvania. There is still no safe place to store their poisonous waste, which remains dangerously radioactive for hundreds of thousands of years. Not thousands—hundreds of thousands. The spent fuel waste ponds at the reactors still in operation today are highly radioactive and could be targeted by terrorists to make so-called dirty bombs, which

could spread radiation far and wide. Eventually, that waste must be moved to a storage facility via trains and trucks—accidents are inevitable and would spill poisonous waste and endanger the public. Plus, the waste trains and trucks become potential terrorist targets.

Nuclear plants at times release radiation into the environment, albeit in small amounts. But the lifetime risk from radiation is cumulative. There is no such thing as a safe level of exposure, as I learned at the time from Dr. John Gofman, one of the first scientists to handle plutonium. Plutonium is the most dangerous substance ever created by humans—one millionth of a gram in the lungs can kill an adult. Uranium mining and milling leaves enormous piles of radioactive waste that have blown around the Southwest for decades, often on or near Native American communities.

Finally, nuclear power is simply too expensive compared to truly clean energy, the sun and wind, which get cheaper every year. The knock on them has been their intermittency, and the challenge of storing the energy they produce. But batteries are getting cheaper, along with other methods of storage and modern grid management techniques. As physicist Amory Lovins has shown, every dollar spent on nuclear energy today is worse for the climate. Instead, those dollars should be spent on power available from cheaper renewables, storage, and efficiency. These also scale to produce power in a year or two, unlike the decade or more it takes to build an expensive nuclear plant. A decade we don't have if we are to maintain a livable climate for humanity.

The *New York Daily News* put an aerial shot of the huge crowd on its front page, headlined "100,000 Rally Against Nukes." That was clearly an underestimate. So, a colleague and I called the editor of the *Daily News* and complained. When the next edition came out later that day, the cover headline said "200,000 Rally Against Nukes." Lesson: Always complain when the media gets it wrong.

So, which lessons are learned from the No Nukes concerts?

First, the name—No Nukes—worked marvelously. Only simple messages work.

Also, the issue of "poison power" speaks to the heart first, mind second. People feel the danger in the words "poison power" more than in detailed facts about meltdowns, waste ponds, and the like. The message "Poison power" frames the issue clearly as a concern for everyone.

Use celebrities. The No Nukes concerts overflowed with them.

Appeal to the culture of the media. The No Nukes concerts were held in New York City, the nation's media capital. Had they taken place in a small city, they would have had much less impact.

While the No Nukes concerts helped turn the public against nuclear power, I left the experience quite disillusioned, vowing never to work with music people again. Celebrities can be very helpful to causes, especially now, with their large social media followings. But some can be difficult to work with.

I retreated to Martha's Vineyard, to a house owned by one of the concert's financial backers. I spent a cold, gray, rainy month there. I had no idea what was next.

ORGANIC AND REGENERATIVE

Soon a series of advertisements on the op-ed page of *The New York Times* caught my eye. Placed by Rodale Press, they outlined how the US food system was completely unsustainable because of its dependence on fossil fuels, neurotoxic and carcinogenic pesticides, and synthetic fertilizers that caused massive nitrogen runoff and such disasters as the "dead zone" in the Gulf of Mexico. Nitrogen runoff initiates a cascade of ecological devastation, including toxic algae blooms, that deprive fish of oxygen.

These ads were unusual, in part for their content and in part because they appeared in the very slot where Mobil and other oil companies ran ads touting the supposed greatness of fossil fuels. Mobil regularly used the spot to intentionally mislead people about global warming.

I wrote a brief fan letter to Robert Rodale, CEO of Rodale Press, praising the series. I also mentioned my PR work for progressive and environmental causes. Unexpectedly, Rodale called and invited me to visit with him at company headquarters in Pennsylvania.

Rodale was a major publisher of books and magazines such as *Prevention, Men's Health, Runner's World,* and *Organic Gardening and Farming*. Rodale's father, J. I. Rodale (originally Jerome Irving Cohen), had brought the word "organic" to the United States, having learned it from the British agronomist Sir Albert Howard. Rodale launched *Organic Gardening* in the early 1940s, when food shortages caused by World War II spurred millions of Americans to plant victory gardens. (I strongly suspect with climate change devastating industrial food crops, victory gardens will become popular again before long.)

Robert Rodale was a shy introvert, almost certainly because his father was an extreme extrovert and a bit of a nutcase. He was an unlikely spokesman for anything. In addition, this was 1980, long before the term "regenerative agriculture" had entered the lexicon. (Rodale coined it.) But Rodale was committed to telling Americans about the dangers and unsustainability of the US food system. I helped him promote his vision in print media and on network TV. He was way ahead of his time. Now we know we must switch to organic and regenerative agriculture to preserve public health and get carbon out of the atmosphere and into the soil.

In 1990, Rodale died in a car accident. He was the opposite of charismatic, but he was a true visionary.

TODAY
Sunny, low 80s

TONIGHT
Cloudy, showers, low 65-70

TOMORROW
Warm, showers, 80-85
Details. Page 2

TV listings: P. 47

NEW YORK POST

© 1980 News Group Publications Inc.   Vol. 179, No. 246

THURSDAY, SEPTEMBER 4, 1980   30 CENTS   R ★   AMERICA'S FASTEST-GROWING NEWSPAPER

AVERAGE DAILY SALES EXCEED 650,000

A POST EXCLUSIVE

Met worker comes clean on slaying of violinist

By CYNTHIA R. FAGEN,
NILES LATHEM and
PHILIP MESSING

METROPOLITAN Opera stagehand Craig Stephen Crimmins made a full videotaped confession of the brutal murder of violinist Helen Hagnes Mintiks during an intensive interrogation by police, The Post has learned.

Police extracted the confession from Crimmins during a gruelling interrogation hours before he was formally charged with the murder.

Sources said law enforcement authorities — worried that they might lose the suspect if he obtained legal counsel — intensified their interrogation in the hours before he was charged.

Sources said they feared they might lose the case due to leaks that a suspect was

Continued on Page 19

HERE'S ABBIE!

Abbie Hoffman, the fugitive Yippie emerged in New York after six years in the shadow of the underground. He booked into a West Side hotel, where he gave The Post an exclusive interview. Minutes later, the incredible hoaxer jumped in a taxi and was again on the lam, going to an unknown destination. As a fugitive he posed as a middle-class environmentalist in a remote upstate retreat. In that time he received a commendation from Gov. Carey and Sen. Moynihan. Today he appears in court to face a drug-peddling charge. After that he will be reunited with old friends at a book-launching party. Full story and more photos on Pages 4, 5 and 31.

Post photo by Hal Goldenberg

CHAPTER 8

BARBARA WALTERS SAVES ABBIE FROM A LONG PRISON TERM

IN WHICH I LEARN...

· FRAME ISSUES YOUR WAY: ABBIE WAS NOT A CRIMINAL; HE WAS EVERY JEWISH MOTHER'S SON.

· STUDY AND APPEAL TO THE CULTURE OF THE MEDIA TO GET COVERAGE.

· THE MEDIA DEFINES REALITY, EVEN FOR THE COURTS.

As you've read, Abbie Hoffman, the yippie agitprop leader of the '60s, was my public relations professor, my media guru, a manic message genius, and funny as hell. Who else would title his books *Steal This Book, Soon to be a Major Motion Picture*, or later, *Steal This Urine Test*? When drug testing first emerged, Abbie went into business selling clean urine—procured from a local convent. By the late '70s, I hadn't seen Abbie in years—not since 1974, when he went into hiding after his arrest for selling three pounds of cocaine to undercover agents. His photograph was plastered on FBI Most Wanted posters at every post office in the United States.

Then one day, his sidekick Jerry Rubin invited me over for dinner in New York, where he introduced me to his friend Barry Fried (like *freed*, get it?) and wife Johanna Lawrenson. It took me about half an hour to recognize that nasally Jewish voice with the Massachusetts accent—it was Abbie! It was hard to tell at first, because he had a nose job and looked different. I was so excited! We hugged and immediately started making a PR plan for getting him back to real freedom.

He gave me a business card with the phone number of an answering service. Under the name Howie Samuels, his firm was Creative Image Associates, or CIA. He was an "agent." (The answering service was eventually busted.) Abbie cracked jokes about life underground, but there was nothing funny seeing him sweat as police cars passed

Abbie turns himself in to the Manhattan District Attorney, September 4, 1980.

or jump when the doorbell rang. The stress contributed to his several nervous breakdowns while in hiding. Fortunately for him, Johanna was there to pick up the pieces.

A few months later, Abbie was in the midst of a massive manic attack. He threw a birthday party for himself at a swank Upper East Side Chinese restaurant—while still a fugitive. I arrived to find him calling the *New York Post*'s Page Six, inviting them to the party. We had to hustle Abbie out of there fast, fearing the *Post* would bring the FBI.

There was never a dull moment with Abbie. He was creatively hilarious, I idolized him, but he was not lovable. Too often he got caught up in a blend of idealism and messianic grandiosity. He was obsessed with pornography and cheated on his amazing, beautiful wife Johanna, who had literally kept him alive while running from the FBI. (He would say, "When you are with a beautiful woman, no one looks at you.") He named his son America, more out of concern with his own mythology than with the boy, who later changed his name to Alan. To Abbie, the cause was everything, so much so that he often ignored his children. He left them none of his significant book royalties, donating them instead to the Black Panthers and other progressive groups.

He was also totally fearless. In the early '60s, he went south to fight segregation in Mississippi and Alabama, risking his life every day in an era when the Ku Klux Klan beat up and sometimes murdered white people who dared to help register Black people in the South to vote. He was arrested

dozens of times. Once, the police broke his nose at a demonstration.

His dedication was inspiring, but like all media celebrities, the attention also went to his head. He was pretty oblivious of other people. This was one complicated dude. I admired him, and we were partners in political mischief-making, but nobody was close to Abbie, except his three wives and his brother.

In 1980, I was doing freelance PR for consumer and environmental groups. By then reconnected with Abbie, I would have helped him beat the cocaine charges for free. Then his publisher actually paid me to arrange the PR for Abbie's return, which coincided with the publication of his autobiography, *Soon to Be a Major Motion Picture*, which he wrote while a fugitive.

BARBARA WALTERS THROWS A FIT

In September 1980, I contacted Barbara Walters and told her I could give her an exclusive scoop—I could take her to see Abbie Hoffman. She asked for details, but I refused to say anything more. She was wary but intrigued enough to agree. I picked Walters up and drove her to the Westchester

Abbie Hoffman with US Senator Daniel Patrick Moynihan after Abbie's testimony to Congress—while he was on the FBI's Most Wanted List. After plastic surgery, nobody recognized him.

RESTAURANT REVIEWER

Abbie was a gourmet cook. His chicken cordon bleu blew me away. While a fugitive, he had posed as a restaurant reviewer for *Playboy*, thereby getting to eat for free in Michelin-starred restaurants in France. It was a ruse, but eventually his reviews appeared in a *Playboy* offshoot, *Oui* magazine, with his accountant sending him the payments in a way that eluded detection.

TOP *Barbara Walters and her ABC News crew on the St. Lawrence River, on the way to meet Abbie.* **BOTTOM** *Jewish mother meets Jewish son. Barbara Walters with Abbie Hoffman at his hideaway.*

County airport, where I had rented a Learjet on the publisher's dime. She badgered me to tell her where we were going. I explained that I couldn't tell her until we were airborne. The cat-and-mouse routine was necessary to keep her TV crew from alerting the FBI while still on the ground. "Young man, I will not get on that plane until you tell me where we are going!" Walters yelled. "Well then you're not getting on the plane, since I can't tell you until we are in the air." Who could blame her? She didn't know me and had no proof I wasn't abducting her. I was sweating profusely.

Abbie using his alter ego, Barry Fried, testifying before the US Senate, all while being sought by the FBI. He had even been appointed to a federal commission on water resources.

The escapade was a huge success. It was Jewish mother Barbara Walters meets long-lost Jewish son. The interview ran the full hour on ABC's *20/20*, with Walters fawning over Abbie. Largely as a result, a week later when he turned himself into the Manhattan district attorney, he served only fifty-four days in jail before being released to spend weekdays in a halfway house and weekends at home.

"YOUNG MAN, I WILL NOT GET ON THAT PLANE," WALTERS SAID.

How could I stand up to a major TV star? But I did, and eventually she gave in.

Right after takeoff, she learned for the first time that Abbie had altered his appearance and assumed a new identity as an environmental activist on the St. Lawrence River in Upstate New York. He and several community groups were fighting the US Army Corps of Engineers' plans to dredge the river, which would ruin the river ecosystem. Getting Walters there safely without tipping off the FBI was a complex undertaking involving thirty-five people, security codes, precise timetables, checkpoints, and fail-safe escape routes. Tight security was essential. If Abbie had been caught, as opposed to turning himself into the authorities, he would have spent many years in prison. On the plane, I showed her photos of

The press leveled the absurd charge that Abbie had turned himself in solely to sell *Soon to Be a Major Motion Picture*. Sure, he was risking decades in prison to sell a book. Right. As Abbie emerged from the courthouse, there was a media riot—over three hundred reporters and photographers jostling each other, with several injured.

It was the ultimate media event. I had helped the master media manipulator manipulate himself out of a long prison term. Yes, public relations also affects the legal system and the courts. The media affects how judges, juries, and prosecutors perceive people charged with crimes. Those perceptions shape their attitudes and behavior. How could it be otherwise? During my career, I've helped quite a few lawyers mount PR campaigns that affected court rulings, prison terms, and financial settlements in controversial cases. Just look at how Supreme Court Chief Justice John Roberts lifts his finger into the winds of public opinion before deciding cases. Roberts is quite conservative and partisan. But sometimes, he votes against his conservative orthodoxy to protect the court's reputation with the public. Activists need to be sure they are the ones blowing the winds.

After his release, Abbie went right back to activism. He worked to oppose the dreadful Reagan wars in Nicaragua and El Salvador. He was arrested with President Carter's daughter Amy while shutting down CIA recruitment at the University of Massachusetts. I still have the button he made for the occasion that says "What's So Intelligent About the CIA?" Indeed. Amy and Abbie turned their trial into a prosecution of the CIA's horrid and counterproductive behavior assassinating foreign leaders and overthrowing governments. The jury acquitted them on all counts.

ONE PERSON CAN CHANGE THE WORLD

Abbie Hoffman and Roger Ailes, the founder of Fox News, were among the first to foresee the impact television would have on American politics. Ailes's use of TV is documented in *The Making of the President 1968*. Abbie used television to attract media attention to himself and his band of yippies, to get kids to rebel against their parents and help his efforts to stop the Vietnam War. Unfortunately, though brilliant, Abbie was an anarchist and mentally ill with bipolar disorder. As he grew older, the disease became increasingly debilitating. Like my mother, he was an early user of lithium for treatment. And like her, he was depressed by the weight gain the drug caused. But

Plotting Abbie's return from underground with him, Watertown, New York, 1980.

for Abbie, there was something worse. Lithium flattens personality, diminishing creativity. In 1989, never having created a tangible or institutional legacy, he killed himself with an overdose of sleeping pills. The evil Ailes went on to create the alternative reality of Fox News and brainwash 30 percent of America, bringing us Donald Trump.

Still, Abbie proved that one person, or a tiny group, could command national media coverage repeatedly with creative satire, stunts, and humor. He knew that if you created events that appealed to the culture of the media, they couldn't help but cover you. This strategy works for both the Left and Right. Consider the emergence of the right-wing Tea Party. Their numbers were tiny, but through creative events managed to loom large. The media blew them totally out of proportion, changing the politics of the early twenty-first century.

Market-Hunting in 'Progressive' P.R.

By CHARLES MOHR
Special to The New York Times

WASHINGTON, April 20 — A press release turned up this month in reporters' mailboxes outlining the schedules and public appearances of 11 European, Latin American and Canadian figures, including a Nobel Peace Prize winner from Argentina and the film maker Costa-Gavras, who had come to this country to protest United States "intervention in Central America" and express solidarity with Nicaragua.

Last month, in the few days before the presidential election in El Salvador, another press release turned up in the same mailboxes.

It gave the locations and telephone numbers where political leaders of the Salvadoran insurgents could be reached in Canada and Mexico for interviews about the election.

These releases, on expensive-looking paper with a black top border, were the work of Fenton Communications, a public relations concern that uses conventional methods to promote some causes that are described as liberal, progressive, left-wing or radical, depending on the perspective of the reader.

A Variety of Clients

The company also works for a variety of publishers, film makers and environmental groups and for groups advocating nuclear disarmament and famine relief.

Fenton Communications once worked for Runner's World Magazine, and it now represents the Greek Government and the League of Women Voters' Presidential primary debates.

It also represents a political action committee in the nuclear freeze movement.

Now the company is splitting up. David S. Fenton, who works out of a New York office on West 57th Street, with six employees, has come to a parting of the ways with Robert P. Pollock, who directed the concern's Washington office in its first two years.

Both men say the disagreement involves business rather than ideology. Mr. Pollock says he will open his own public relations company in Washington, commenting, "Now there will be two progressive public relations firms." Mr. Fenton plans to retain his Washington office.

They Say There Is a Market

But both insist they have proved that a market exists for "progressive P.R."

Mr. Fenton said his company had survived solely on client billings, without investment capital. He said he charged about $4,000 to $6,000 a month for long-term clients, a fee he estimates is only about 30 to 40 per-

The New York Times/Marilynn K. Yee
David S. Fenton

cent of the monthly retainers of large commercial public relations concerns.

"Our clients don't have a lot of money," Mr. Pollock said.

The Fenton company, which will continue to work on some projects with Mr. Pollock's new company, handles numerous "one shot" projects, described as not especially profitable.

An example was getting news media exposure for a coalition of members of the clergy who wanted to dispute the findings of President Reagan's commission on hunger, which had reported that hunger was not widespread in America.

Another example was briefly representing a group boycotting the Nestlé Company because of its sales of infant feeding formula in third world nations.

From the Vietnam Era

Both Mr. Fenton and Mr. Pollock are in their early 30's and are products of Vietnam era causes. Mr. Fenton was once a photographer for the Liberation News Service. In Michi-

gan he joined an effort to help take over Ann Arbor's City Council. He has also been the publicity director of Rolling Stone magazine. He later helped organize antinuclear rock concerts at Madison Square Garden.

Mr. Pollock was a co-author of a book published in 1973, "Vietnam: What Kind of Peace?" He then worked at the Indochina Research Center.

After that, for five and a half years, he directed Critical Mass, the antinuclear project of Ralph Nader, the consumer advocate.

Mr. Fenton and Mr. Pollick use nearly identical language, saying they "learned the skills of professionally dealing with the press," something they say many public interest groups have never really mastered.

Both men characterize most public relations operations as "sleaze, hype, manipulation and distortion." They say that their work is an effort to provide journalists with useful, trustworthy facts and figures.

Brochure on Guerrillas

Although Fenton Communications produced a glossy brochure about the Salvadoran leftist Opposition this year, Mr. Fenton and Mr. Pollock said they had never been employed by the guerrillas or the Opposition political figures. The money for that job, they said, came from a San Francisco foundation dominated by the leftist National Lawyer's Guild.

In 1982, Mr. Fenton represented the Nicaraguan Government for a month, escorting the Foreign Minister, the Rev. Miguel d'Escoto Brockmann, on a monthlong trip in the United States. On an evening television program, Father d'Escoto staged a spirited debate with Jeanne J. Kirkpatrick, the chief United States delegate to the United Nations.

The only measure of success, Mr. Pollock said, "is do you get your client's story out."

Earlier this year, when Mr. Pollock was still working for Mr. Fenton, he arranged lunches in Washington for Guillermo Manuel Ungo, one of the Salvadoran leftist leaders.

'Do It Right,' and in Style

Mr. Pollock says he favors good restaurants and press breakfasts at expensive hotels like the Hay-Adams, near the White House.

"The conservative foundations and P.R. firms are the people we are going head to head with," he said. "Why should we surrender the Hay-Adams? We want to be professional and to do it right."

"Public relations," Mr. Fenton said, "is actually very simple work. Ours involves hard news and gaining exposure. We don't give clients a list of all the press releases we wrote for them."

CHAPTER 9

PUTTING ABBIE'S LESSONS TO WORK BY FOUNDING FENTON

IN WHICH I LEARN...

- **THE RIGHT ROUTINELY INFLUENCES MEDIA WITH FRAMING: PROGRESSIVES MUST LEARN HOW.**

- **STORIES AND MOVEMENTS NEED EFFECTIVE, APPEALING SPOKESPEOPLE.**

- **NEVER OVERPROMISE AND UNDERDELIVER.**

- **PEOPLE LEARN FROM ENGAGING CHARACTERS AND MORAL STORIES.**

- **BE CREATIVE: ABC'S THE DAY AFTER IS REALLY SCARY.**

- **BE NIMBLE: AVOID BUREAUCRACY AND PAY FOR TALENT.**

Fighting a tendency to depression, I took refuge in cannabis and smoked too much. One day, my body started shaking uncontrollably. I couldn't make it stop, which was scary. My girlfriend, Jill Bullitt, suggested I talk on the phone to her therapist, Dr. Nathan Ross, who had been the head of the American Psychoanalytic Association. As I shook, she put Dr. Ross on the phone with me.

I don't recall what he said, but his soothing tones calmed me, and, remarkably, the shaking stopped. I was impressed, to say the least.

Dr. Ross inquired about my parents, especially my bipolar mother. "I think you'd benefit from seeing a mature woman therapist," he said. Thus began seven years of seeing his wife, Dr. Edith Ross, who largely cured my depression by helping me see—and feel—that I was emotionally shutdown. While growing up, I had learned to "not feel" the impact of my mother's illness. At first, I couldn't see it, but once I did, the realization opened my heart like never before. Talk therapy doesn't solve everything, but it made an enormous difference in my life. I doubt I could have built a successful company without it.

Meanwhile, my lawyer, David Lubell, kept urging me to rent an office, hire a staff, and start a progressive PR firm. The prospect terrified me financially. There were no such firms, and I recoiled from assuming the financial obligations. But I was getting gigs and outgrowing working from my bedroom. I also felt apprehensive about the growing influence big corporate PR firms had on the media.

The first New York Times article on founding Fenton Communications, April 21, 1984.

Even the most fair-minded reporters couldn't help but be affected by these firms' effort to influence them. When only one side is meeting with journalists or sending them story ideas and information, that side automatically gains more influence. The major PR firms mostly represented the wrong side—big, often-polluting companies and, increasingly, such murderous dictators as Mobutu Sese Seko in Zaire and Ferdinand Marcos in the Philippines. This was really bad for democracy.

A progressive alternative to these "will lie for money" types seemed imperative. But I had no idea if it could be financially successful. I was also wary of the designation "PR firm," which in our culture—especially among progressives—stands for paid deception and deceit. A PR firm for social good seemed like a good alternative.

I was afraid of failure, but David Lubell persisted. David had become my second substitute father, after John Sinclair. David and his twin brother, Jonathan, were nearly thrown out of Harvard Law School in the 1950s for taking the Fifth Amendment and refusing to tell the House Un-American Activities Committee if they were members of the Communist Party USA. They were—and their contribution to civil rights, social justice, and constitutional and First Amendment law remain a beacon to this day.

So, in February 1982, just before my thirtieth birthday, I listened to David and took my meager $10,000 in savings, bought office furniture, rented two rooms on West 57th Street and opened Fenton Communications Inc. as a for-profit business. I felt so anxious that I immediately tried to sublet one room. That proved unnecessary—Fenton grew

PR FOR THE RIGHT

Speaking of PR for the Right, one particularly bad actor was Black, Manafort, Stone, and Kelly, a Republican lobbying firm that worked for some of the world's worst human rights abusers, notably Angola's rebel leader and apartheid ally Jonas Savimbi. You might recognize "Stone" as Trump loyalist Roger Stone, whose crimes the president pardoned. Paul Manafort is in jail as I write, having sold his access to Trump while managing his campaign. Charlie Black, for a while head of the Republican National Committee, perfected so-called black ops, or the intentional spreading of false information to damage political opponents. They tried to portray the murderous Savimbi as some kind of freedom fighter, right when he terrorized the population in alliance with apartheid South Africa. Other big corporate firms, including Hill + Knowlton, Edelman, and Burson-Marsteller, were just as sleazy—and often still are. They help fossil fuel companies deny their role in ruining the climate. The giant PR firm Edelman is under pressure as I write to stop working for the oil companies on climate grounds.

quickly. After just one week I hired a brilliant natural publicist, Cathy Saypol, who had been Gloria Steinem's head of PR at *Ms. Magazine*. Six months later, in the summer of 1982, we opened an office in Washington, D.C.. Today, Fenton employs almost one hundred people in four cities. One hundred percent of its work involves progressive causes, mostly nonprofits, foundations, and some government agencies. And Fenton has spawned several imitators.

ARE NONPROFITS ALWAYS THE BEST VEHICLE FOR CHANGE?

Over the years, many people have asked me two questions: Why did I found Fenton as a for-profit enterprise? And could we make money working almost exclusively for nonprofits? I'm a lifelong activist, but I've always questioned some elements of the nonprofit model, especially their layers of bureaucracy. Of course, for-profit companies can also become mired in bureaucracy, but compared with nonprofits, for-profits are usually nimbler. At Fenton, we had to be nimble. If we didn't perform for clients, we got fired. If we didn't work efficiently, we lost money. If we didn't return people's phone calls promptly, we risked going out of business. One big problem with many of today's big nongovernmental organizations (NGOs, meaning a voluntary group or institution with a social mission not run by the government) is that they become bureaucratic and lose their founders' flair for taking risks and getting things done. At many NGOs, people get what amounts to tenure, whether or not they keep innovating and help the organization grow. It can take twenty-five people five meetings to reach decisions—or postpone making them. For-profit

David Fenton.

Communications.
Twelve Charles Street, No. 6D, New York, N.Y. 10014 (212)929-1331

My first business card after founding my company, 1982.

firms cannot afford to act this way. I sometimes sympathize with conservatives who correctly despise the sloth of overly bureaucratic government agencies. Most NGOs pay no bonuses for performance, which just plain goes against human nature. At Fenton, from day one, I did. Rewarding people incentivizes them to do their best. I believe some kind of hybrid of the for- and nonprofit model would serve the progressive movement better.

Nonprofits have another big problem—they don't pay people enough to stay in movement careers as they get older, start families, buy homes, etc. NGO leaders often say they "can't afford" to pay more—but sometimes paying more attracts better talent, so you can get more done with fewer people. This, however, is not how most NGOs think. There are some great NGO leaders that I admire. But too many of them make large salaries with no performance measurements and, frankly, without much success at times.

TOTALLY NUTS FOR BEN & JERRY'S

Since business pretty much controls the world, I wanted to help the newly emergent "socially responsible" companies do actual good, as opposed to greenwashing. We promoted the first ethically screened progressive investment fund, Calvert, then ice-cream chain Ben & Jerry's and cosmetics company The Body Shop. I met their key people after joining the Social Venture Network (SVN), a trade organization of progressive business activists and progressives who had inherited substantial wealth. In 1992, SVN launched a bigger, more mainstream group, Business for Social Responsibility (BSR). I'm proud to say Fenton was a founding member.

We had a blast working with Ben Cohen, cofounder of Ben & Jerry's. In 1996, he decided to release a new flavor to protest the unbelievably bloated defense budget. But his new flavor had no name. Following the precept "keep things simple," our creative director suggested "Totally Nuts." It became quite popular.

Anita Roddick of The Body Shop was a force of nature and a real pioneer in sourcing ethical fair-trade ingredients, paying living wages, and eschewing animal testing. She did have one problem, however. She was such a visionary that she sometimes made announcements in speeches as if they had already happened—when they were still just ideas in her head. Eventually, one tenacious journalist criticized her for these dreamy pre-announcements. Poor Anita took this hard and withdrew from much of her socially responsible work, I suppose to avoid risking more criticism. Lesson for activists: Never overpromise and underdeliver. Do the opposite.

STEALING RONALD REAGAN'S SPOTLIGHT

In its early days, Fenton took significant risks and got into what the great Black activist and congressman John Lewis called "good trouble." One early cause involved opposing the Reagan administration's murderous interventions in the civil war in El Salvador and against the Sandinistas in Nicaragua. This period will go down as a shameful episode in our nation's history, in which the Reagan administration funded death squads that tortured and murdered thousands of activists fighting against oligarchy—close to fifty thousand in El Salvador alone. Reagan claimed that we were fighting Communism. Actually, we were protecting the economic interests of US companies and

their partners among the ruling and land-owning gentry in those small poor countries. At Fenton, we were determined to counter the administration's media manipulation and tell the public the truth.

Bill Zimmerman, a longtime activist and author of the important memoir *Troublemaker*, was running a controversial humanitarian effort to send medical supplies into the rebel-controlled areas of El Salvador. Bill introduced me to a Salvadoran guerilla commander, whom I knew only as Rene. Rene, whose last name I never learned (or if Rene was even his first name), was fluent in English, with an easy, trusting manner. He could somehow regularly visit the United States and was good at remaining in the background. We discussed the need to counter the Reagan administration's propaganda by arranging for a US TV crew to visit the rebel-controlled zones. Rene assured me he could guarantee their safety, even in the midst of an all-out civil war. I decided to trust him.

I visited Howard Stringer, the executive producer of the CBS *Evening News* (and later the head of Sony), and persuaded him to send the first US TV crew into rebel-controlled areas. Producer David Gelber and correspondent Mike O'Connor met Rene in New York and also decided to trust his assurances of their safety. They were about to risk their lives. I felt profoundly responsible for their fate. Just weeks before, a Dutch TV crew had been murdered by Salvadoran government death squads as they'd attempted the same thing.

Thankfully, Gelber and O'Connor emerged safely. Their reports on CBS were the first to show the rebels in a human light, serving their population and protecting people from right-wing death squads. This infuriated the White House and the State Department, whose propaganda machine

TOP *Crossing a bombed-out bridge with journalists to reach rebel-controlled areas of El Salvador during the civil war, 1984.* **BOTTOM** *Salvadoran rebel commanders Shafik Handel and Joaquin Villalobos meet journalists from rebel-controlled territory, 1984.*

had depicted these mostly former schoolteachers and labor organizers as terrorists instead of who they really were: fighters for social justice who had been driven to take up arms rather than become victims of US-supported death squads. To get Americans' support for murdering these people, they had to be demonized first.

As thoroughly documented in Mark Hertsgaard's 1988 book, *On Bended Knee: The Press and the Reagan Presidency*, the Reagan administration was accustomed to having the media all to itself. So, when Fenton arranged fair media treatment for the "enemy," the government came after my staff and me big time. For daring to distribute a simple press kit explaining why rebel leaders could not run in the Salvadoran elections without risking their lives, Deputy Secretary of State Elliot Abrams denounced Fenton by name several times at the televised daily State Department briefings. (Abrams was later convicted of withholding information from Congress in the Iran-Contra affair. In my opinion, he is a war criminal.) The *Wall Street Journal* ran a lead editorial that also excoriated our efforts.

Next, I personally shepherded a group of reporters from *The New York Times, Washington Post, Associated Press,* and others into rebel-controlled El Salvador. This truly was dangerous. We had to cross a bombed-out collapsed bridge and stay completely undercover. When we finally arrived at our destination in the middle of nowhere, the guerilla leaders served us a five-course steak dinner. Clearly, the United States was not winning the war against them. The charismatic rebel commander, Joaquín Villalobos, showed us a video they had recently shot of a US Army helicopter crashing nearby. The United States lied,

of course, claiming it crashed accidentally far from combat areas. (Later, the *Financial Times* called Villalobos "the true master of 20th-century Latin American guerilla warfare, above even Che Guevara." He eventually helped negotiate the peace accord that ended El Salvador's civil war and became a leading politician and intellectual.)

Most of the US press corps covering Nicaragua and El Salvador were based in Mexico City. The five Salvadoran rebel groups also had offices there. To combat White House media demonization of the rebels, I threw a series of parties in Mexico City, where the reporters and the guerilla commanders could eat, drink, and mingle. Over time, these get-togethers and the relationships they engendered helped change the reporting on Central America. Key lesson for PR activists—throw lots of parties for journalists, with plenty of booze.

One of the most popular figures at these events was Rubén Zamora, the mild-mannered, university-educated head of the Social Democratic Party in El Salvador who had become allied with the rebels. His brother had been murdered by right-wing death squads. He feared he was next, so he left the country. In Europe, Zamora would have been viewed as an ordinary social democratic politician, but to the Reagan administration, he was a "dangerous communist."

On the same day Congress required Reagan to report whether or not the Salvadoran military was "making progress on human rights," we organized a press conference to counter the president. It featured spokespeople for several human rights groups that insisted there had been no progress. That death squads continued to operate. Many major media gave us equal TV billing with the president. We rained on Reagan's parade pretty well.

The murder and mayhem the United States spread to Central America remains among this country's worst and most shameful hours and directly resulted in the immigration crisis today by destabilizing those small poor nations. The former US ambassador to El Salvador, Robert White, later told me that the CIA had literally chosen death squad victims in the basement of the US Embassy.

One of the most shameful episodes in the history of TV journalism in United States occurred when all three network anchors broadcast their government hired Fenton to arrange a series of press briefings for d'Escoto, the first time I had to register as a foreign agent. But most of Fenton's work opposing the Reagan wars in Nicaragua and El Salvador was underwritten by human rights groups, churches, and a young woman who had inherited a Texas oil fortune from her father. Several times during the war, Fenton staff and I traveled to Nicaragua to visit villagers who had been terrorized by the US-backed forces, the Contras. In the far back country, we had to travel armed to protect ourselves from the US-paid mercenaries. It was scary.

IT WAS ONE OF THE MOST SHAMEFUL EPISODES IN THE HISTORY OF TV JOURNALISM.

news shows from El Salvador on their election day. The anchors interviewed presidential candidate Roberto D'Aubuisson from a hotel rooftop, fawning over him as some kind of democrat. In fact, he ran El Salvador's death squads, as has been well documented. (For more on our crimes in Central America, I recommend former *New York Times* reporter Raymond Bonner's seminal book *Weakness and Deceit: U.S. Policy and El Salvador*.)

Attending my first congressional hearing on the war in Nicaragua, I was astonished to hear Boston University President John Silber denounce Fenton by name for helping the media meet Nicaragua's Sandinista leaders. Knowing the history of the McCarthy era, this was worrying. I had gotten to know the Sandinista leadership through Nicaragua's foreign minister, Miguel d'Escoto, a Roman Catholic priest whom I'd met in New York at progressive antiwar events. The Nicaraguan

When my staff arranged for Sandinista leader Daniel Ortega and his wife, Rosario Murillo, to appear on the widely syndicated *The Phil Donahue Show* (a precursor of *The Oprah Winfrey Show*) and meet with the three network news anchors, the Reagan White House went berserk. We never glorified the Sandinistas, who were a mixed bunch with some bad apples, like most movements, but we were 100 percent opposed to the United States backing oligarchs and spreading terror in those countries. Only the poor suffered from these misadventures. (Unfortunately, as I write, Ortega, the current president of Nicaragua, has turned out to be a terrible disappointment—and brutal despot.)

Reagan once called Contra terrorists "the moral equivalent of the founding fathers." Hardly. While in Nicaragua, I met a US attorney, Reid Brody, who produced scores of signed, handwritten, first-person, multiple-eyewitness accounts of horrible Contra atrocities against villagers. They attacked children and pulled out their parents' fingernails, spreading terror to try to topple the Sandinista government. I brought Brody's yellow legal paper signed affidavits to John Darnton, then the deputy foreign editor of *The New York Times*, and challenged him to send a reporter to Nicaragua to investigate. He did, the reporter verified it all, and the resulting front-page story helped galvanize Congress to cut off aid to the Contras for good.

In response, Reagan illegally sold arms to Iran, surreptitiously funneling the proceeds to the Contras, clearly violating the will of Congress. Reagan tapped the notorious Colonel Oliver North to run the operation. For his efforts, North was eventually indicted on three felony charges.

We used basic public relations techniques against Reagan's war. We built relationships with reporters and introduced them to the people under attack, humanizing them. We counterprogrammed to block the White House's ability to control the narrative. Fenton and other activists organized a massive campaign that succeeded in finally cutting off all funding to the Contras.

WE TRY TO STOP REAGAN FROM INVADING TINY GRENADA

One war we failed to prevent was Reagan's 1983 invasion of the Caribbean nation Grenada, which the United Nations denounced as "a flagrant violation of international law." The official—and totally false—story was that Cuban soldiers had supposedly taken over the island and were building a military airbase there. Americans studying to be doctors at the medical school there were allegedly in danger until cowboy Ronald Reagan swept in and saved them. The lasting image of the invasion was American students kissing the ground when they landed back home in Miami.

This was all propaganda.

A few months before the US invasion, I'd met Grenada's tall, handsome, and compelling prime minister, Maurice Bishop. He wanted to ensure good relations with the US, as Granada's economy was wholly dependent on tourism. Bishop showed me a report from US engineers that recommended extending Grenada's sole airport runway so that jumbo jets full of tourists could land on the tiny island. Bishop's government contracted with Cuban construction workers to build the longer runway. Reagan was already making a stink about the airport, claiming it would become a Cuban military base. This was nonsense.

Prime Minister Bishop visited Washington, D.C., and Fenton staff took him around. Not one member of the Reagan administration agreed to meet with him. Not one was interested in the real purpose of the runway. They preferred war to boost Reagan's image. (The idea that the Cubans would provoke the US with a new military base is fanciful.) So, instead, we took Bishop to meet journalists and editorial writers to make his case. Later, we learned the Reagan administration had already decided to invade little Grenada to prove the United States was over its Vietnam-induced syndrome of avoidance of military intervention.

To its credit, at first the media did a good job presenting Bishop's evidence that the runway

---

The 1983 ABC TV movie The Day After *helped reverse the nuclear arms race.*

UNTHINKABLE . . .
NUCLEAR WAR . . .
APOCALYPSE . . . THE
END OF THE FAMILIAR . . .
THE BEGINNING OF
THE END . . .

THE DAY AFTER

was being built to boost tourism. But then, when he returned to Granada, Bishop was overthrown by ultra-leftist crazies in his own party and soon killed. This provided Reagan's excuse to invade. For those of us who have been to Lilliputian Granada, the idea that this was some big military victory for the United States is laughable. It's really a shame about Bishop, who was setting a new example in the Caribbean, helping poor people, like former Jamaican Prime Minister Michael Manley, who introduced me to Bishop.

SIMPLE "NUCLEAR FREEZE" CONCEPT HELPS REVERSE THE ARMS RACE

We didn't stop that invasion, but in the early days of Fenton, our small firm managed to have a disproportionate impact on the escalating nuclear arms race between the Soviet Union and the United States. Both nations were stockpiling more nuclear weapons of every kind, including so-called tactical nuclear weapons that could be launched against opposing armies on the battlefields of Europe. Even worse, both sides' growing arsenals were kept on "hair-trigger" alert, programmed to "launch on warning." At the first sign of incoming missiles, they could be launched with no questions asked. And if they were, within twenty minutes, hundreds of millions would die and much of the Earth would become uninhabitable.

Ronald Reagan's plan was to bankrupt the Soviet Union by frightening the Kremlin into spending all its limited resources on an expanded nuclear arsenal. It was insanely dangerous. He even joked about it, saying in a live interview that "the bombs will start falling in five minutes."

Reagan's nuclear moves right after taking office in 1981 terrified the public, fueling the explosive growth of a movement to reverse the nuclear arms race. This movement was funded in part by members of the Rockefeller family. Through Wade Greene, a former *New York Times* reporter who had become a philanthropic consultant to the Rockefellers, Fenton received funding to work with several arms control groups. We advised them how to increase their media savvy and impact. I owe so much to Wade, who passed away in 2019. He was a gentle soul. Luckily, as a former journalist, he understood the importance of communications. Back then, hardly any funders did.

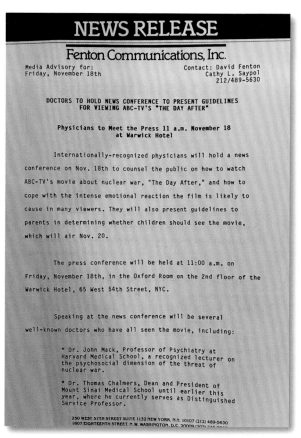

A press release that got 100 million people to watch The Day After. *It was the most-watched made-for-TV movie in history.*

Working with the telegenic Dr. Randall Forsberg of MIT, we helped the idea of a "nuclear freeze" become a household phrase. Forsberg created the "freeze" concept—freeze the production and deployment of new nuclear weapons. The concept's simplicity and common sense, combined with Forsberg's warmth and communication skills on television, resonated with Americans.

As I've mentioned, only simple, moral, emotional messages, repeated over and over again, change public opinion (and the brain). Freeze nuclear weapons. That's easy to understand. A nuclear freeze. It's common sense and goes straight to the heart. Trump is a master of the simple message repeated endlessly. "Make America Great Again." Like it or not, that's what our brains respond to.

The nuclear freeze movement, and the resulting million-person antinuclear rally on June 12, 1982, in New York's Central Park (publicized by guess which PR firm), forced Reagan to change direction and negotiate historic arms reduction agreements with the new Soviet president, Mikhail Gorbachev. The Left won one by reframing the issue and transforming public opinion, which moved the government. At one point, Reagan and Gorbachev even discussed phasing out all nuclear weapons entirely. Of course, the political and military establishment shot that one down right away.

Another event that galvanized public opinion against the nuclear arms race was the November 1983 ABC broadcast of the made-for-TV film *The Day After*. This gripping, frightening film showed the effects of a dramatically created "limited" nuclear war. In the film, the United States uses tactical nuclear weapons against the Soviet Union,

MORAL STORIES

Every movement needs a few strong, likable, effective spokespeople. We had a great one in Dr. Randall Forsberg. People learn from engaging characters and moral stories. Today, too many progressive leaders bore the public with endless facts, scorning simple moral stories. And too many activists also scorn the very idea of leaders and spokespeople altogether. Based on fifty years of progressive PR, that's not just sad, it's stupid.

and the Russians retaliate with nuclear missiles that hit the Midwest. It is still the most watched made-for-TV film in history. And it scared the country to death.

Months before its broadcast, Josh Baran, an ace progressive publicist working for the antinuclear wing of the Rockefeller family, showed me a bootleg advance copy of the film. We immediately realized its importance and created a strategy to get everyone to watch it.

Working with the antinuclear doctor's group, Physicians for Social Responsibility, we decided to scare people into watching it. We sent out a number of unusual press releases.

The first one was headlined "This Movie Is Really Scary. Don't Watch It Alone."

The second said "This Movie Is Really Scary. Talk to Your Doctor before You Watch It."

Another warned "This Movie Is Really Scary. Don't Let Your Children Watch It."

That's a big part of why one hundred million Americans watched it. At first, ABC excoriated us. But eventually they changed their tune. Our efforts vastly boosted the film's audience. Sure, I know, our tactics smacked of P. T. Barnum, the circus huckster. But it was for a good cause. It worked.

JESSE JACKSON AND CARL SAGAN FIGHT NUCLEAR WEAPONS

The film and nuclear freeze movement changed the context for the first Reagan/Gorbachev summit in Geneva in 1985. I met the new Soviet leader while accompanying Rev. Jesse Jackson to the event. Gorbachev had just assumed power and was still an enigma to the West. Most previous Soviet leaders were opaque, angry, dull, defensive, and massively repressive, so expectations were not high. The Berlin Wall was still up, and most of Eastern Europe was still under Soviet domination.

We were hired by the National Committee for a Sane Nuclear Policy (SANE) to help the Reverend Jackson represent the peace movement

Reverend Jesse Jackson asks Soviet leader Mikhail Gorbachev about the plight of Soviet Jews, November 19, 1985.

at the Geneva summit. When word came that Gorbachev would meet with Jackson, the reverend insisted on bringing fifteen television crews with him. A private tête-à-tête was not for him. Around this time, Rev. Jackson had gotten into big trouble with the Jewish community for mentioning that, during his youth, Black people bought clothes from Jewish stores in a neighborhood they called "Hymietown." Many Jews considered this a slur. As a Jew myself, I can attest there is not an anti-Semitic bone in Rev. Jackson's very spiritual body. But his remark was a big mistake. It hurt his credibility.

Jesse Jackson is very tall—Gorbachev is very short. As we stood in a circle, surrounded by at least thirty journalists with cameras, Jackson looked down on Gorbachev, and as we had agreed earlier asked, "What about the plight of Soviet Jews? Why won't you let them leave Russia?" Gorbachev ignored him. I whispered in Jackson's ear, and he asked the question again. Gorbachev exploded, saying "There is no problem with Jews in our country! Here is comrade Arbatov, the head of our US research institute—he's a Jew." This exchange helped Jesse partially repair the damage done by his previous thoughtless remark.

Rev. Jesse Jackson might be the most articulate person I've met. He is certainly the fastest on his feet, speaking with absolutely no preparation, no writers, no rehearsals, no role-playing. He makes powerful points in poetry and rhyme. Talk about a natural orator. He's among the best. People rarely remember that he assembled a rainbow coalition and ran for president in 1984 and 1988. He won enormous numbers of white working-class votes in key primaries. Jackson was truly a pioneer, decades before President Obama came along.

In fighting the nuclear arms race, we also had the privilege of working with astronomer and TV personality Dr. Carl Sagan, who hired us to publicize his protests against underground nuclear testing in Nevada. We publicized his civil disobedience arrests as he blocked the entrance to the Nevada nuclear test site. Sagan was one of the most important scientists of his generation. He was also gracious and a frequent pot smoker. Maybe that helped him contemplate the universe. He helped select the human artifacts carried by the *Voyager* interplanetary probe to explain us to distant aliens. He also coined the phrase "one pale, blue dot" to describe Earth as seen from outer space. His *Cosmos* series on PBS showed the public the "billions and billions" of stars and galaxies that surround us. And his protest against underground nuclear tests bore fruit. The United States and Russia concluded a treaty that banned them forever. Thank you, Carl Sagan!

Sagan consciously used his celebrity to help humanity. He was that rare scientist willing to engage the public using simple, clear language. I wish he were still here helping us with climate change today!

My lawyer, David Lubell, had pushed me to leave my bedroom and open a progressive PR firm. He was right beyond anything I could have imagined. The firm had impact, and became profitable, right away. Fenton Communications became an important force in the media and on the left. It remains so to this day.

CHAPTER 10

FIGHTING TO FREE NELSON MANDELA AND CONFRONTING FIDEL

While visiting Nicaragua to attend Daniel Ortega's 1984 inauguration as president, I developed a fever and became very ill. Late one night while I was sick, Ortega showed up at our guesthouse and insisted out group of *norteamericanos* come with him on an unexpected journey. So, off I went, thinking I should stay in bed. As our convoy pulled into a heavily armed military base on the outskirts of Managua, there loomed large the six-foot-three figure of Fidel Castro in his famous freshly starched green army uniform. There were no chairs, so we stood up and listened. For three hours. In Spanish, with simultaneous translation. His monologue was so riveting, I forgot how sick I was.

Our group wasn't easy to impress. Hollywood producer Bert Schneider had made the classic films *Easy Rider* and *Five Easy Pieces*. Attorney Michael Kennedy had represented Abbie Hoffman, antiwar protestors, and major pot dealers. Los Angeles activist and media consultant Bill Zimmerman had personally broken the FBI's blockade of the American Indian Movement takeover of Wounded Knee, South Dakota, on the Pine Ridge Indian Reservation. A pilot, he dropped supplies to the protestors so they wouldn't starve. During the 1970s, Zimmerman ran Tom Hayden's unsuccessful campaign for US Senate and launched Medical Aid for El Salvador, which supplied medicines to rebel-controlled areas of the country. Zimmerman later masterminded the ballot initiatives

Meeting with Fidel Castro in Havana, Cuba. From left: me, Madeline Eisner, Fidel, and Bill Zimmerman.

that successfully legalized medical marijuana in California and other states. A true American hero.

My girlfriend, Jill Bullitt, was also there. Jill was the black sheep of a famous Seattle family that had founded the biggest TV and radio chain in the Northwest, KING Broadcasting. Her father, Stimson "Stim" Bullitt, was the first owner of a US TV station to oppose the Vietnam War on the air. For that, his mother, Dorothy, who controlled the company, sacked him.

Castro riveted us. He had an incredible grasp of history and explained in great detail how his poor Caribbean island had ended malnutrition, greatly reduced infant mortality, and brought health care to the entire population. But after an hour and a half, I asked him a question. He *exploded*, turned beet red, and accused me of "interrupting him." After ninety minutes! The unquestioned dictator had been questioned. That was my last question that night.

I had asked why restaurants in Cuba didn't offer lobster and high-quality fish. After all, Cuba is an island surrounded by water filled with both. Castro went into a long, detailed explanation. Compared with lobster, there was much more protein in condensed milk. So, he explained, it made more sense to sell the lobster abroad and buy condensed milk on the international market to feed Cuban children. He knew the protein content and market prices of each down to the gram. Bill Zimmerman told me later that Castro was the "smartest man I've ever met."

Toward the end of our three hours of standing up listening to Castro, at around three in the morning, he asked what we all did in the United States. After he learned that Zimmerman was a political consultant and that I did progressive

PR, he said "I really want to learn more about American politics and media to help improve Cuba's relations with the United States. Please visit me in Havana." We agreed.

ANOTHER CASTRO MEETING

A few months later, I found myself in Cuba, arranging press coverage for a congressional delegation investigating the origins of the Reagan wars in Central America. Reagan had castigated Castro for supporting the insurgencies—which of course was true. Bill Zimmerman flew in, too, and one morning we visited Castro in his spacious but down-to-earth, wood-paneled office with high ceilings and beautiful abstract paintings of revolutionary commanders. This time we had a two-way conversation, starting in the morning, continuing all day and then through dinner. (His aides kept reminding him he had other appointments, but he brushed them away.) It was remarkable how few security people accompanied him as we went out to eat, especially given how many times the CIA had tried to kill him with poisoned cigars and poisoned food. Castro truly had ninety lives. Back in 1953, when he landed the yacht *Granma* crammed with fifty revolutionaries on a beach, only he and five others survived being machine-gunned from the air by the forces of Cuban dictator Fulgencio Batista.

At his office, I urged Castro not to wear his trademark green military fatigues when he traveled abroad. His aides recoiled in horror. Nobody talked that way to El Comandante, apparently. "To the rest of the world, it doesn't mean what it means to your supporters in Cuba," I explained. "Here, it reminds people that you liberated them from a brutal military dictator and the Mafia and gave everyone free education and health care. Abroad, it communicates that you're a military dictator." Castro was getting the "use symbolism" lesson backward. His military uniform was the wrong symbol outside Cuba.

There was a long silence. Castro laughed and came back at me with "Next, you are going to tell me to dye my beard black!" I said no, the beard was okay, but the green army uniform had to go. Castro never wore that uniform on a foreign trip again. From then on, he always wore a suit and tie.

We spent most of the day talking about the political situation in the United States. Castro could quote the congressional record on the course of every debate having to do with Cuba. On every vote, he knew who voted for and against. Never before nor since have I met anyone with such an extraordinary command of detail. Castro seemed to think he could manage every detail of the Cuban economy by the sheer force of his personality. Having spent time with him, I could see how he suffered from that delusion.

Returning from Cuba, the FBI called. An FBI agent offered to take me to lunch.

"What do you want to talk about?" I asked.

"We'd rather not talk about that on the phone."

"Why not? You're the people who tap the phones."

"Well, I work for the counterintelligence division of the FBI. We note your recent visits with Fidel Castro and Daniel Ortega and want to know if you'd like to serve your country?"

They wanted to recruit me as a counterintelligence agent.

In Fidel Castro's private office in Havana, Cuba. From left: Madeline Eisner, me, the translator, Bill Zimmerman, and Fidel.

My heart racing, I told them to call my lawyer and never spoke to them again.

Through my later friendship with Jamaican Prime Minister Michael Manley, I spent more time with Castro in the 1980s, as he and Manley were friends from neighboring islands. Castro is perhaps the most complicated figure of the twentieth century. He was a horrible human rights violator. He inexcusably kept dissidents in prison long past their sentences and relentlessly crushed dissent. At the same time, we will never know what his government would have been like if the United States had not been so committed to overthrowing and killing him. That could make anyone sufficiently paranoid to suppress opposition and seek support from another superpower. Every time I came to Cuba from an impoverished Central American nation, it was astonishing to see the level of literacy, education, and medical care available to everyone at that time. Yet, the upper classes had left the country as their property was brutally seized and redistributed. Certainly Castro was one of the most spellbinding, charismatic, flawed, and dogmatic people I have ever met. Years later, I worked with Nelson Mandela, who said that without Castro, he might well have died in prison. More on that later.

I realize it will be easy to distort my comments here about Castro, who remains a highly polarizing figure in our country. When Bernie Sanders ran for president in 2020, he condemned Castro's crackdowns on the opposition, while also mentioning that Castro had introduced many reforms, including a massive literacy program, that proved remarkably successful for reducing poverty and improving Cubans' quality of life. Critics mercilessly attacked Bernie for that, but he was right.

Castro did both horrible and good things, as history will undoubtedly show. President Barack Obama was certainly right to open diplomatic relations with Cuba, as the cruel previous policy of isolation never worked and never will.

WORKING WITH NELSON MANDELA

Nelson Mandela is the only saint I've ever met.

Somehow after twenty-seven years of imprisonment by the white apartheid South African regime, the man had transcended anger. I saw this firsthand. In 1994, while in South Africa volunteering for his first campaign for president, Madiba, as he was affectionately known, took me to a meeting in Johannesburg with his former jail guards. He wanted their input into the design of the new home he was building. He wanted it to be an exact replica of the house he'd inhabited while confined at Pollsmoor Prison. There was the tall, slender, regal Mandela, backslapping his former jailers, joking and trading stories. No anger. It was astonishing.

I first started working for Mandela's political party, the African National Congress (ANC) in the mid-1980s, while Mandela was still in prison. My introduction to the ANC came from antiwar activist Cora Weiss, an heir to the Fabergé cosmetics fortune who knew the ANC's ambassador to the United Nations, Johnny Makatini.

A lawyer, Mandela had spent years organizing peaceful and legal protest against South Africa's racist apartheid system, which forcibly separated white and Black. Getting nowhere, he eventually decided apartheid could be overthrown only by guerilla warfare. For this he was hunted down and imprisoned for almost three decades,

Working with Nelson Mandela during his first US tour, Washington, D.C., June 1990.

along with dozens of ANC colleagues. In 1990, with Mandela still in prison, the combination of international sanctions and increased popular resistance inside the country—both peaceful and armed—forced the apartheid regime to negotiate a transition to Black majority rule. This included releasing Mandela from prison that year.

In the mid-1980s, with funding from David Rockefeller's rebel daughter, Peggy Dulany, Fenton staff brought ANC officials to Washington to meet with journalists. Among them were ANC President Oliver Tambo and future South African President Thabo Mbeki. The Reagan administration was firmly on the side of racist apartheid and falsely portrayed everyone in the ANC as "dangerous communists and terrorists." We worked to dispel that lie.

People forget that Ronald Reagan was firmly on the side of racist apartheid. His administration was actively engaged in a military alliance with the apartheid regime. Working together with genius organizer and lawyer Randall Robinson, founder of TransAfrica, the Black foreign policy lobbying group in Washington, we helped

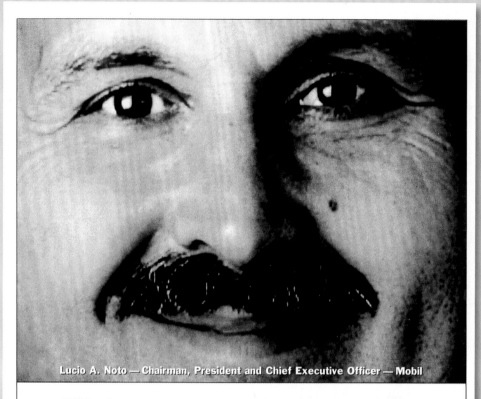

Lucio A. Noto — Chairman, President and Chief Executive Officer — Mobil

This man can actually change the weather.

Severe storms. Floods. Temperature extremes. Unchecked, global warming will mean catastrophic climate change. Mr. Noto and the CEO'S of the other oil companies could help prevent that catastrophe.

Here's the message Mobil Oil should be running today: *We at Mobil recognize that the burning of fossil fuels — oil and coal — is the major cause of global warming. Global warming is now an accepted scientific fact. It would take over fifty years to burn the proven reserves of oil at the current rate of use. If we were to burn all that oil, along with even moderate amounts of coal, the resulting change in climate would create a world wide catastrophe. We must pursue a safer, saner course: NO NEW OIL.*

Instead of exploring and drilling for even more oil — as our fellow oil companies are foolishly proposing to do off Alaska's north coast — we pledge instead to stop further exploration. We also pledge to devote our research and development dollars to promoting energy efficiency and implementing solar and other renewable energy sources. We have more than enough reserves, more than enough time to prevent disruptions in the lives of the American people while we provide an orderly shift from oil and coal to renewable energy. Again, our motto will be: NO NEW OIL.

Unfortunately, this message is not forthcoming from Mobil and the other oil companies. Until these companies have leadership that understands that substantial profits can be made from solar and other renewable energy sources, it is up to each of us to act. We at Greenpeace are leading the fight to stop the oil companies from further exploration. Join us.

GREENPEACE

You can reach Greenpeace at 800-326-0959 or www.greenpeaceusa.org

pass congressional sanctions against South Africa. Reagan vetoed the bill. But we successfully lobbied Congress to overturn his veto. Presidential vetoes rarely get overturned. It takes a two-thirds majority vote in both the House and Senate. But the tide was turning against apartheid, and we succeeded.

I took several trips to Angola to meet with ANC leaders in exile, including their military chief, Chris Hane, later assassinated by the apartheid regime. These were tense, frightening trips deep into Angola's war-torn countryside. I'm a nervous flyer to begin with, so being piloted by teenagers in an Angolan air force plane with the windows blacked out was not fun. To land, in a thunderstorm no less, we descended in a sharp corkscrew spiral—to avoid ground fire. I was so terrified I wrote a goodbye letter from the plane to my second wife, Beth Bogart.

I met Beth when I hired her for a job at Fenton's Washington office. She was a brilliant writer and publicist who had been among the first women to attend Princeton. She could also be a bit impulsive—she quit Harvard Law School after only five days, deciding the school valued the law more than actual justice.

To push US companies to withdraw from South Africa, Randall Robinson came up with an advertising campaign that juxtaposed the faces of American corporate CEOs with photos of the South African police beating up children. "Meet IBM's CEO," the ad read, "A Face Behind Apartheid." Or "Meet Senator Bob Dole: A Face Behind Apartheid." This personalization of the issue proved remarkably effective at putting

Climate ad for Greenpeace by Pacy Markman of Zimmerman/ Markman, early 1990s.

prominent Americans on the defensive. Soon after those ads ran, increasing numbers of companies withdrew from the country.

Attention activists: Whenever possible, get personal. All the policies you hate—there are people behind them, people whose photos are usually readily available. Stories need characters. Focusing on them helps the public understand the issue. Plus, this approach generates news—and pushback, which can generate more news. For example, in the 1990s, Fenton produced a climate change ad for Greenpeace that ran in the *Washington Post*. It featured a photo of the CEO of Mobil above the headline "This Man Has the Power to Change the Weather." I happened to once sit on a bus next to a top executive of the corporate PR firm, Burson-Marsteller. Learning who I was, he said "David, every time your anti-apartheid ads attack another corporate leader, we get another client."

Robinson's other inspiration was arranging arrests at the South African embassy in Washington, D.C.. Every day for months, he escorted members of Congress, business and church leaders, and celebrities of all kinds to the embassy of apartheid, where they sat down and got arrested. These demonstrations started small, but they grew and grew, putting enormous pressure on the Reagan administration to act against apartheid. Soon, there was a waiting list for celebrities and politicians to get arrested. Randall Robinson was an organizing genius.

Those demonstrations succeeded because they happened *every day*. Repetition is critical. It's a crucial source of political power. People in power know they can usually ignore one-day news stories. After twenty-four hours, they go away. Politicians rarely pay attention until stories persist for several days. After a week or so, they appoint task forces and presidential commissions. That's how it works.

So, the challenge for activists is to devise scenarios that guarantee their story gets repetitive play. Don't say or reveal everything at once. For maximum impact, stage a series of events. Announce endorsements serially and add surprise announcements later. Keep the pot boiling.

The brain learns best from repetition of simple messages. If you hear something once, it does not usually stick in your head. We progressives hate simple slogans like "Make America Great Again," but through massive, intentional repetition, they work to change public opinion. Repetition, repetition, repeat after me. This is why advertisers repeat their messages until you are sick to death of them. Only then do they work.

After the anti-apartheid campaign, Randall Robinson told me he hired Fenton because he thought I was Black. I'm not—but I'd just returned from Jamaica and had a hell of a deep suntan. I'm so glad he made that mistake. Tall, proud, and with regal bearing, Robinson had grown up in segregated Richmond, Virginia, and worked hard to suppress his understandable anger about racism. In 2000, he published *The Debt: What America Owes to Blacks*, the first detailed call for reparations. The book opens with a description of how slaves built the White House and the US Capitol. Who got paid for the work? Their owners.

Moderating an anti-apartheid news conference in Washington with Harry Belafonte and Bishop Desmond Tutu.

Because of Robinson, not long after Mandela was released, Fenton staff and I helped organize Mandela's first visit to the United States. We worked with the great singer and activist Harry Belafonte, tennis legend Arthur Ashe, South African Archbishop Desmond Tutu, and many others. It was the first time I used a cell phone— of course in the early '90s they were huge and weighed a ton, which is hard to believe now.

Mandela toured eight US cities. The highlight was his speech to an overflow crowd at Yankee Stadium. Dressed in the team's uniform, he told the crowd, "I am a Yankee." That guy knew how to make headlines.

In 1994, I spent weeks in South Africa helping Mandela handle international press coverage of the presidential election, which he won handily. Between interviews, I was privileged to spend time alone with him. One day, I asked if he knew that at that very moment activist Randall Robinson was on a hunger strike to the death in Washington, demanding that President Clinton intervene militarily to restore the duly elected government of Haitian President Jean-Bertrant Aristide, who had been overthrown in a military coup.

"Why didn't anyone tell me?" Mandela asked an aide. "Get me Clinton on the phone right now." In front of me, he called the president and said, "Don't you let anything happen to Randall. I'd still be in prison without Randall Robinson." A few days later, Clinton invaded Haiti and restored Aristide to power. Such are the accidents of history. (I also worked with Aristide, who showed great promise but turned out to be a bit of a nut case.)

CUBANS PROTECT AMERICANS FROM AMERICAN MERCENARIES

On one of my trips to Angola, I took a helicopter to see the oil fields of Cabinda, on the country's far northwest Atlantic coast. As I landed, all around me were good ole boys from Texas in ten-gallon hats and cowboy boots working the rigs. But they were under military threat—from their own American government. What?

In 1974, after a long, brutal war, Angolan patriots kicked out the ruling colonial power, Portugal. The Portuguese had been particularly brutal in Angola and nearby Mozambique. The founder of modern Angola, Agostinho Neto, was a doctor whose People's Movement for the Liberation of Angola (MPLA) Party had forged an alliance with the Communist Party against their common enemy. After winning independence, Angola became a Communist country, supported by the Soviet Union. This was the height of the Cold War, and the Reagan administration wanted the Neto government overthrown, even if it meant working with apartheid South Africa. Reagan and South Africa backed a guerilla war led by Jonas Savimbi, who Reagan called a "freedom fighter." He was actually a South African mercenary.

I had brought a group of US journalists to see the situation's absurdity firsthand. After visiting with the Texas oil men working the offshore rigs, we drove a mile down the road to a Cuban military camp. The Cubans were guarding the US workers against the US-funded guerilla insurgency of Jonas Savimbi.

At the Cuban camp, large billboards with photos of Marx, Lenin, and Engels exhorted the Cuban soldiers to do their best to guard the US oil

Angolan refugees walked hundreds of miles to this UN camp to escape war. They danced to celebrate our visit.

workers. Talk about a twisted foreign policy. The reporters were shocked. Thanks to my Cuban connections, we were the first and only delegation of journalists allowed into the Cuban camps.

In the agricultural fields of central Angola, Savimbi's forces planted US-supplied land mines so people could not farm. It was part of a murderous strategy to create chaos and make the country ungovernable. That strategy had turned Angola into the country with the most amputees per capita on Earth. I brought journalists from CBS, *Newsweek*, the *St. Louis Post-Dispatch, The New York Times*, and others to witness the carnage. We were all in tears watching so many women and children hobbling around on missing legs, often with missing arms as well, and usually with no prostheses. Impoverished, war-torn, and corrupt Angola is beyond a doubt the most disturbing place I have ever visited, with poor, suffering Haiti next.

But it wasn't all distressing. We visited one refugee camp, where people had walked barefoot for hundreds of miles to find safety from Savimbi's attacks. They had nothing and had suffered decades of war. Yet they were so excited that some Americans had come to pay attention to them that they broke out into the most intense, rhythmic, joyous, spirited, and moving dances I have ever seen anywhere. In the face of adversity, the human spirit can be breathtaking.

In the Angolan civil war, apartheid South Africa had much at stake. South Africa had no oil. Its goal was to seize the country's oil fields. Without oil, the apartheid regime could not withstand international sanctions. So South Africa invaded Angola with regular ground troops. Few Americans know that Fidel Castro and his little country of only ten million stopped South

Africa from gaining that oil by sending a whopping seventy thousand Cuban soldiers to repel the South African military invasion. This was the equivalent of the United States, with 330 million people, sending an army of 2.5 million US soldiers to Africa. At the time, Cuba was supported by the Soviet Union, but the Cuban people made a great, expensive sacrifice to fight apartheid. The Cubans turned back the South African army at the Battle of Cuito Cuanavale. Mandela certainly knew that he owed his freedom to Castro's determination not to let South African apartheid win Angola's oil. We discussed it several times. Despite US pressure, Mandela insisted on visiting Cuba upon his release to thank the Cuban people for their sacrifice.

In addition to Ronald Reagan and the Republican Party, Jonas Savimbi had another key US ally, the notorious mercenary Washington "public affairs" firm of Black, Manafort, Stone, and Kelly. They portrayed Savimbi as a "freedom fighter" and brought him to the Reagan White House, where they dined with all the trimmings. I'm happy to say we defeated their efforts. Amnesty International included the despicable Black, Manafort firm in its report "The Torturer's Lobby" for the firm's work for Savimbi and South Africa, and for various dictators: Ferdinand Marcos in the Philippines, Mobutu Sese Seko of Zaire, and Mohamed Siad Barré of Somalia. In our nation's Capital, representing murderous thugs is considered normal. I founded Fenton to chart a better, more honest, progressive path.

Angola was, and sadly still is, among the most corrupt countries on Earth. Its leaders have siphoned off billions in oil profits while the country has starved. While I remain confident that helping them repel South Africa's attempted oil grab was the right thing to do, I became increasingly troubled by the corruption, with comically bejeweled ministers hosting lavish spreads at the only luxury hotel in Luanda, the nation's capital. Not to mention the government rarely followed our advice. So, once we ended US aid to Savimbi, Fenton quit in protest, which astonished them, as they were paying us a lot of money. It was the right thing to do. I had founded the firm to do honest, progressive public relations, not the sleaze of "PR" firms. To be true to our values, we had to get out of there. Of course, the mainstream corporate PR firms would never quit like we did, which is why the Angolans were so surprised.

THE IMPORTANCE OF DRINKING WITH REPORTERS

Meanwhile, in the early 1980s, Cora Weiss, the heiress and activist who'd introduced me to the African National Congress, also introduced me to the fascinating former Jamaican Prime Minister Michael Manley. She sponsored a series of lectures he delivered at Columbia University on the history of US imperialism in the global South.

Manley remains one of my heroes and was one of the most dignified, brilliant, and caring world leaders I have known. He was also incredibly handsome. I'll never forget walking down the streets of Manhattan with Manley, Harry Belafonte, Randall Robinson, and Arthur Ashe. Women were practically falling down in the street.

Manley paid a big price for supporting Fidel Castro in Angola. Henry Kissinger had pressured Manley while he was prime minister to vote in the United Nations to condemn Cuba's intervention in Angola. Manley refused, telling Kissinger

Me with Jamaican Prime Minister Michael Manley. Kingston, Jamaica, 1989.

the United States should have stopped the South Africans from invading, but since it didn't, then hooray for little Cuba for stepping in. Kissinger was furious. In 1979, Kissinger directed the CIA to take revenge on Manley. The agency took over Jamaica's main newspaper, the *Gleaner*, and spread the absurd lie that Manley, a longtime social democrat, was a communist. Manley lost due to this campaign and his own mistakes. I met him soon after.

I loved Michael Manley and miss him to this day (he died of prostate cancer in 1997). Sophisticated, elegant, educated at the London School of Economics, and a compelling orator and writer, he spent many years as a militant union organizer representing Jamaica's bauxite miners before he ran for national office. His books explain how the wealthy northern countries used the International Monetary Fund and its false promises of "development" to exploit and impoverish the global South. His father, Norman Manley, was the George Washington of Jamaican independence, while his mother, Edna, was an important painter and sculptor who had a profound impact on Jamaican art and culture. The Manley family helps explain why little Jamaica has had such an outsized impact on global music, culture, sport, and language.

Manley asked Fenton to help regain power. One important element of the plan called for me to drink excessively with the US reporters in Miami who covered Jamaica. Once they were plastered, I would push them to stop referring to Manley as a communist. "He's a social democrat! Don't you know what that is?" I would say. "He's a member of a democratic parliament. He supports free enterprise. When he lost the election, he left office in a peaceful transition. How, pray tell, is he a communist? Just because you have good relations with your neighbor Cuba doesn't make you a communist."

The alcohol—and persistent cajoling—worked. The United States and international media stopped smearing Manley. This helped Jamaicans see he had learned from his mistakes and was a "new Manley." The lesson for activists is crystal clear: Get to know journalists personally. Build relationships with them. Had we just sent them emails, Manley's global image would never have been resurrected.

Manley returned to power in 1988, hiring Fenton to represent Jamaica in the US. Tough duty :). The best part was frequent trips to the island. I had honeymooned in Jamaica in 1973, when I was all of twenty-one. We stayed in Negril, on the island's western tip. Unlike today, it was totally undeveloped. On the seven miles of beach there was just one small hotel. Our little cabin was surrounded by open-pit latrines, but we didn't care. It was so beautiful. Locals offered us great cannabis for almost nothing and kids held out buckets of psilocybin mushrooms asking, "Hey, mon, want some mushrooms?" A true hippie paradise. I still return every year or two.

During Manley's 1988 election campaign, he and I traveled together to the island's remote central mountains. One day we heard gunshots and hit the floor of the van fast. Luckily, it was a false alarm. He was unfazed—it took me half a day to calm down.

Manley had extramarital affairs. I found it remarkable that in Jamaican politics, the more rumors swirled of Manley's liaisons, the more popular he became. Maybe it was the famous family name, but it sure was the opposite of what happened in the United States, where Gary Hart was forced to leave the presidential race because of his affair with Donna Rice.

Once re-elected, Manley faced an enormous problem. His profligate predecessor, Edward Seaga, had run up a huge pile of debt to the United States and other countries. This was truly an anvil on Jamaica's back. So, in advance of his first meeting with George H. W. Bush, we helped him write an op-ed article in the *Wall Street Journal* arguing that Jamaica's debt should be forgiven to enable the country to buy more US products and services. Bush read it and told Manley he would forgive much of the debt. And he did.

Manley and I became close friends. To remember and honor him, my youngest son, Theo's, middle name is Manley. As his prostate cancer advanced, I helped Manley and his fifth wife, Glynn, rent a summer house in the Berkshires and visited him frequently. His death was a great loss to the world. In Jamaica today, mention his name and people smile, especially the poor. No wonder—he built thousands of units of low-income housing, more than any other Jamaican prime minister.

SOMETHING TO CHEW ON

CARBARYL
neurotoxin, carcinogen

ENDOSULFAN
endocrine disruptor

ORTHO-PHENYLPHENOL
probable human carcinogen

CAPTAN
probable human carcinogen

CHLORPYRIFOS
developmental neurotoxin

METHYL PARATHION
developmental neurotoxin

METHOXYCHLOR
endocrine disruptor

GUTHION
neurotoxin

10 YEARS AFTER ALAR, APPLES STILL NEED A CLEANUP

An apple a day... exposes your child to more than 30 pesticides over a year. An average of four per apple, with six or eight not uncommon. Some apples have 10. AFTER they are washed and cored.

Apples are among the most contaminated foods. With pesticides that can damage the human brain and nervous system, disrupt hormones, and cause cancer.

Apples should be a symbol of health. Instead, they symbolize a regulatory system that fails to protect children, whose developing bodies are far more vulnerable than adults.

And apples aren't the only problem. More than a million preschoolers consume at least 15 pesticides a day in food, according to our latest study of government data.

Some 324,000 kids age 5 and under exceed federal safety standards EVERY DAY for just one neurotoxic insecticide, methyl parathion. It's mainly on apples, peaches and other produce. Nearly half get their unsafe dose JUST BY EATING ONE APPLE.

Some apples and peaches are so contaminated with methyl parathion that a kid can exceed the government's daily limit with just TWO BITES. Long term exposure to this chemical can impair the nervous system and brain development at low doses.

Ten years ago this week, apple sales plummeted after the news media exposed the cancer risk of the pesticide Alar. Pesticide

APPLES SYMBOLIZE A REGULATORY SYSTEM THAT FAILS TO PROTECT CHILDREN.

companies have called the Alar episode an unfounded "food scare." They don't mention that the Bush Administration banned Alar in 1990 as an unacceptable cancer risk, years after government scientists first raised a warning. The American Academy of Pediatrics supported Bush's ban.

Kids are safer with Alar gone. But apples still need a cleanup. So do other foods.

Congress passed a food safety law in 1996 that was supposed to clean up food for kids. Yet not one pesticide limit has been lowered to protect children, as the law requires. Pesticide levels are actually increasing in fruits and vegetables heavily consumed by children.

You can help us change things. At home, where you shop, maybe even in Washington.

Visit our web site: *www.foodnews.org*. You'll see the startling amount of pesticides in your food, and what the risks are.

You'll find simple ways to cut back on pesticides. Fruits like watermelon, kiwi, pineapple, bananas, oranges, and domestically grown melons have fewer pesticides. Red raspberries, strawberries, peaches, pears — and apples — have the most. Organic produce is the safest by far.

We'll help you send a message to food companies and Washington. Alar is gone today because concerned citizens made their voices heard. Let's take another bite at that apple.

ENVIRONMENTAL WORKING GROUP

www.foodnews.org

1718 Connecticut Avenue NW, Suite 600, Washington, DC 20009

CHAPTER 11

ALAR, APPLES, AND THE AGE OF DISINFORMATION

I founded Fenton to preserve the environment, protect public health, and advance human rights. Sometimes, we combined these, for example, in our work against pesticide use, an environmental issue with enormous public health consequences.

Ask Professor Google about me, and what comes up are right-wing attacks stemming back to 1989. They claim a campaign I organized that year against the pesticide Alar (a trade name for daminozide) on apples was a "scare" based on "no science." Many people—even some decent journalists—believed this nonsense, due to the effectiveness of a phony, right-wing smear campaign, coupled with the failure of the Natural Resources Defense Council (NRDC) to defend its findings to the media when they were sued over the issue.

For me, the battle over Alar marked the beginning of our current age of lies and disinformation, a media strategy peddled by Fox "News" and other right-wing outlets for power and profit.

Alar was a "growth regulator" used to ripen and redden apples for harvest at the same time. It was the most carcinogenic chemical in the food supply. For many years, consumer groups, the American Academy of Pediatrics, and several state attorneys general had sued the US Environmental Protection Agency (EPA) to ban it, to no avail. The EPA had stalled action on Alar in "special review," a bureaucratic euphemism for going nowhere because of industry pressure (otherwise known as "regulatory capture" or just plain D.C. corruption).

Newspaper ad showing that apples still contain other poisons ten years after NRDC's 1989 campaign against the pesticide Alar.

One day in 1988, John Adams, the executive director of NRDC, one of the nation's preeminent environmental groups, asked me for a meeting. Adams was a former prosecutor and a trusted natural leader. He told me he was tired of the fact that the Environmental Defense Fund (EDF), a rival environmental group, and its leader, Fred Krupp, kept getting more media attention. He wanted me to find a way to get more coverage for NRDC.

Adams handed me an advance copy of a report called "Intolerable Risk" which NRDC planned to release in a few months about pesticide residues polluting the diets of infants and children. Not long before, the National Academy of Sciences had issued an alarming report on this same subject, by the great environmental physician Dr. Philip Landrigan of Mount Sinai in New York. The report showed that children, with their still-developing brains and bodies, were particularly susceptible to chemical exposures, especially the neurotoxic compounds in most pesticides.

The NRDC report showed that the most dangerous chemical was Alar in apples (although there were, and sadly still are, many others). Alar was highly carcinogenic. Relative to their weight, children consume large quantities of applesauce and apple juice, so much that they were overdosing on Alar. The NRDC had done its homework. They'd taken two years to prepare the report, then had it reviewed by noted scientists.

You didn't have to be a PR expert to see that this could and should have been a big story. Parents want to protect their kids, and the symbolism was powerful: A poisoned "apple a day" was not going to keep the doctor away. As I've mentioned, symbolism is one of the most powerful communications tools.

THE PUBLIC BANS ALAR

As discussed previously, to change policies, one must change public opinion. The only way to do that is to change people's thinking, to change their brains. We know from cognitive science that the only effective way to do that is through simple messages aimed at the heart and repeated endlessly. So, I set out to construct a media strategy that would change people's minds and *guarantee* enormous repetition of NRDC's story. We planned the campaign so news about Alar's harm to children would hit the public in wave after wave, overwhelming the agrochemical industry's attempts to ridicule the story and bury it.

Months ahead of our planned release date, I approached a broad spectrum of media, especially magazines and broadcasts aimed at moms, including all the then-major women's magazines known in the trade as the Seven Sisters: *Redbook, McCall's, Woman's Day, Family Circle, Good Housekeeping, Ladies' Home Journal,* and *Better Homes and Gardens.* We insisted on an embargo, meaning they couldn't publish before a certain date. In exchange, we gave them plenty of time to investigate and fact-check the story. This guaranteed the story would not disappear upon release, no matter what the American Chemical Society and agribusiness interests did.

NRDC had arranged for the actress Meryl Streep to help the effort. Our partner advertising firm, Zimmerman & Markman, filmed a TV ad featuring Streep at her kitchen sink, urging people to wash their fruits and vegetables to remove the pesticide residues. "What's wrong with our food that the government recommends we wash it?" she asks. "What's in the food?" We coordinated the ad's release and TV interviews with Streep to come right after the story was launched in other media.

Finally, the lynchpin of our strategy was CBS's *60 Minutes*, then the highest rated, most trusted show on US television. At the time, many more people watched network TV than today, so a *60 Minutes* story was likely to have major public impact. We took the story to producer David Gelber, who immediately realized its importance. When *60 Minutes* reporter Ed Bradley asked the head of EPA pesticide regulation about Alar, this bureaucrat admitted that if Alar was a "new" chemical and its manufacturer applied for EPA approval, it would be banned. But because

THE CORPORATE RESPONSE

To agribusiness, the chemical companies, and their highly paid right-wing agents, this was way too much power to the people. These forces pressed the Washington State apple growers association to sue *60 Minutes*, NRDC, and Fenton Communications for "knowingly and maliciously" using false information to slander their apples. Of course, this bogus charge ignored all the evidence—the peer-reviewed science we had relied on and the American Academy of Pediatrics' years of efforts to ban Alar.

THE NRDC HAD ARRANGED FOR THE ACTRESS MERYL STREEP TO HELP THE EFFORT.

it was an "old" chemical, he claimed the EPA's hands were tied. "Bingo," Gelber told me just after the interview. He was outraged. Parents would be, too.

The *60 Minutes* report aired on Sunday, February 26, 1989. Sitting in front of a skull and crossbones drawing of an apple, Ed Bradley told the story of government failure, under industry pressure, to remove the carcinogen Alar from the food supply.

Even I could not have imagined what happened the very next morning. From coast to coast, Americans stopped buying apples. In an instant, the bottom fell out of the apple market. Within a week, Uniroyal, Alar's manufacturer, was forced to take it off the market to restore the apple trade. The public banned Alar—without lawsuits or regulatory or legislative action.

The growers' legal action was a classic slap suit, a lawsuit filed for purposes of harassment. Slap suits usually have little chance of success, but industry files them to bankrupt nonprofits. The best defense against them is to play offense by showing the public the nonprofit was righteously defending public health.

Unfortunately, NRDC—made up largely of lawyers—freaked out. They took the lawsuit way too seriously. Instead of doubling down on the findings of its own report, NRDC's lawyers advised the organization to go completely silent. We begged them to publicly defend their report and everything we had done to promote it, but their lawyers wanted to wait—years—until the case came to trial.

I warned John Adams that if the organization remained silent, the agrochemical industry would rewrite the story to say we had launched a baseless scare. To make that case, the apple growers and their henchmen paid the corporate PR firm Hill + Knowlton millions of dollars to smear us. NRDC remained silent for two years while the case worked its way through the courts. This was a horrible decision, even from a legal viewpoint, as years of one-sided debate would mean a biased jury. No use. NRDC folded and Hill + Knowlton prevailed in the media because it had the media largely to itself.

The slap suit went nowhere. In 1993 a federal judge ruled that the apple growers had not proved their case. The bad apples then appealed. The US court of appeals ruled against them. Industry then appealed to the Supreme Court, which declined to review the ruling. Luckily, I'd found a *pro bono* lawyer to defend us.

A few months after the campaign, an EPA scientific advisory board decided that "long-term exposure to Alar posed unacceptable risks to public health." The EPA banned it. It's illegal to apply any amount to any food crop. But to this day, conservative media, which is all over the internet, never mentions the EPA ban. It doesn't fit their ideological and propaganda agenda. Alar was a "scare" with no basis, and it was all Fenton's fault.

Our efforts to ban Alar earned yours truly a cover story in Rupert Murdoch's right-wing D.C. rag, the *Weekly Standard*. Entitled "The Scaremonger," it claimed "the Alar story caused the culinary equivalent of Orson Welles' War of the Worlds radio panic, with school cafeterias pulling apple juice from their shelves and mothers running after buses to retrieve apples from children's lunchboxes." It featured a cartoon of me sitting in front of a portrait of Karl Marx. In true Murdoch disinformation style, almost nothing in the article was true.

A while later, I wrote a private memo for environmental leaders outlining how we organized the campaign and urging them to use similar tactics. It was leaked to the *Wall Street Journal*. Their right-wing editorial page published it under the blazing headline "How a PR Firm Executed the Alar Scare." That's not what the memo said, but looking back, it did come off as too much of a victory lap, fueling charges that we had "manipulated the media." If that means we managed an accurate story for maximum impact to protect public health, then I plead guilty. I haven't written anything similar since. Until now.

Upset at their loss, the agrochemical and industrial food interests organized many state legislatures to pass so-called veggie hate crime bills. These laws made it a crime to disparage foods. For example, the meat industry used the Texas version to sue Oprah for reporting on E. coli poisoning related to hamburgers. She was acquitted. These laws are a clear violation of the First Amendment. They have all been ruled unconstitutional.

But poor Meryl Streep. At first, she was gracious and down-to-earth, clearly eschewing any special treatment, the opposite of a diva. She even helped start a new organization called Mothers and Others for Pesticide Limits. But she had no idea how vicious industry harassment could be, and it understandably unnerved her. She was harassed by industry stooges. Then her home was burglarized. Upset, she disparaged me as her "grade B movie director." Yikes, that stung. The greatest actress of our time. Imagine. But I knew she was under tremendous stress, and that together we had all done a great service for public health.

After watching this 60 Minutes broadcast, the public stopped buying apples because of Alar.

For Our Kids' Sake

How to Protect Your Child Against Pesticides in Food

Foreword by
T. Berry Brazelton, M.D.

Published by
Mothers and Others
for Pesticide Limits,
a project of the
Natural Resources
Defense Council

One aspect of chemical industry propaganda continues to confuse people. The claim that "you'd have to eat a million pounds of apples (or other foods) to get the dose that caused cancer in laboratory animals; therefore, this food is safe for humans at typical doses people are exposed to." Industry knows this is deceitful. The gold standard in mainstream science is to feed large doses of a chemical to a small number of animals to find carcinogens. To detect statistically significant effects at small doses requires hundreds of thousands of animals. No lab can handle that many. Let's say a chemical causes cancer in one hundred out of every million animals exposed. The human equivalent in a population of three hundred million would be thirty thousand people—that's an unacceptable risk. Most importantly, the vast majority of industrial chemicals do not cause cancer in lab animals *at any dose*. Of course, the industry never mentions this. Those few chemicals that do should not be permitted in food.

The chemical industry—and the EPA—also ignore the fact that we ingest many chemicals all at once. Do they have additive or synergistic effects? We don't know, because the EPA doesn't study combinations of chemicals in food. They also rarely conduct studies in baby animals. Compared with adults, babies are often more chemically sensitive.

Despite all the attacks, ridding the country of Alar was worth it. The campaign also had another benefit. It helped spur the sale of organic foods. You can clearly date the rise in organic sales from the Alar *60 Minutes* story. They've been increasing every year since, a boon to health and the planet. Years later, author Michael Pollan wrote "the Alar episode is a watershed, marking the birth pangs of the modern organic industry."

The Alar campaign worked because its symbolism hit the heart. In the depths of their souls, Americans believe that apples are good for you. "An apple a day keeps the doctor away." But apples covered with poison? That violated the symbolism, offending the public. As Malcolm Gladwell explained in *The Tipping Point*, some symbols are "sticky." They stay in your brain, activating powerful, existing circuitry. Activists should always look for sticky symbols to convey lasting meaning. For example, most people don't know that all the world's tuna fish carry high levels of toxic mercury. Why? Coal burning power plants. Coal contains mercury. As coal burns, its mercury goes up the smokestack and lands on the ocean, where it works its way up the food chain. Top predators like tuna wind up with high levels. Many health organizations already urge pregnant women not to eat tuna. Meanwhile, tuna fish sandwiches are sticky symbols of child-rearing. I bet a PR campaign focused on toxic tuna sandwiches would help speed coal's demise.

A few years after the Alar campaign, the Environmental Working Group (EWG) and its founder, Ken Cook, hired Fenton to publicize a

Meryl Streep helped NRDC start "Mothers and Others for Pesticide Limits," which published this booklet showing parents how to protect their kids.

In 2006, the Centers for Disease Control (CDC) found that synthetic estrogens even played a role in risk for type 2 diabetes, which has become epidemic. Experiments show that the offspring of mice exposed to these chemicals can be born grotesquely obese. Europe has moved against some of these chemicals. But almost twenty-five years after Myers, Dumanoski, and Colborn sounded the alarm, the United States has not moved against them. The EPA has been "studying" the issue, but, fearful of industry attacks, it moves slower than frozen molasses.

Frankly, a big concern about these chemicals is one I hesitate to mention. But hormone disruptors may also contribute to gender confusion (dysphoria). Gender should be a personal choice, not the result of something your mother ingested while pregnant with you. I recognize how fraught gender politics have become. However, given what we know about xenoestrogens, it's hard to remain silent. Whenever possible, we should try to buy organic food. It's true that it costs more than conventionally grown food, but the price differential is falling. If the US Department of Agriculture encouraged the production of organic food, its price would fall further.

Before the 1940s, all food was organic. It should be again. Organic soils retains much more carbon, so organic food helps prevent climate change. Avoid plastic baby bottles, and don't heat or microwave anything in plastic. Steer away from Teflon pans, which leak chemicals into food, especially at high heat. When you use plastic wrap, make sure it is on the top of a bowl, not touching the food. Or use wax paper. These basic steps can protect your family's health.

report showing that baby foods, including Gerber, the most popular brand, were contaminated by pesticides. Everyone should eat clean food, but especially babies, whose growing brains and nervous systems are particularly susceptible to pesticides' neurotoxic effects. We held a press conference to release the report, which brought the issue so much media attention that 2 percent of the baby food market shifted overnight to the sole organic producer, Earth's Best. That may not sound like much, but Gerber and the other baby food makers could read the writing on the wall. They soon announced policies to greatly reduce—and eventually eliminate—pesticide residues in baby food altogether. Without the media pressure, this never would have happened.

Another controversial food and health issue is genetic engineering. That technology first emerged in the early '80s. In 1983, Fenton helped leading GMO critic Jeremy Rifkin promote his anti-GMO book *Algeny*. We also helped publicize a lawsuit Rifkin brought that stopped the very first outdoor experiment with gene-editing technology.

HORMONE DISRUPTING CHEMICALS: A PUBLIC HEALTH THREAT

One of the few client decisions I regret came shortly after promoting *Algeny*. Fenton helped an agricultural biotech firm obtain federal permits to test placing a gene from soil bacteria into corn to kill caterpillar pests. We thought this could reduce the pesticide load in the environment. Rifkin begged me not to take this job, but I ignored him, arrogantly convinced we had to use this technology to reduce toxic chemicals in food. Bad decision for two reasons. First, sadly, Rifkin stopped speaking to me. Second, our efforts helped legitimize the GMO industry and its successful quest to avoid regulation. This is an industry that has gotten away with falsely claiming its food is "just like any other." BS. Genetic engineering produces novel proteins, unknown in nature before and rarely tested. Recent research suggests that the increasing prevalence of GMO soybeans may partly explain why nut allergies in particular are rising in children.

By the way, the corn protection technology was never marketed, as it reduced yields.

If you go back to Professor Google, you'll find another attack on me for exposing the dangers of chemicals in plastics, cosmetics, and even Teflon cookware.

One day, biologist Peter Myers told me that men were being feminized by chemicals in the environment. He explained that these "hormone disrupting" chemicals were accumulating in the food chain, wreaking havoc with many animals, including humans. The chemicals of particular concern were synthetic estrogens (xenoestrogens), which mimic the female hormone estrogen. Myers said these chemicals were at least part of the reason why, in the industrialized world, sperm counts had declined dramatically. Scientists also suspected these same chemicals helped explain increasingly early menstruation and breast development in girls, increasing penile and urethra deformities in baby boys, increased rates of breast and prostate cancers, and feminization of wildlife to the point that some species—reptiles, for example—were having difficulty reproducing. Evidence also indicated that in utero exposure to these chemicals could cause gender identity confusion in newborn animals and increase autism-like symptoms. Animals have hormonal systems similar to humans. Low doses could be unusually dangerous, since they can bind to hormone receptor sites in the body better than large doses. (The body produces hormones in tiny doses.)

Myers hired us to promote his 1996 book on the subject, *Our Stolen Future*, coauthored by journalist Dianne Dumanoski and, one of my personal heroes, the late biology researcher Theo Colborn. Al Gore wrote the introduction, which brought the book considerable attention. At the time, this was a brave act, given all the industry attacks that were bound to come. They certainly did.

Pete Myers felt confident that when men learned they were being feminized by these chemicals, they would demand action. It hasn't happened yet at the scale needed. Unfortunately, we are all still being exposed to these chemicals in products that contain Bisphenol A (BPA) or similar compounds: plastic baby bottles, water bottles (watch out for the large five-gallon, polycarbonate, water-cooler bottles at your office), food wraps, microwaveable plastics, anything that's coated with Teflon, anything that comes in plastic-lined cans, and many common cosmetics and other everyday items. Certain pesticides and fungicides used on foods are hormone-disrupting. Strawberries, for example, make the list of the "dirty dozen" foods contaminated with pesticides every year.

David Gelber of *60 Minutes*, who produced the Alar story, still tells me he considers it the most significant story he was ever involved in. Maybe he's right. Now he heads The Years Project. He's working full-time making effective content against climate change, as am I. I hope that becomes our most successful campaign. Otherwise, civilization might just collapse, and we won't get to make progress on anything else.

A MESSAGE FROM NORTH ATLANTIC SWORDFISH:

As our appetite for North Atlantic swordfish has gotten bigger and bigger, the fish being caught have gotten smaller and smaller. The average fish caught in 1960 weighed 266 pounds. Today, the average fish caught weighs just 90 pounds. The majority of swordfish caught are too young and too small to reproduce.

The swordfish population in the North Atlantic is declining at a dangerous rate. That's why leading chefs like Nora Pouillon of Nora in Washington, DC, Lidia Bastianich of Felidia, Eric Ripert of Le Bernardin and Rick Moonen of Oceana in New York have joined with SeaWeb (a project of the Pew Charitable Trusts) and the Natural Resources Defense Council to ask you to give North Atlantic swordfish a break in 1998, the Year of the Ocean.

If you see swordfish on a menu or at your fish counter, ask where it comes from. If it's from the North Atlantic, order something else. Just don't eat swordfish from the North Atlantic. It's that simple. You'll be doing something wonderful for the environment. And you'll get this message from the swordfish of the North Atlantic: thank you.

SeaWeb and the Natural Resources Defense Council are working together to protect the living ocean.

For information about this campaign, call 1-888-4-SEAWEB.

SeaWeb • 1731 Connecticut Ave., NW • Washington, DC 20009
Natural Resources Defense Council • 40 W. 20th St. New York, NY 10011

CHAPTER 12

SAVING SWORDFISH, WHAT WOULD JESUS DRIVE?

In the 1990s our work to protect the environment went into warp speed with a couple of high-profile and effective campaigns.

SAVING SWORDFISH FROM EXTINCTION

In the mid '90s, the Pew Charitable Trusts asked Fenton and our sister organization, Environmental Media Services, to dramatize the worldwide decimation of fish stocks. When we interviewed marine experts, we kept hearing that swordfish were on the verge of extinction. Only baby swordfish were being caught, too young to reproduce. The situation was dire. The species was about to disappear.

Working with Pew's new marine group, Sea Web, we decided to focus on the poignant plight of this one species, rather than the generic issue of overfishing. People relate to swordfish more than most other fish species—they hang on the walls of many seafood restaurants. Sure, people care more about whales and dolphins, but swordfish are next in popularity.

We asked Nora Pouillon—of D.C.'s Restaurant Nora, the first certified organic restaurant in the country—to help organize a coalition of the nation's top chefs to pledge not to serve swordfish until the government protected swordfish spawning grounds. With these areas off-limits to fishing, the species could recover. Many top chefs agreed, including Eric Ripert at Le Bernardin and Lidia Bastianich at her namesake restaurant in New York. Then

"Try the pasta." Our New York Times *ad to save swordfish from extinction, January 20, 1998. Ad by Pacy Markman.*

Fenton staff organized a press conference for the activist chefs, who also appeared on TV. We only had enough money to buy one *New York Times* ad. It featured a sticky note on the end of the fish's sword. The note said, "Try the pasta."

Immediately, people stopped buying swordfish. Sales plummeted and its price crashed. This was pre-internet, but even so, cruise lines, airlines, hotels, and restaurant chains all stopped serving swordfish—and we didn't even organize or contact most of them! We had hit a nerve. The fishing industry originally opposed our campaign but had a sudden change of heart to save their livelihoods—and the species. They helped us push the US Department of Commerce to make the spawning grounds off-limits for fishing—and the fish recovered. Swordfish are fine today (although they are high in mercury, mostly from coal-fired power plants, and overfishing remains a huge problem with large factory ships strip-mining the ocean.)

This viral, yet pre-internet, campaign worked for several reasons. We named it "Give Swordfish a Break." We did not use the word "boycott," which sounded like a traditional left-wing effort without contemporary pizzazz. Plus, we had no ability to pull off a real boycott.

Our slogan led to an interesting conflict with a marine scientist at the NRDC, which was part of the campaign. While swordfish were threatened everywhere, she pointed out that the situation was most acute in the North Atlantic. So NRDC insisted we call the campaign "Give North Atlantic Swordfish a Break." This is a

prime example of what former Fenton star Kristen Grimm calls "literal sclerosis," a common affliction of people steeped in science and policy who understandably focus on the details to the point of diluting the message. Adding "North Atlantic" sounded clunky and reduced the slogan's stickiness. We patiently explained that simple is memorable, complex less so.

We showed that celebrity chefs can carry a message to the public to change habits and policy. And focusing on one charismatic species works better than bland overly general pronouncements like "we are overfishing."

Swordfish had become a symbol of overfishing. Symbols drill into the brain, and are important PR devices. The repetition of simple, symbolic messages and images changes awareness—and public opinion. UC Berkeley linguistics professor George Lakoff, an expert on messaging, has demonstrated this over and over. And Trump has proven it, too—with MAGA.

Another thing that can change public opinion is humor. The Left can be so *boring*, rhetorical, literal, and dull. Many environmental groups would have headlined their ads something like: "Don't You Dare Eat Swordfish." No wonder the Right attacks us as purveyors of the nanny state. On the other hand, "Try the pasta" is light and humorous. A spoonful of sugar to help the medicine go down. *The Daily Show with Jon Stewart* became the number one news show (that is not a misprint) because it was also *funny*. Abbie taught me this long ago. Lucky for the swordfish campaign, we worked with genius copywriter Pacy Markman, who could turn a humorous phrase while still helping to save the world.

Ad for the Evangelical Environmental Network, 2002. "Transportation is a moral choice."

What Would Jesus Drive?

To some, the question might seem amusing. But we take it seriously. As our Savior and Lord Jesus Christ teaches us, "Love your neighbor as yourself." *(Mk 12:30-31)*

Of all the choices we make as consumers, the cars we drive have the single biggest impact on all of God's creation.

Car pollution causes illness and death, and most afflicts the elderly, poor, sick and young. It also contributes to global warming, putting millions at risk from drought, flood, hunger and homelessness.

Transportation is now a moral choice and an issue for Christian reflection. It's about more than engineering—it's about ethics. About obedience. About loving our neighbor.

So what *would* Jesus drive?

We call upon America's automobile industry to manufacture more fuel-efficient vehicles. And we call upon Christians to drive them.

Because it's about more than vehicles—it's about values.

Rev. Clive Calver, Ph.D.
President, World Relief

Rev. Richard Cizik
Vice President for Governmental Affairs, National Association of Evangelicals

Loren Cunningham
Founder, Youth with a Mission
President, University of the Nations

Rev. David H. Englehard, Ph.D.
General Secretary, Christian Reformed Church in North America

Millard Fuller
Founder & President, Habitat for Humanity International

Rev. Vernon Grounds, Ph.D.
Chancellor, Denver Seminary

Rev. Steve Hayner, Ph.D.
Past President, InterVarsity Christian Fellowship

Rev. Roberta Hestenes, Ph.D.
International Minister, World Vision

Rev. Richard Mouw, Ph.D.
President, Fuller Theological Seminary

Rev. Ron Sider, Ph.D.
President, Evangelicals for Social Action

Sponsored By THE EVANGELICAL ENVIRONMENTAL NETWORK

10 East Lancaster Ave., Wynnewood, PA 19096 **www.WhatWouldJesusDrive.org**

Partial list of signatories. Affiliations listed for identification only.

DEFEAT COMPLEXITY WITH SIMPLICITY

"Regulatory reform" doesn't sound too exciting, does it? But it doesn't sound like a bad thing, either. During the '90s, Republicans deceptively touted it as a benefit, when really it was the cornerstone of their scheme to stymie public health and environmental regulations. They were on the verge of passing it when a brilliant campaigner, the late Phil Clapp, introduced us to a group of parents whose children had died from eating hamburgers contaminated with E. coli at a Seattle Jack in the Box restaurant. Calling themselves STOP (Safe Tables Our Priority), the parents were furious. Regulatory reform would have delayed for a decade their efforts to protect children by cleaning up the meat supply. So we arranged for the parents to appear all over the media. Instead of the story being "regulatory reform," it became "dead kids." I knew we had won when Republican Senate leader Bob Dole took to the Senate floor, exclaiming "last night Peter Jennings of *ABC News* called me a purveyor of tainted beef!" Bingo: Terms of debate changed. Regulatory reform died, and the meat supply was made much safer.

Had we used the other side's language and called it "regulatory reform," we would have lost. This is a common mistake activists can make, adopting the frame of the other side, which only reinforces it. Linguist George Lakoff has begged progressives not to use terms like "entitlement reform," which he believes should instead be called "earned benefits." He makes this clear in his seminal book, *Don't Think of an Elephant!* Now try not thinking of one.

The denuded, clear-cut national forests in Washington state, as seen from a Lighthawk small plane.

In another environmental effort that touched the public zeitgeist, we created a campaign for the Evangelical Environmental Network against gas-guzzling SUVs called "What would Jesus drive?" The campaign slogan was "Transportation is a moral choice." The launch ad in evangelical publications featured Jesus looking out over traffic with text saying, "Of all the choices we make as consumers, the cars we drive have the single biggest impact on all of God's creation. Car pollution causes illness and death. It also contributes to global warming, putting millions at risk … Because it's about more than vehicles—it's about values."

"What would Jesus drive?" exploded all over the news. It even appeared in the monologues of all the late-night talk show hosts. Frankly, we should probably relaunch this campaign now. There are more huge, polluting SUVs on the road than ever. Most people don't even think for a moment about how their cars cause asthma and rising sea levels.

Of course, the automobile companies were pissed at us. And then even more so, when we helped promote Arianna Huffington's controversial TV ad pointing out that filling up your SUV at the gas pump helps fund terrorist nations.

Thankfully, hybrid, plug-in hybrid, and all-electric cars are gaining in popularity—although this is the early days of what will be a massive transition to clean transportation.

CLEAR-CUT FORESTS FROM THE SKY

To solve the climate crisis, we need not only to eliminate dirty cars and power plants, but also to end deforestation. In fact, reforestation is a remarkably cost-effective way to reduce planet-heating carbon in the atmosphere. Trees absorb carbon. Biodiverse old-growth forests aren't only being destroyed in the Amazon. It's still happening in the United States. But Fenton helped activists slow it down by working with the environmental air force.

Back in the early '90s, a group of environmentalist pilots organized as the nonprofit LightHawk contacted us. Their mission was to fly influential people in small planes at low altitudes to see first-hand the devastation wrought by the clear-cutting of old-growth temperate rainforests in the Pacific Northwest. You can't see the carnage on these public lands from commercial airliners flying at high altitudes.

We joined forces with LightHawk and the Native Forest Council and took many important journalists to the skies to see for themselves. They were shocked to see the ugly clear-cuts from the air, where enormous forests were cleared down to stumps. Often, these cuts eliminated all the trees on very steep hillsides, causing massive soil erosion, with the soil frequently clogging the narrow streams where salmon spawn. The massive cutting also threatened the clean water supply that trees provide and the habitat of the spotted owl.

Activists filed lawsuits against the timber companies and the US Forest Service for violating the Endangered Species Act. Industry tried to frame the issue as timber jobs versus the spotted owl: "These environmentalists only care about this dumb bird, not humans dependent on the forests for their livelihoods." But, thanks to LightHawk, as journalists flew low over the almost lunar landscapes where giant trees had recently stood, they became infuriated. This helped shift the issue from obscure birds to the massive forest devastation—subsidized by taxpayers who paid for the construction of US Forest Service logging roads, without which the trees couldn't be brought to market. We also showed that protecting the measly 5 percent of US virgin forests still standing would provide more jobs than logging thanks to fishing, tourism, recreation, and other industries. Forest protection also helps prevent flooding and water pollution caused by excessive logging.

This narrative shift helped environmentalists win in the court of public opinion, which helped them win in Congress and the courts. Many of the worst clear-cuts were stopped.

AN ENVIRONMENTAL MEDIA HERO

The late Arlie Schardt was an inspiration. Schardt was personal friends with both Martin Luther King and Duke Ellington. He started the ACLU's "Impeach Nixon" campaign—before the Watergate break-in even happened. An Olympic swimmer, Schardt swam the freezing Colorado River through the Grand Canyon, rapids and all. He was *Time* magazine's bureau chief in Atlanta at the height of the civil rights movement.

Schardt was also a big environmentalist, having been executive director of the Environmental Defense Fund in the 1970s. In the early '90s, we joined forces to start a new nonprofit, Environmental Media Services (EMS), to help environmental causes gain more media coverage. At the time, few of the environmental groups even had press secretaries.

EMS started a regular press breakfast series in Washington, D.C., where journalists heard from leading scientists and activists. This was a prime example of the benefit of getting to know journalists personally. These events led to many stories and helped grow the field of environmental reporting. EMS released the United Nations Intergovernmental Panel on Climate Change report in 1994. EMS still exists as a nonprofit PR firm for the environment, although now it's called Resource Media.

Schardt was a smiling, inspirational troublemaker. His life is proof that you can make a difference in this world. My son Cole's middle name is Arlie in tribute.

I WANT YOU
TO INVADE IRAQ

Go ahead. Send me a new generation of recruits. Your bombs will fuel their hatred of America and their desire for revenge. Americans won't be safe anywhere. Please, attack Iraq. Distract yourself from fighting Al Qaeda. Divide the international community. Go ahead. Destabilize the region. Maybe Pakistan will fall – we want its nuclear weapons. Give Saddam a reason to strike first. He might draw Israel into a fight. Perfect! So please – invade Iraq. Make my day.

TomPaine.common sense

Osama says: 'I Want You to Invade Iraq.'
TomPaine.com *features reasons why we shouldn't.*

CHAPTER 13

LAWYERS, DEATH SQUADS, AND EFFECTIVE ADVERTISING

Besides Nelson Mandela, the only other saint I've known is Bryan Stevenson—whose best-selling book *Just Mercy* was made into a Hollywood film starring Jamie Foxx. How Stevenson keeps his amazing tranquility while working within the heinously racist Alabama court system is beyond me. We met Stevenson in 1990, when John "Rick" MacArthur gave birth to the Death Penalty Information Center (DPIC) to expose the many problems with capital punishment. These include prosecutors tampering with evidence, incompetent court-appointed defense lawyers who sometimes fall asleep at trial, Southern judges campaigning for reelection who boast about the number of people (almost all of them Black men) they've executed, and institutional racism at every level of many states' "justice" systems. People can be sent to death row without any physical evidence—sometimes they go with only jailhouse testimony coerced by the police. It's a nightmare.

In *Just Mercy*, Foxx portrays Walter McMillian, an innocent man who spent many years on Alabama's notorious death row. There was zero evidence against McMillian—just the uncorroborated testimony of one inmate who had been threatened by the cops. He had recanted, but McMillian rotted on death row anyway. What finally forced the Supreme Court of Alabama to reexamine the evidence and let McMillian out? As the movie shows, a *60 Minutes* segment with Ed Bradley. When the most popular news show on television featured McMillian's ordeal, the resulting national pressure freed him. Our firm took the story to *60 Minutes*. We did the

Bin Laden Wants You to Invade Iraq. Print ad and poster, 2002.

public relations on several other death row cases with Stevenson, which led to the release of several other innocent prisoners. When we started work to stop legal executions, 80 percent of Americans supported the death penalty. The figure is now much lower—54 percent—in large measure because of Stevenson and others like him.

WHY THE CAMPAIGN WORKED

Why have activists been able to change public opinion on the death penalty so dramatically?

Here are the ingredients. First, DPIC organized the facts into morally compelling stories featuring real victims of a racist criminal justice system. We also had real heroes in Stevenson and other lawyers, among them Stephen Bright, who fought for truth, justice, and the American way. People learn from stories and characters, not from just facts or legal or policy briefs. And we made it easy for journalists to cover these stories. We deluged reporters relentlessly with press releases, desk-side background briefings, press conferences, and road shows to meet with lawyers and exonerated inmates. Over time, with repetition, we made heartrending tales of death row injustice increasingly visible and changed public opinion.

DPIC has had an enormous impact and still does. This is largely thanks to the persistence of Rick MacArthur, the philanthropist and publisher of *Harper's Magazine*. When MacArthur approached Fenton in 1989, asking how to end the death penalty, we suggested starting the media project that became DPIC. MacArthur has supported that effort now for three decades, a commitment that's highly unusual for liberal foundations and philanthropists. They often go with the latest fashion for two or three years, then move on to something else.

Working to end the death penalty was just one of many legal issues in which Fenton helped organize media and thereby inspired the public to pressure the legal system. We helped the Campaign for Tobacco-Free Kids fight the tobacco companies' strategy of intentionally addicting children to nicotine. They used Joe Camel and other cartoon characters to hook kids early, often for life. Their defense? Freedom of speech. This was a case where "free speech" was successfully banned and for good reason—to protect children from being preyed upon for profits.

TAKING DOWN THE BIG GUYS

Fenton also worked in the 90's with some of the trial lawyers who became the Republican Party's *bêtes noires*. These lawyers made questionably high fees while performing a great public service—suing companies that polluted the environment or engaged in fraud or discrimination. With their millions, the trial lawyers became big supporters of the Democratic Party. I never thought they should become so rich, but their work stands as an important check and balance on power.

One swashbuckling Houston law firm, O'Quinn Laminack, hired us to expose the large proportion of silicone breast implants that ruptured and leaked, spreading silicone into the lymphatic system and throughout the body. This was one tough assignment. The implant industry—manufacturers, plastic surgeons, medical centers—had a huge head start on us. For years, they'd marketed breast implants as safe and aiding women's self-esteem. From their PR, you'd never know that after receiving breast implants, many women complained of autoimmune diseases. In recent years, scientists have shown that the silicone in the

Walter McMillian (left) and his wife, Minnie (center), celebrate with attorney Bryan Stevenson (right), who got him released from Death Row in Alabama, March 2, 1993.

implants caused these diseases, but way back in the 1990s, we had no proof of that. All we had was the fact that, over time, implants ruptured and leaked, which required women to undergo multiple surgeries at great expense—and often with pain. Few plastic surgeons warned women of the likelihood of rupture and repeat surgery. Their financial incentives compromised their ethics. The implant industry pushed journalists to dismiss the possibility that implants contribute to autoimmune disease. We focused on the high rate of rupture and its consequences—pain and more costly surgery. We tried, but the lawyers had hired us too late to turn this issue around. We publicized the work of other trial lawyers who filed class-action securities lawsuits. These were brought against executives who illegally misled investors through forgery, the back-dating of stock options, or inflating their stock prices by putting out falsified financial information.

You may recall the 2007 collapse of the Texas energy company Enron. It turned out to be a giant Ponzi scheme. At one point, to hype its move into selling broadband, Enron even created a mock trading room to hoodwink analysts and investors into believing the company was coining money trading rights to build fiber cables across the country. But it was entirely fraudulent. The trading room looked real, but nobody was actually trading. We helped plaintiff's lawyers win a large settlement against that blatantly fraudulent company and their executives.

To dramatize the case, we invited the media to see our client, attorney William Lerach, hold up a box of shredded documents taken from Enron offices. Here's how writer Jeffrey Toobin reported the incident in the *New Yorker*: "On the morning of January 22nd, a lawyer named Bill Lerach got out of his van in front of the Houston federal courthouse and presented a cardboard box full of shredded documents to the cameras of a waiting press corps. At the time, the implosion of Enron was still leading the news, and Lerach had filed a lawsuit against the company on behalf of its aggrieved shareholders. 'It's a smoking howitzer,' Lerach told reporters that day. 'It doesn't get any worse than this. Call the cops. Something has to be done here.'"

The pictures of Lerach and the shredded documents became the lasting, sticky image of Enron's collapse. "I thought I was going to be run over by the media," Lerach recalled months later. A picture is worth a thousand …

THE JENNIFER HARBURY CAMPAIGN

One day in 1995, another courageous lawyer showed up at Fenton's offices unannounced—without an appointment or even a phone call. Her name was Jennifer Harbury, and she insisted on seeing me. Harbury was a crusading Harvard-trained US lawyer who worked on immigrant rights issues. She had married Commander Everardo, a Maya-descended leader of the Guatemalan insurgency against that nation's land-owning oligarchy. They wanted him dead. Shortly after their wedding, Everardo disappeared. Harbury told us she planned to start a hunger strike to the death in Guatemala to force the government to reveal her husband's whereabouts—or fate. She was one determined woman.

"When do you plan to travel to Guatemala to start your hunger strike?" I asked.

"Tomorrow," she said.

Alarmed, we suggested she wait a week so we could introduce her to key journalists before she started her fast. Brilliant, charming, and a great storyteller, Harbury was an instant hit with reporters in New York and Washington, D.C.. Those in-person meetings attracted considerable media coverage for her hunger strike and quite likely prevented her murder. The Guatemalan military was known for political assassinations. There is no substitute for personal relationships. Had those reporters not met her, there would have been far less coverage, if any.

After some weeks, as Harbury became painfully pale and thin in front of the White House, consuming only fruit juice, I called Mike McCurry, who was President Clinton's press secretary. He had been a college friend of Beth. "Mike, Jennifer is serious," I said. "If you don't make something happen, you'll have a dead woman in front of the White House."

At this moment, *The New York Times* mysteriously obtained secret documents proving that Harbury's husband had been murdered by Guatemalan military commanders who worked

THE SHREDDED DOCUMENTS BECAME THE IMAGE OF ENRON'S COLLAPSE.

At one point during her fast, media coverage trailed off. "Call me when she's near death," some reporters actually told us. In response, Fenton's talented writer and publicist, Beth Bogart (who was also my second wife), invented a new PR tactic. When journalists turned her down, Beth sobbed into the phone. "What do you mean you won't cover Jennifer till she's near death," she cried, bawling her eyes out. It worked. Reporters traveled to Guatemala to interview Harbury, including *60 Minutes'* Mike Wallace.

We eventually convinced Harbury she'd be safer—and get more media attention—if she switched her hunger strike to the White House gate. After all, the CIA was almost certainly involved in what happened to her husband. The agency works for the White House. And she was much more likely to be ignored or even killed in Guatemala.

for the CIA. Tragically, the United States was once again there to help the local ruling class. (The *Times'* source was later revealed to be the State Department's Richard Nuccio, who was fired and stripped of his security clearance for doing the right thing.)

Harbury's hunger strike and Fenton's publicity efforts revealed the truth. Soon, Clinton offered an historic apology to Guatemala for CIA involvement in death squads and torture in that poor, suffering nation. The mess the United States helped make in Guatemala is a big reason so many Guatemalans have immigrated to the United States. Shame on us. After the truth emerged, Harbury shunned celebrity, returning to her work as a *pro bono* lawyer for indigent immigrants seeking asylum in the United States. She's still at it. Bravo, Jennifer!

USING ADVERTISING TO GET THE WORD OUT

Thank goodness Harbury showed up at my office, appointment or not. She was featured in no less than twenty-seven front-page stories in the *New York Times* and two *60 Minutes* stories with Mike Wallace. The legal system—lawyers, judges, and prosecutors—pretend to be immune to public opinion and news coverage. But they're not. *Everyone reacts to the information they receive.* The only question is: What information?

In addition to arranging news coverage, Fenton buys strategic advertising, which has tremendous power to create news stories and drive media coverage. Advertisements can be media bombs that attract attention. This can sometimes work, even if you only have enough money to run the ad once. But no matter how many times your ads run—the more, the better—they must be creative, sticky, memorable, and newsworthy. Boring, predictable, rhetorical, wonky, long-winded lefty ads don't work.

Fenton used advertising while working for lawyers who sued German and US companies that employed slave laborers in Nazi work camps during World War II. We ran full-page ads, created by Pacy Markman, in major newspapers that made news themselves. In one ad, we featured the Mercedes logo against a black background with the headline "Design. Performance. Slave Labor." That got Mercedes pretty upset. Above a photo of a Ford assembly line with workers in prison garb, the headline called out "The Assembly Line Ford Would Like You to Forget."

Before the advertisements, the companies offered far too little compensation to exploited Holocaust survivors. After the ads appeared, the companies suddenly raised their compensation offers many times over. They were worried we might organize boycotts. We didn't have that power—but the ads helped magnify the myth that we might. Our law firm clients credited the ads as decisive in the negotiations.

Part of our campaign in the 1980s against Ronald Reagan's war in Nicaragua included advertising. Reagan called Nicaragua's murderous Contras "freedom fighters," which gained them credibility in the United States. We made a TV ad about the Contras that asked "Heroism or Terrorism?" It aired on all the news networks for free, as part of coverage of the Contra war and the congressional fight to cut off their US funding. We only had enough money to run it a few times, but it helped defund the Contras.

Here's another example. In 2002, when NBC threatened to end the voluntary fifty-year network taboo against broadcasting hard liquor advertisements, the American Medical Association (AMA) hired Fenton to stop them. A great deal of research showed that liquor ads have an insidious influence on young people's behavior and health. Advertising that depicts drinking as seductive and cool increases underage drinking, and compared with young people who start drinking at twenty-one, those who booze at fifteen are four times more likely to become alcoholics.

In response to NBC's announcement, we placed one full-page ad in *The New York Times*. It showed a TV set with a surgeon general–type warning label across the screen, like the labels on cigarettes: "WARNING: Watching NBC May

Pacy Markman of Zimmerman/Markman's ad helped push Mercedes to pay reparations to their slave laborers who survived WWII.

Mercedes-Benz

DESIGN.
PERFORMANCE.
SLAVE LABOR.

"I was 15 when Daimler-Benz selected me from a concentration camp to work in its factory. My father, mother, two brothers and sister had all already been murdered."

Irving Kempler

When Daimler-Benz purchased Chrysler in 1998 for $36 billion, the company could point to a long history of efficient craftsmanship. What the company does not want to talk about is its equally efficient exploitation of tens of thousands of forced and slave laborers during World War II. Leased from the Nazis, these concentration camp inmates and abductees have never been compensated by Daimler-Benz for their labor, suffering and inhuman treatment.

Daimler-Benz owned or supervised factories throughout occupied Europe, including motor vehicle and tank facilities for the Nazi army, with many of the plants relying on slave labor for at least half their labor force, sometimes more.

German companies were not required to use these people. They chose to use them. And to obtain workers from concentration camps, companies had to initiate formal bids. Many companies declined. But Daimler-Benz aggressively sought and received as much "disposable" forced and slave labor as possible. Daimler-Benz supervisors, in league with members of the SS, committed ongoing atrocities against these people, including imprisonment, torture and murder. Many were put to

work digging out tunnels for underground facilities designed to protect Daimler-Benz equipment from Allied bombs. The death rate at Daimler-Benz was staggering.

Today, survivors of slave or forced labor at such companies as Daimler-Benz, BMW, Ford and Bayer await compensation for their work and suffering. Meanwhile, Nazi overseers received, and continue to receive, their salaries and pensions. Even some convicted war criminals collect their payments in prison.

No meaningful proposal to compensate these victims has yet been put forward. Time is running out. The survivors are dying. On October 6, negotiations between German companies and representatives of their victims will take place in Washington, D.C. Germany and those companies that used slave labor have a moral and legal obligation to pay these victims for their work, suffering and inhuman treatment. Surely, DaimlerChrysler, with $143 billion in assets, can afford to pay its debt to those it so brutally exploited.

From the makers of Mercedes-Benz, that's the level of performance we expect.

JUSTICE. COMPENSATION. NOW.

B'nai B'rith International • American Jewish Congress • Claims for Jewish Slave Labour Compensation
German Association for Information and Support to Nazi Persecutees • Federation of Polish Slave Laborers during the Third Reich
The Polish American Congress • Federation of Polish Americans • Citizens' Foundation of the Victims of World War II

B'NAI B'RITH INTERNATIONAL • 1640 Rhode Island Avenue NW • Washington, DC 20036-3278 • cpp@bnaibrith.org

THE ASSEMBLY LINES FORD WOULD LIKE TO FORGET

"We had no names, only numbers. They demanded total obedience. We were treated like animals."

Elsa Iwanova, forced to labor at a Ford plant as a 17-year-old girl

For years, Ford proudly advertised that it had "a better idea." But during World War II, Ford's German subsidiary, Ford Werke AG, was a willing participant in one of the worst ideas in human history—the exploitation of forced and slave laborers. Now, 55 years after the war, those who worked for Ford and other German companies under the most inhuman conditions imaginable are still waiting for compensation for their labor and their suffering.

From 1940 (even before the U.S. entered the war) to 1945, Ford Werke AG profited greatly from the forced labor of thousands of captive people from occupied countries like France, Poland, Russia, Czechoslovakia and the Ukraine. The company also leased inmates from the Buchenwald concentration camp for slave labor. By the end of the war, these laborers accounted for over half of the work force at the Ford plant in Cologne.

The workers were subjected to horrific treatment. They were expendable. Workers who disobeyed or tried to escape were either shot on the spot or sent to the Gestapo for execution. Many who failed to meet production quotas were beaten with rubber truncheons. The plant doctor performed involuntary abortions on pregnant laborers. He retained his position after the war, as did Ford Werke CEO Robert Schmidt, a member of the Nazi party.

Though Ford Motor Company denies any involvement with Ford Werke AG during the war, the record tells a different story. Henry Ford was a Nazi sympathizer whose notorious anti-Semitic tract, *The International Jew, a Worldwide Problem*, was published in both the U.S. and Germany. A great admirer and personal friend of Adolf Hitler, he gave Hitler annual birthday gifts of tens of thousands of dollars. In turn, Hitler awarded Ford "The Great Cross of the German Order of the Eagle."

Not surprisingly, then, Ford was one of the few foreign companies permitted by the Nazis to retain its own management during the war. Supervisors at Ford Werke AG are believed to have been in continued contact with Ford management in Dearborn, Michigan, throughout the war. And at war's end, Ford received its share of the wartime profits from its German subsidiary.

Today, survivors of slave or forced labor who worked at such companies as Ford, BMW, Daimler-Benz and Bayer await reasonable compensation for their work and suffering. Meanwhile, Nazi overseers received, and continue to receive, their salaries and pensions. Even some convicted war criminals collect their payments in prison.

No meaningful proposal to compensate these people has yet been put forward. Time is running out. The survivors are dying. On October 6, negotiations between the German companies and representatives of their victims will take place in Washington, D.C. Germany and those companies that used slave labor have a moral and legal obligation to pay these victims for their work, suffering and inhuman treatment. Ford has chosen not to participate in talks even though it has an obligation to pay its former slave workers. Surely, with $237 billion in assets, Ford can afford to pay its debt to those it so brutally exploited.

For Ford, that would surely be the best idea of all.

Henry Ford receiving Hitler's "Great Cross of the German Order of the Eagle" in July 1938

Polish civilians being rounded up to serve in Germany as forced industrial laborers

JUSTICE. COMPENSATION. NOW.

B'nai B'rith International • American Jewish Congress • Claims for Jewish Slave Labour Compensation
German Association for Information and Support to Nazi Persecutees • Federation of Polish Slave Laborers during the Third Reich
The Polish American Congress • Federation of Polish Americans • Citizens' Foundation of the Victims of World War II

B'NAI B'RITH INTERNATIONAL • 1640 Rhode Island Avenue NW • Washington, DC 20036-3278 • cpp@bnaibrith.org

Top photo: slave laborers assembling V-2 rockets. Workers like these were used by Ford Werke AG and other leading German companies.

Be Hazardous to Your Children's Health." The morning after the ad ran, the president of NBC called the head of the AMA. Soon after, NBC announced it would keep liquor ads where they belong: off the airways.

A 1993 full-page ad in the *Washington Post* helped stop planned Disney's America theme park in suburban Virginia. Nearby residents were concerned about the big increase in traffic the park would cause, adding to already long commute times. Our ad showed a huge traffic jam on the way to the proposed theme park—with every car driven by Mickey Mouse. The ad helped kill the project. It defined the terms of the debate and, along with an intense grassroots organizing campaign, put Disney on defense. It canceled the park.

During the run-up to the 2004 presidential election, we scored a major ad coup. MoveOn, the grassroots online democracy group, held a contest for the best ad to use to defeat George W. Bush. The contest was called Bush in 30 Seconds. This was the first crowdsourced video contest. MoveOn promised that the winning ad would air during the Super Bowl. MoveOn knew, however, that it was unlikely CBS would accept an "issue" or political ad for a Super Bowl time slot. When CBS turned down the winning ad, we turned the moment into a giant news story. Stories about the ad getting turned down generated many more views of the ad than it would have received had it run during the Super Bowl. And all this for free.

Exposing Ford Motor's use of slave labor, October 1999. Ad by Pacy Markman.

I am most proud of the ad we ran on the eve of the Iraq invasion. It featured Osama bin Laden's face in the classic "Uncle Sam Wants You" format, pointing while saying, "I Want You: To Invade Iraq." "Go ahead, send me a new generation of recruits," the copy read. "Your bombs will fuel their hatred of America and their desire for revenge. Americans won't be safe anywhere. Please, attack Iraq. Distract yourself from fighting al Qaeda. Divide the international community. Go ahead. Destabilize the region. Maybe Pakistan will fall—we want its nuclear weapons. Give Saddam a reason to strike first. He might draw Israel into a fight. Perfect. So please—invade Iraq. Make my day."

We placed this full-page ad in several newspapers for the social commentary site TomPaine.com. It instantly went viral, and not only on the internet. Spontaneously around the world, people turned it into posters. One family in Berlin hung it as a twenty-foot banner on their apartment building. Unfortunately, the ad's prediction came true, most especially in the creation of ISIS.

Except for the bin Laden ad, Fenton staff didn't usually create the ad creative concepts or write the copy. We edited the best ideas dreamed up by brilliant copywriters like Josh Gold, Pacy Markman, his partner Bill Zimmerman, and others. Markman created Miller Lite's iconic "Everything you ever wanted in a beer …. and less" campaign. Always get a gifted copywriter—their brains are wired differently than yours and mine. They can pull genius from the atmosphere in uncanny ways.

"SMOKE AND MIRRORS" ADVERTISING ONLINE

Digital banner and social media ads can be used exactly the same way—to make news, create stories, define the terms of the debate, and put bad actors on the defensive. And TV isn't dead quite yet—the audience remains huge—and can be very useful. But today, the microtargeting features of contemporary digital advertising create new opportunities. For example, we tried something new to stop the giant Korean electronics firm LG from building a huge office tower on the west side of the Hudson River. The planned monstrosity would have been the only building to rise above the tree line. It would have ruined the iconic view of the New Jersey Palisades, a view that has been adored for centuries.

We bought Google search ads for the names of top LG executives and board members. When they searched for their own names, or their assistants or PR firm searched for news about them, up popped our ads demanding they protect the Palisades. Then we put a digital cookie on them, so for weeks wherever they went on the internet the ad appeared. You're undoubtedly familiar with this experience. You shop online for a mattress—and suddenly mattress ads follow you everywhere. The catch was the LG executives didn't know that hardly anyone else saw those ads. Just them.

One digital ad firm specializes in buying ads on smart TVs and cable set-top boxes. Not only can they target a particular home address, but a specific screen. For example, if they see the basement TV is only used to watch cartoons, they don't put your ad there. This should probably be illegal, but until it's banned, you are free to use this approach to pressure particularly bad actors.

During the mid-1990s, when the World Wide Web first emerged, it seemed obvious it would forever change communications—and activism. At one of the first World Internet conferences, I saw the first aggregator website (from O'Reilly Associates). It was a web table of contents that easily linked to many other sites. It was like a magazine. We created a similar site to drive people to a variety of activist campaigns.

In 1996, we launched InterActivism, the second site for activists online (the first launched a month earlier, Real Active by Real Audio). Back then, hardly anyone had email, so the site featured a "fax gate," where you could send faxes to CEOs of polluting or racist companies, or push members of Congress to vote the right way. We called it digital disobedience and felt gratified when one campaign generated ten thousand faxes. The site was beautifully designed by Sparky Rose. It only took one full-time person to choose and write up the various actions. It also seemed likely that soon secure credit-card transactions would come to the internet, allowing us to do fundraising for worthy causes big time.

But the majority of the Fenton board of directors objected to InterActivism. It earned no money to offset our costs. They voted to shut the site down. I listened to them. Had we funded it for another year, I bet we could have sold it for $10 million. Oh well, at least Fenton was the first PR firm with a website. Soon, almost all communications would be on the internet, for better, worse, or both.

Soon after this ad, NBC stopped hard-liquor ads on TV. The New York Times, *February 27, 2002. Ad by Zimmerman/Markman.*

A Message to Parents from the American Medical Association

WARNING: Watching NBC May Be Hazardous To Your Children's Health.

NBC has let down America's children. And their parents.

By dropping its fifty-year voluntary ban on hard liquor advertising, the network is guaranteeing that our children and teens will be bombarded with such advertising throughout their formative years.

The serious health and safety risks of alcohol consumption by young people – including death – are well established.

And research clearly shows that exposure to alcohol advertising makes kids more likely to start using those products.

Children and teens watch, on average, more than a thousand hours of television per year. About a fourth of American families even have a TV set in a child's bedroom.

No amount of "responsible advertising" can change these facts.

ABC and CBS continue to set an example by refraining from hard liquor advertising. We implore the management of NBC to reconsider its actions and do the same.

Please. Don't trade our kids for cash.

Visit www.LiquorFreeTV.com to learn more and make your feelings known.

American Medical Association

Physicians dedicated to the health of America

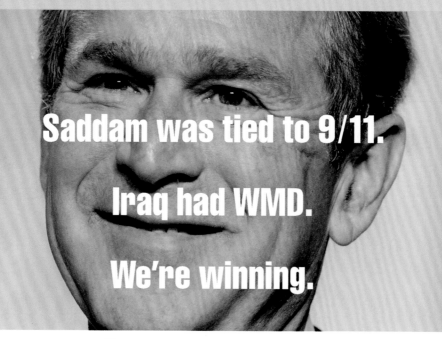

Saddam was tied to 9/11.

Iraq had WMD.

We're winning.

George Bush:
Still Misleading

With so much at stake, isn't it time for the President to admit an obvious truth? The experts – even his experts – are already saying it.

"I don't think you can kill the insurgency." *(W. Andrew Terrill, top Iraq expert at the Army War College)*

"Right now, we are not winning. Things are getting worse. We are in deep trouble in Iraq." *(Senator Chuck Hagel, R-Nebraska)*

The death toll is mounting. The financial costs are staggering. The insurgency is getting stronger, not weaker. It's dangerous for George Bush to keep insisting, as he did last week, that "our strategy is succeeding."

Or maybe the President is right. Maybe he knows something we don't. To prove it, he ought to make public two extraordinary documents whose existence has just come to light.

In July, the CIA sent Bush a formal "National Intelligence Estimate" on the situation in Iraq. By all accounts it is a depressing document. Its prognosis for Iraqi democracy is grim. When the report's existence became public, the President dismissed it as a "guess." Later he upgraded that to an "estimate," but one he disagrees with.

More than 150,000 MoveOn members have already signed a petition calling on the President to make this report public. Senators John McCain (R-AZ) and Bob Graham (D-FL) agree with this idea. Add your name at **www.MoveOn.org**.

Another document that needs to be released is an earlier assessment by the same CIA team. Its author says the CIA warned the President, before the war, that a quagmire was in the making.

Please Mr. President, it's time to face facts.

MoveOn.ORG™
Democracy in Action.

YES! I WANT TO HELP.

NAME _____ EMAIL _____

ADDRESS _____ CITY _____ STATE _____ ZIP _____

CHAPTER 14

MOVEON RISES, MURDOCH AND ZUCKERBERG RUIN AMERICA

During the late 1990s, online organizing and protest developed into a new art. Nobody was better at it than the democracy advocacy group MoveOn. The name derives from Bill Clinton's 1998 impeachment, based on the progressive slogan of that time: "Censure the president ... and move on." The organization was founded by two software pioneers, Joan Blades and Wes Boyd, whose firm Berkeley Systems invented, among other things, the Flying Toaster screen saver.

In late 2002, George W. Bush was threatening to invade Iraq, and Blades, Boyd, and MoveOn's executive director, Eli Pariser, hired us to try to stop it. That campaign proved that the internet could be harnessed for high-impact digital organizing. It helped grow MoveOn from a People's Republic of Berkeley dream to eight million members and, at the time, the country's most important progressive organization.

MoveOn pioneered a host of digital organizing and fundraising techniques. At the touch of a button, we could mobilize tens of thousands to turn out for candlelight vigils across the country to oppose the invasion or demonstrate at Congressional offices. We organized a "virtual march" on Washington, where MoveOn members reserved time slots to call their representatives. For the first time in history, small donors poured money into MoveOn to run TV advertising opposing the war. The campaign urged Bush to "let the inspections work." Sadly, the bombs fell instead, based on false claims of nuclear mushroom clouds and other official lies. We named Bush the "Misleader in Chief."

George Bush: MISLEADER. A campaign for MoveOn. Ad by Pacy Markman.

In 2008, MoveOn raised $75 million from small donors to support Barack Obama's presidential campaign. Some of the MoveOn talent later created Bernie Sanders's digital fundraising juggernaut. This enabled Bernie to become the first viable presidential candidate financed by only small donors—no fat cats. Before the internet and digital organizing, that simply was not possible. It changed politics forever—but not enough. Big money still has too much power. Democracy is supposed to be one person, one vote. But in the United States, too often it's one *dollar*, one vote.

At its peak, MoveOn was equally focused on its grassroots organizing and on its image, or what one could call its mythology as a progressive juggernaut. MoveOn regularly bought advertising to keep it in the public—and media—eye as an important voice. At Fenton, we directed the ads at opinion leaders, the so-called chattering classes. This increased MoveOn's clout with the political elite in D.C. and elsewhere, because our advertising kept the organization visible and talked about.

For example, in 2004 we created a MoveOn newspaper ad attacking Fox News. "The Soviets had Pravda," the ad read, "Republicans have Fox." It's still true! Fox is truly a source of evil in this country. Their big-name on-air personalities intentionally spread falsehoods for ratings, power, and profit. Ads like these kept MoveOn front and center in the news. Had we only communicated with the membership by email, we would have had far less visibility, and therefore less clout.

Sadly, compared with MoveOn in its early days, few of today's activist groups pay as much attention to this important aspect of social change impact. As Abbie Hoffman taught, *your myth is as important as your reality*. In the modern world,

perception *is* reality. The "soft power" of advertising and PR is real power, too. When combined with shoe-leather grassroots organizing, the amalgamation of "air war and ground war" can be potent indeed.

At first, the internet transformed politics for the better. But soon its early promise turned into poison—the spread of intentional disinformation, hatred, and foreign interference in our democracy. Social media platforms have cleaved the country into warring tribes, creating compelling but false realities for large segments of the public. During the COVID-19 pandemic, vaccine disinformation contributed to tens of thousands of deaths. Climate disinformation, left unchecked, will cause environmental devastation, swamping our coastal cities—in just a few decades. We now face monopoly domination by a few big companies that control the public square but don't give a hoot about the public.

FACEBOOK AND THE RISE OF DISINFORMATION

Facebook has become a giant cesspool of misinformation. It rarely takes down false material at scale. Conservative groups (which should be called radical right-wingers) and Republican members of Congress, keep working the refs. They pressure Facebook to include more "conservative news." This "news" is frequently inaccurate on purpose: Climate change isn't real. Masks can cause COVID-19. Obama is a satanic Muslim. Democrats want to raise taxes on the middle class. And other flat-out lies. Due to conservatives' constant pressure, Facebook has even hired right-wing

Sadly, this 2004 ad for MoveOn is still true. Ad by Pacy Markman.

The Communists had PRAVDA. Republicans have FOX

Fox News calls itself "fair and balanced." But in the words of our greatest living newsman, Walter Cronkite, Fox has always intended to be "beyond conservative, a far-right wing organization."

Cronkite was interviewed as part of a disturbing new documentary called "OutFoxed: Rupert Murdoch's War on Journalism." Through additional interviews with former Fox journalists—and extensive use of archival footage—Fox is proven to be virtually "G.O.P. TV."

On its self-proclaimed "signature news show," for example, five Republican guests are interviewed for each Democrat, and five conservatives for every liberal.

All the Fox news programs get daily marching orders from the top, specifying the day's stories and slant [see sidebar]. Says Cronkite: "I've never heard of any network, or any other legitimate news organization doing that."

And so George Bush is defended and John Kerry demeaned. Bad news from Iraq is minimized, while the patriotism of war opponents is questioned. Divisive social issues, from abortion to gay rights, are continually emphasized.

This conservative ideology is effectively being packaged in Fox's "high-tech tabloid" style, where commentators and reporters are interchangeable, sarcasm and hyperbole commonplace, and fear mongering is the order of the day.

Ultimately, Fox doesn't really do the news; they are state of the art mass propagandists. That's why MoveOn.org is proud to have helped underwrite Robert Greenwald's documentary. That's also why we're petitioning the Federal Trade Commission this week—to deny Fox permission to use the slogan "fair and balanced."

It's a simple question of false advertising.

MoveOn.ORG
Democracy in Action.

YES! I WANT TO HELP.

NAME   EMAIL

ADDRESS   CITY   STATE   ZIP

The Party Line

Recent excerpts from the daily instructions given to Fox News reporters and producers by senior management:

"The so-called 9/11 commission has been meeting. Do not turn this into Watergate." (3/23/04)

"Today is likely to be the apex of the so-called 9/11 commission hearings. Remember that while there are obvious political implications for Bush, the commission is looking at eight years of the Clinton Administration versus eight months . . . for Bush." (3/24/04)

"Do not fall into the easy trap of mourning the loss of U.S. lives [in Iraq] and asking out loud why are we there." (4/4/04)

"Ribbons or medals? Which did John Kerry throw away after he returned from Vietnam? His perceived disrespect for the military could be more damaging to the candidate than questions about his actions in uniform." (4/26/04)

"Also, let's refer to the US marines we see in the foreground as 'sharpshooters,' not 'snipers,' which carries a negative connotation." (4/28/04)

"The President and VP are MEETING with the 9/11 commission. They are NOT testifying . . . " (4/29/04)

"The President goes to Michigan [today], accompanied by a powerful campaign asset, the first lady." (5/3/04)

THE CONSERVATIVE MEDIA'S ALTERNATIVE REALITY

You can trace the rise of conservative "news," which is often intentional lying and distortion, to 1976, the day the evil Australian media mogul Rupert Murdoch bought the *New York Post*. He has lost many millions on that paper ever since. But that doesn't matter to Murdoch, since his plan all along was to do what he'd done in Australia—use the *Post* to begin to create an alternative reality of nonfacts in the United States. His goal was to gain power and profits by pushing right-wing ideas and false memes into the mainstream. With Fox News, he has succeeded brilliantly. There was no better place for Murdoch to start his takeover of the American mind than New York City, home to the bulk of the media. Right away, the *Post* started spinning the entire media slowly to the right by influencing what they viewed as the news agenda, blaring from huge tabloid *Post* headlines on the desks of every newsroom in the city.

At around the same time, the right-wing groups spawned by various billionaires out to protect themselves from higher taxes and regulation started "working the refs." They pushed media decision-makers to include more conservative "news," the facts be damned. Among the first and most successful of these groups was the so-called Accuracy in Media, which published regular attacks on the mainstream media. They were loud, obnoxious, highly persistent, and attacked Fenton frequently, too. Reed Irvine, the group's head agitator, held meetings with many decision-makers, including the publisher of *The New York Times*. This didn't affect *The Times*, which has a long history of resisting such pressure. But it sure worked insidiously at other media.

Murdoch, along with the fossil-fuel billionaire Koch brothers and Accuracy in Media, became part of a sophisticated right-wing infrastructure. This also included such conservative think tanks as the Heritage Foundation, American Enterprise Institute, and the Cato Institute. They installed right-wing judges on the courts through the Federalist Society. To take over state legislatures, right-wing heavyweights founded the American Legislative Exchange Council (ALEC). All these groups worked together to push the narrative that government was the problem. They

bellowed that lowering taxes on the rich would increase prosperity. (It never has. Our greatest periods of prosperity have coincided with higher taxes on the wealthy.) They say all regulations are bad—especially when they protect workers, public health, or the environment. Sadly, these fabrications and exaggerations are now mainstream American lore, due to their consistent, organized, and concerted efforts to brainwash and deceive.

Some of this rightward media drift grew out of a memo Lewis Powell wrote in 1971 for the US Chamber of Commerce. Powell was concerned that consumer activist Ralph Nader and others had succeeded in putting business and free enterprise on the defensive in the media, and among young people. (He was right.) Powell urged the creation of new institutions to mount a systematic counterattack that has largely succeeded. He later became a Supreme Court justice.

As *New Yorker* writer Jane Mayer put it succinctly in her seminal book *Dark Money*: "what the Koch brothers really did was pay to change how Americans think." Sadly, with few exceptions, the progressive community hasn't done the same. We haven't effectively promoted the need for collective action to reduce income inequality and invest in infrastructure, health care, and other public goods. Of course, the Left espouses these ideals. But progressives have rarely developed the language and ideas—or spent the media dollars—to guarantee effective engagement with the broad public.

During the '60s, progressive civil rights and antiwar activists targeted the media creatively, made that a priority, and changed public perceptions of racism and Vietnam. But starting in the '80s, the Right used these same tactics to push falsehoods—and sweep our ideas off the table. Meanwhile, the Left paid less attention to the media and instead focused on policy and legal work. Accuracy in Media launched in the '70s, but the progressive answer, Media Matters for America, wasn't founded until 2004. Media Matters has done excellent analysis, but compared with the right-wing groups, it has rarely been in the face of media decision-makers, so has rarely had as much clout.

groups as "fact-checkers." Facebook has become an accessory to hundreds of thousands of deaths as a result of COVID-19 vaccine disinformation spread on its platform.

Decades ago, Supreme Court Justice Louis Brandeis warned "you can have a democracy, or you can have great concentrations of wealth. But you can't have both." One can update this to "you can have a democracy, or you can have unregulated social media companies boosting false and hateful content. But you can't have both." A democracy requires an informed electorate. Facebook, other social media, Fox News, and the rest have given us a misinformed, brainwashed one.

Newspaper editors and publishers decide what to print and which advertisements to accept. The good ones keep out fake, false, and tasteless material, as is their right. But the algorithms of social media boost the worst, most divisive, often intentionally false material to keep eyeballs glued to their platforms, all to make money. On YouTube, for example, the powerful recommendation engine home page often boosts climate change disinformation and hate speech that in the old days was hard for people to find. Now it's just a tap or click away.

In the run-up to the 2015 Paris climate talks, a company called Planet Labs hired us to help create the first Facebook page for the Earth and its fragile climate. Facebook gave the Earth Page a large amount of free advertising. With this resource, almost overnight we created the largest climate change science information platform on Earth, with a huge number of followers. But right after the Paris talks, Facebook suddenly killed the entire project. Why? Republicans in Facebook's Washington, D.C., office convinced the company the project endangered their relationships with

Our billboard near Facebook headquarters for Climate Power, 2020.

Republicans in Congress. So the Earth lost its voice to conservative pressure.

Fenton once made a huge error and handed the Right our head on a silver platter. Perhaps my biggest communications mistake was helping create an ad in 2007 for MoveOn that attacked Army General David Petraeus. Its headline exclaimed, "General Petraeus or General Betray Us." It correctly called out Petraeus for misrepresenting the situation in Iraq, but the headline backfired. It provoked a huge right-wing counterattack that culminated in both the House and Senate passing resolutions specifically denouncing the MoveOn ad. It's the first time in US history that Congress censured an advertisement.

We had misjudged how calling the General "Betray Us" would offend many patriotic and promilitary Americans, regardless of their position on the Iraq War. I suggested that MoveOn apologize for the headline. The organization disagreed, worried this might appear weak and reduce its future clout. We understood but disagreed with this decision. In PR, and in life, it's better to admit your mistakes right away, before the damage grows worse.

For quite some time, MoveOn dominated online politics. It still does many good things, but is no longer as powerful. The influence of protest petitions has waned. Progressives used to be way ahead in using the internet, but now the Right is far outpacing us, both with online fundraising and microtargeted digital persuasion. Compared with progressives, the Right just pays more attention to marketing ideas.

BILL MOYERS VS. FOX

Bill Moyers, the great television commentator and producer, saw this coming long ago. As Roger Ailes and Rupert Murdoch were starting Fox News, Moyers warned several progressive billionaires—philanthropists George Soros, Peter Lewis of Progressive Insurance, and others—that unopposed, Fox News would push American society to false beliefs and right-wing ideological dominance. He urged them to counter Fox with a truly progressive national TV network. Unfortunately, his warnings went unheeded. If his advice had been followed, our country might be very different today.

When Fenton Communications opened in 1982, the whole country could only watch three TV networks, which meant the public generally shared the same information. But today, media fragmentation on cable and the internet has given us hundreds of media outlets, and we have lost much of this shared reality. Worse, with Fox's Roger Ailes and Rupert Murdoch, we now have the intentional creation of a false reality for millions of people, boosted by the subliminal power of television and video of all kinds.

Pollsters used to report that Americans had different opinions about the same set of facts. Now people have their own facts. We can and must reverse this tragedy so democracy can function again.

The only advertisement ever formally censured by both houses of Congress. For MoveOn, September 10, 2007.

GENERAL PETRAEUS OR GENERAL BETRAY US?

Cooking the Books for the White House

General Petraeus is a military man constantly at war with the facts. In 2004, just before the election, he said there was "tangible progress" in Iraq and that "Iraqi leaders are stepping forward." And last week Petraeus, the architect of the escalation of troops in Iraq, said, "We say we have achieved progress, and we are obviously going to do everything we can to build on that progress."

Every independent report on the ground situation in Iraq shows that the surge strategy has failed. Yet the General claims a reduction in violence. That's because, according to the New York Times, the Pentagon has adopted a bizarre formula for keeping tabs on violence. For example, deaths by car bombs don't count. The Washington Post reported that assassinations only count if you're shot in the back of the head — not the front. According to the Associated Press and National Public Radio, there have been more civilian deaths and more American soldier deaths in the past three months than in any other summer we've been there. We'll hear of neighborhoods where violence has decreased. But we won't hear that those neighborhoods have been ethnically cleansed.

Most importantly, General Petraeus will not admit what everyone knows: Iraq is mired in an unwinnable religious civil war. We may hear of a plan to withdraw a few thousand American troops. But we won't hear what Americans are desperate to hear: a timetable for withdrawing all our troops. General Petraeus has actually said American troops will need to stay in Iraq for as long as ten years.

Today, before Congress and before the American people, General Petraeus is likely to become General Betray Us.

EDWARD SNOWDEN FOUGHT FOR OUR FREEDOM.
IT'S TIME HE HAD HIS OWN.

Platon 2014

Before leaving office on January 21, President Obama should grant a pardon to Edward Snowden. Here's why it's the right thing to do for America:

Edward Snowden is a whistleblower who acted to expose a mass surveillance system that violated the U.S. Constitution and our values. His actions led to reforms that strengthened our democracy and security.

Because of Snowden, a federal court ruled the National Security Agency had violated the law by collecting data on all of our phone calls. Congress imposed limits on NSA surveillance, asserting checks and balances against the abuse of power. President Obama agreed that there was too much secrecy about these programs, and that some had overstepped their bounds.

Technology companies increased security and encryption, making the internet safer from hackers, and dissidents safer from repressive governments.

Former Attorney General Eric Holder believes that Snowden "performed a public service by raising the debate that we engaged in and by the changes that we made." He also said Snowden should come back to face trial.

But that trial would be a farce. Under current law, Snowden would not be allowed to tell a jury of his peers why he acted to protect our freedoms. That WWI - era "Espionage Act" makes no distinction between whistleblowers like Snowden and spies who sell secrets for profit. Snowden wouldn't be given a trial - he'd be given a sentencing to decades in prison.

The petition to pardon Snowden has already been signed by notables such a law professors Lawrence Lessig and Erwin Chemerinsky, digital pioneers Steve Wozniak, Esther Dyson and John Perry Barlow, writers Joyce Carol Oates and Eve Ensler and prominent figures such as George Soros and Martin Sheen. Please add your name to the petition to tell President Obama that pardoning Edward Snowden is the right thing to do.

"When someone reveals that government officials have routinely and deliberately broken the law, that person should not face life in prison at the hands of the same government."
The New York Times Editorial board

H U M A N
R I G H T S
W A T C H

GO TO PARDONSNOWDEN.org

WORKING WITH WHISTLEBLOWER EDWARD SNOWDEN

In 2015, the American Civil Liberties Union (ACLU) hired Fenton to create a campaign urging Barack Obama to pardon Edward Snowden, the whistleblower who alerted the United Stated that the National Security Agency (NSA) was illegally spying on citizens. We coached Snowden to speak in shorter, crisper sentences, so his ideas would be stickier. Nerds, engineers, scientists, and policy people like Snowden dislike simplifying things, which is Communications Principle

Gore. They pushed them to use language found effective in polling and focus groups, rather than speaking authentically from the heart. Big mistake. Audiences respond best to authentic characters, even when they disagree with them.

I remember the moment Al Gore lost his first presidential debate with George W. Bush. After Gore repeated a rehearsed and flat-sounding explanation of tax policy, Bush simply said, "I trust the American people with their own money." And repeated it several times during the debate. When will Democrats learn?

PEOPLE ONLY LEARN FROM REPETITION.

One. They often also hate repeating themselves (Communication Rule number four) and tend to lose or even bore people with lengthy explanations. But people only learn and the brain (and therefore public opinion) only changes with repetition and simplicity. We media-trained him remotely, as he lived in exile in Russia. Fenton staff and I sat at a conference room table in New York with Ed, who was virtually there in the form of a digital robot with a TV-screen head. We practiced over and over again, with his attorney from the ACLU, the talented Ben Wizner. It was weird talking to a robot, but we made it work. He could even move it around the room.

By media training, I mean we helped him more effectively communicate what he truly believed, so the audience could clearly understand his motivation. This is different from how pollsters and consultants advised Hillary Clinton and Al

Another important part of good media training is to help the trainee understand how to set the agenda in interviews. People being interviewed should decide in advance what they want to discuss. You only have five minutes (often less) and can only make maybe three points, so it's important to decide them in advance. During the interview, don't talk about anything else or the audience won't absorb your main messages.

Another important lesson is to prepare one or two short, pithy sound bites that resonate with journalists. Say them over and over, no matter what you are asked. This gives you more control over the news, rather than simply leaving it only to the reporter. Strong, memorable sound bites are those most likely to make it into the story.

Edward Snowden is an earnest, selfless guy who made a huge sacrifice for privacy and freedom. I think he's a hero and a patriot. He should be pardoned and allowed to return to the country he served and loves.

Print ad for campaign to pardon Edward Snowden. September 2016 ad by Josh Gold.

HOW TO FIX OUR BROKEN PUBLIC SQUARE

At some point, I expect public and government pressure will make the social network companies act more responsibly. Personally, I think we need laws to force them to stop boosting false material on climate, politics, science, vaccines, the virus, and so much else that threatens to destroy our country and planet.

Current law shields internet platforms from responsibility for what people post. So they have no incentive to remove harmful, false material. A proposed law now before Congress would make the companies liable when their algorithms boost false content to large audiences. This makes sense. We should protect the right of people to post what they please, with prohibitions against hate speech and personal threats. But when Facebook and other social networks choose to boost false posts to millions, they are acting as publishers and should be held responsible.

When it comes to Fox and right-wing talk radio, we should reinstate two rules that used to govern broadcasting—the Equal-time rule and the Fairness Doctrine of the US Federal Communications Commission (FCC). The Equal-time rule required that broadcast station owners licensed to use the public airwaves give equal time to all significant candidates for public office. Had this still been the law in 2016, it may well have prevented Trump from becoming president. Right-wing talk radio couldn't have shunned Hillary Clinton while giving Trump such lopsided airtime. The Fairness Doctrine required broadcasters to air competing points of view. They couldn't feature only one perspective. Of course, the radio and TV industries challenged these rules, but they were upheld by the US Supreme Court.

I'm a big supporter of the First Amendment. But there have always been limits on free speech. For example, you can't yell "Fire!" in a crowded theater, and a public company can't publish false information to hype its stock price without risking prosecution for violating laws governing the securities markets. The Federal Trade Commission polices false advertising, but not enough. There is no absolute free speech, nor absolute anything else.

Ronald Reagan and his nefarious allies repealed both the Equal-time rule and the Fairness Doctrine, expressly to allow the Right to dominate the airwaves. Soon after their repeal, Rush Limbaugh's radio show spread hate and falsehood nationwide. The result has been a disaster for our country.

We should reinstate these rules and extend them to also apply to cable TV and the monopoly social media companies. After all, while cable and the internet don't use the public airwaves, they depend on cable lines strung through our communities. They use our common property, and we should have the right to insist they be fair on issues and candidates that affect our lives. Yes, this means someone has to make decisions about what is fair and accurate, just like newspaper and magazine editors do. Yes, this will be imperfect, as all human systems are. Lawyers will argue about the feasibility of reinstating and expanding these common sense rules. But the alternative is unfettered monopoly private control that intentionally boosts falsehoods to divide our country. Balanced media regulation can be significantly—but not perfectly—isolated from government and politics, as is the Federal Reserve, the British Broadcasting Corporation (BBC), and other institutions.

The United Kingdom deemed Rupert Murdoch not "fit and proper" under their laws to buy a controlling interest in Sky News, the big cable news channel in London. Had Murdoch acquired Sky, he would have turned it into another Fox News. This would have ruined the UK even more than it has been already thanks to false information (Brexit was significantly driven by a false social media campaign, probably boosted by the Russians). Thank goodness the laws of the UK prevented this. We need to consider some basic media regulation in our country, or kiss democracy, public health, and the planet goodbye. The Europeans have more media regulation than we do, in part because they witnessed the role propaganda played in fueling fascism and World War II.

George Soros, August 2009.

MAKING CRITICISM OF
THE ISRAELI RIGHT KOSHER

I had moved back to New York and was divorced from Beth Bogart by the time George Soros invited me to see Barack Obama speak in Connecticut one spring evening in 2007. Afterward, we returned to Soros's home for dinner. I had brought a date. Meanwhile, George neglected to inform me that someone else would be joining us for dinner. When the tall, beautiful, and sophisticated Swiss osteopath Sylvie Erb walked in, I was instantly smitten. That was the end of my date! Sylvie and I have been together ever since. When you meet George Soros, you

figure it must be about money or philanthropy. It turned out to be about love.

In 2002, when I met him through MoveOn, Soros was a climate denier. Surprised, I arranged for Al Gore and climate scientist Professor John Holdren (later President Obama's science advisor) to spend a day briefing him. Soros is one of the smartest people in the world. By the end of the briefing, he announced that "climate change is an even bigger issue than open society," his term for democracy and his life's work. He's right. If we don't reverse climate change, there may not be any kind of human society, never mind one that's open, democratic. But alas, he hasn't made investing in the issue a priority for his Open Society Foundations.

Soros has done *so* much good for democracy, human rights, criminal justice, drug reform, and fighting facism, racism, and mass incarceration, to name a few. I very much admire him. Unlike the Koch brothers, who use philanthropy to benefit their polluting business empire, Soros seeks no personal financial gain from his philanthropy. Soros is a hero for ignoring the incredibly anti-Semitic attacks and conspiracy theories directed at him, while continuing to devote his fortune to the public good. Yet I wish he did more to alert the global public to the imminent dangers of climate change.

In 2007, Soros played an important role providing funding to help Fenton start J Street, an organization of American Jews advocating a two-state solution to the Israeli-Palestinian conflict. For years, the American Israel Public Affairs Committee (AIPAC), the dominant Jewish American lobby, made it hard for members of Congress to criticize Israel's unending occupation of the West Bank. But to increase Israel's security, to bring real peace there, criticizing the right-wing Israeli government's policies had to be made "kosher." War-driven occupations aren't known for long-term stability and security. Likud, the right-wing party of longtime Israeli Prime Minister Benjamin Netanyahu, doesn't deserve blind support from the United States. Nobody does.

My first exposure to the Palestinian cause came in 1969 at Liberation News Service. This led me to try, as only an eighteen-year-old would, to convince my paternal grandfather that the Israeli-Palestinian conflict was best settled with a two-state solution. I tried this despite his being a top fundraiser for Israel in Montreal. In a letter I still have from him in 1970, Grandpa says that my father told him I said "that the Jewish people are usurpers in Israel, or as the Black Panthers call it 'Palestine.' I want from you a plain answer, yes or no, did you or did you not tell your father the above statement? After I receive your honest reply, I will decide if I want to remain estranged or not."

No, I don't think Jews are usurpers—I support Israel *and* a Palestinian state. But that didn't go over too well with Grandpa Harold.

In 2005, Jeremy Ben-Ami interviewed for a job at Fenton. Over lunch, we bonded instantly and discovered we both had the same idea to create a new progressive, pro-peace, pro-Israel Jewish American organization. Ben-Ami was born in the United States, but his grandparents had helped found Tel Aviv. Never before have I hired someone the same day as meeting them. But Ben-Ami was an obvious choice. We agreed he would work for Fenton for some time and then, once funds were raised, leave us to start what became J Street.

When we were ready, I asked Soros to contribute. He was understandably cautious. Israeli Prime Minister Yitzhak Rabin had been assassinated by a fundamentalist right-wing Jew for negotiating peace with the Palestinians. But to his credit, Soros came through with the grant that launched J Street. As planned, Ben-Ami left to start it. J Street now has hundreds of thousands of American Jews as members and has become an important—and necessary—balance to AIPAC. Jeremy Ben-Ami has done an outstanding job. Check it out at Jstreet.org.

A 2015 ad protesting the Wall Street Journal *editorial page's climate science denial, a position which they maintain to this day.*

THE INCONVENIENT AL GORE

In 2002, MoveOn was a major Fenton client. That year, Al Gore approached MoveOn for help returning to public life after the December 2000 Supreme Court decision denied him the presidency.

Gore was among the first to see how the internet would change politics, activism, and fundraising. MoveOn assigned Fenton to help Gore with his comeback. We arranged for Gore to speak repeatedly to thousands of MoveOn members at Constitution Hall in Washington, D.C.. With Fenton's help, MoveOn bought full-page newspaper ads featuring excerpts from Gore's speeches. The program worked, putting Gore back in front of the press and public, providing him a platform to influence events once again.

In 2004, while in Boston helping the former vice president write his Democratic Convention speech, word came down from Bob Shrum, the media director of John Kerry's Presidential campaign that nobody speaking at the convention was to criticize the sitting president, George W. Bush. The explanation: Patriotic concerns in the aftermath of September 11, 2001.

In his speech, Gore planned to come out swinging against Bush's disastrous decision to invade Iraq, calling it "the greatest foreign policy blunder in modern American history." Now, he was supposed to take that out of the speech. Every Gore advisor present urged him to delete the criticism of Bush—except me.

Poster for Al Gore's 2006 film An Inconvenient Truth.

"Al, this is the stupidest advice I've ever heard, and you know it," I said. "How are we supposed to defeat Bush if we can't use a prime-time speech to attack him?" This was a big night for Gore. He had been unfairly denied the presidency less than four years earlier by a politicized Supreme Court. The entire nation would be watching.

Media director Shrum had previously advised Kerry not to respond to the phony "swift boat" attacks on him from veterans, arguing they would fade quickly. They didn't, and the attacks hurt Kerry badly. Gore, in my view, correctly ignored Shrum's edict. At the convention, only Al Gore and Al Sharpton criticized Bush in their speeches.

This was the final straw for me with the "palace court" around Gore. His advisors decided I was a dangerous radical who had to be banished. They whispered that I was taking advantage of him to boost my firm and career. This was more than ironic, since several of them had used their Gore connections to become big-time corporate lobbyists. One of Gore's top advisors helped Big Tobacco delay FDA regulation for years and torpedoed all efforts to empower Medicare and Medicaid to negotiate drug prices with Big Pharma. Before long, they succeeded, and I was history.

All public figures have palace courts around them. The term originates from the court of Louis XIV, the monarch who was overthrown in the French Revolution. Power comes from your proximity to the king and your ability to control the information the king receives—or doesn't. Not surprisingly, members of these entourages usually avoid telling the emperor he's wearing no clothes. They can often be suck-ups. I really didn't fit in with that crowd.

I had also clashed with Gore's advisors while helping him write previous MoveOn speeches. They had worked with him for years, and viewed MoveOn and the Fenton staff as interlopers. Al Gore was a brilliant speechwriter, but his process was always a marathon. He would stay up all night before a speech, fueled by a dozen Diet Cokes. (What an astonishing metabolism. I'd never seen anyone drink that much caffeine before.) We could never get him to write his speeches at any decent hour. Once, in the middle of an all-night speech writing session, I fell asleep for a couple of hours. I awoke around 3 a.m. to see Gore stuck with writer's block, mad as hell, and lashing out at those around him. Eventually, he got back on track, and the speech turned out fine. But sometimes we weren't sure what would happen.

At one such marathon, we were writing a speech at Tipper and Al Gore's suburban Virginia home. It charged that George W. Bush's warrantless wiretapping in the aftermath of 9/11 was illegal, a clear violation of the constitution. As usual, I conked out to take a nap around 3 a.m. When I returned at 5 a.m, the speech had changed and no longer condemned the wiretaps as illegal. Some of his former national security advisors had insisted that presidents had to reserve the right to wiretap without a warrant for national security purposes. They wanted, I suppose, to keep Gore from going on the record in case he became president again and wanted to wiretap. So, Gore changed the speech.

It was 5 a.m. We had two thousand people set to arrive at Constitution Hall, along with the entire international media, for Gore's 9 a.m. speech.

New York Times ad based on Al Gore's 2004 speech in Washington, D.C.

Our World is Facing a Climate Crisis

by Al Gore

ALTHOUGH THE EARTH IS VAST, its most vulnerable point is the atmosphere, which is surprisingly thin. As the late Carl Sagan used to say, it's like a coat of varnish on a globe.

Today, there is no longer any credible basis for doubting that our atmosphere is heating up because of global warming caused by human activities. The earth's environment is sustaining severe and potentially irreparable damage from an unprecedented accumulation of pollution in the atmosphere. The evidence is overwhelming and undeniable.

Glaciers are melting almost everywhere in the world. Within 15 years there will be no more snows of Kilimanjaro. In our own Glacier National Park, most of the glaciers have already melted. Soon it will be "the park formerly known as Glacier."

The Arctic ice pack has thinned by 40 percent in the last half century, and is still receding. Scientists project that within another 50 years, we may well see the complete disappearance in summertime of the Arctic ice cap.

At present, this massive ice cap works like a giant mirror, reflecting 95 percent of the sun's energy. But without it, 90 percent of that energy will be absorbed. Since temperature variations between the equator and the poles help shape ocean currents and jet streams, polar melting threatens massive disruption of our entire global weather pattern.

Indeed, there is evidence this is already beginning to happen: Skyrocketing losses from extreme weather events; and more frequent record heat waves, as in Western Europe last summer, when 15,000 people died.

Even more ominous is the predicted evaporation of soil moisture from our nation's most productive agricultural areas, and the flooding of low-lying coastal regions around the world, causing millions of environmental refugees.

The Climate Crisis is real. It is unfolding right now.

MEANWHILE, THE BUSH WHITE HOUSE represents a new departure in the history of the presidency. The current Administration has explored new frontiers in cynicism by consistently appointing to high government positions the principal lobbyists and lawyers of America's biggest polluters, where they are now administering the laws their clients abhor.

> ### "In the presence of large campaign contributors, President Bush is a moral coward."

EPA's enforcement budget has been slashed for three years in a row. The Superfund for toxic cleanups has dwindled from $3.8 billion to a shortfall of $175 million. The president has worked tirelessly to open up oil drilling in the Arctic National Wildlife Refuge, and has gutted the protections of the Clean Air Act.

These are not just swings in the political pendulum, or small changes. These are dramatic, radical shifts – the kind of change a fanatic in sheep's clothing would make. Indeed, it seems at times as if the Bush-Cheney Administration is wholly owned by the coal, oil, utility and mining industries.

While President Bush likes to project an image of strength and courage, the truth is that in the presence of his large financial contributors he is a moral coward – so weak that he seldom if ever says "no" to them on anything, no matter what the public interest might mandate.

OUR WORLD IS CONFRONTING a five-alarm fire that calls for bold moral and political leadership from the United States of America. With such leadership, there is no doubt whatsoever that we could solve the world's Climate Crisis.

In doing so, we will in the process strengthen our economy with new generations of advanced technologies. We will create millions of good new jobs. And we will once again inspire the world with a bold, moral vision of humankind's future.

*These remarks are excerpted from a recent speech by former Vice President Al Gore. It was delivered to members of MoveOn.org in New York City. A full text of his speech is available at **www.MoveOn.org**. More information on the Bush Administration's environmental record may be found at **www.BushGreenwatch.org**.*

Recently, scientists drilled through nearly two miles of Antarctic ice. By analyzing small bubbles of atmosphere trapped in the ice, they created an astounding 400,000-year timeline of the earth's historic temperature (bottom graph line) and carbon dioxide levels (top line).

A Note the close correlation between rising carbon dioxide levels and increased temperatures. Note also that in 400,000 years, spanning four ice ages and all of recorded history, CO_2 levels never exceeded 280 parts per million – until our modern industrial age.

B Today's CO_2 levels are already 25% above recorded highs.

C Projected CO_2 concentration in 2050, assuming no decrease in the burning of fossil fuels. This represents a doubling from recorded highs, and unless action is taken soon, we are headed toward a quadrupling. What will happen to temperatures then?

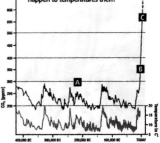

Temperature and CO_2 levels rise and fall together over 400,000 years.

"Al," I said bleary-eyed. "The audience has been told you are going to call the wiretapping illegal. The press corps has been invited with the understanding you are going to condemn it as illegal. And you know darn well it's illegal, which is why you decided to give the speech in the first place. You can't back down now."

To his great credit, Al ignored his advisors and gave the speech condemning illegal, warrantless wiretapping. The media gave him big headlines.

Al Gore is imperfect like the rest of us and can at times be subject to the pull of groupthink's conventional wisdom in Washington, D.C.. But he is a true progressive with a big heart and giant intellect, and he cares. I truly like and admire him, warts and all.

TRUMP VS. GORE

Donald Trump and his minions continue to spread lies about the 2020 election, calling it "stolen." You want a real stolen election, just look at Al Gore's narrow loss in 2000. The Supreme Court stopped the recount in Florida, throwing it to George W. Bush, one of our worst presidents. I do believe that had Gore been true to himself in that campaign, he would have become president. Instead, he listened to his pollsters and consultants, who made him overthink his every word, robbing him of authenticity with the public. The over-calculating made him appear stiff, robotic, and unsure of himself—which he isn't at all in person. It's a similar story for Hillary Clinton. When you meet her in person, Clinton radiates warmth and brilliance. But during her presidential campaign, she was stiff. She overthought her pollsters' and media consultants' advice, instead of being her warm and brilliant self. The public responds to authenticity, even if they disagree with some of what the person says.

GORE TAKES THE CLIMATE CHANGE PATH

One day, Gore called from Florida, saying he was confused about which issues he should pursue. I said, "Please, focus exclusively on climate change. It's your issue. As you've said, it's the most important crisis facing humanity. If you focus on several issues, you will have far less impact." He had already been developing the climate slide show that would become the Academy Award–winning documentary *An Inconvenient Truth*. When Fenton staff and independent publicist Josh Baran organized a New York City town hall meeting to screen the slides, Laurie David, Larry David's wife, moderated. She decided then and there it should be a film. Laurie became one of the historic documentary's producers.

That town meeting was part of a campaign we organized that Gore initially opposed. A Hollywood film had just been released that used climate change as a backdrop. *The Day After Tomorrow* used very cool special effects to show how climate change might shut down the Gulf Stream, the Atlantic current that warms western Europe. In the film, Europe gets thrown into a new ice age. In Earth's geologic history, the Gulf Stream has shut down before from melting glaciers. If it shuts down again, Europe will freeze, and agriculture in places like France and Germany will become very difficult. Recently, renowned climate scientist Dr. James Hansen predicted the Gulf Stream may actually shut down by 2050.

I suggested that we position Gore in the media to react to the movie.

He was aghast at first: "I can't associate with that film. Some of its science is incorrect."

"You can be the one to tell the public what's true and what isn't," I urged. "It's a Hollywood

A scene from An Inconvenient Truth, *2006.*

movie—of course it isn't entirely accurate, but it is a teachable moment for the culture." To his credit, Gore relented, appeared on many TV shows, and spoke at the town meeting in New York. If he hadn't, *An Inconvenient Truth* might never have become a film.

Al Gore should probably have been a college professor. His grasp of science and technology is astonishing. He also loves to lecture, and, unfortunately, he's sometimes unconsciously condescending. Yet he's deeply earnest and entirely true to his convictions. While he sometimes lacks typical politician charisma, he is totally incorruptible. When he left office, Gore refused to become a corporate lobbyist shill, like so many other former senators. He left Washinton altogether and returned home to Tennessee. I'm not the first to point out he has lived much of his life in the shadow of his father, revered Senator Al Gore Sr. That has left Gore Jr. with an undercurrent of insecurity. Even so, this would be a very different country had he become president. We wouldn't have wasted trillions on the Iraq War, which sparked ISIS and more terrorism. And most of all, I am certain we would be well on our way to solving climate change.

A PARTING OF THE WAYS

I admire Al Gore, but he can also be a control freak. In 2004, before *An Inconvenient Truth* became a movie, I invited Gore to present his then-unknown slide show at billionaire philanthropist George Soros's home in Southampton, Long Island, to an audience of several other billionaires. After Gore's presentation, we planned to make a pitch for a multimillion-dollar campaign to raise public awareness about the urgency of climate change. Gore knew this was the plan. Instead, the night before the event, Gore stopped us cold. If we presented the public education plan, he threatened to tell the donors he did not support our effort. Shocked, I huddled with Stephen Heintz, the head of the Rockefeller Brothers Fund, and his associate Michael Northrop, who had both collaborated on the presentation. Heintz decided we had to back down. The next day, the billionaires saw Gore's slide show about the problem, but they heard nothing about helping to solve it. What a wasted moment!

Another time, at the Aspen Institute, Gore screamed at me in public after I proposed a public information campaign on climate. Apparently, he felt it might compete with a similar campaign he was planning. Later, Gore urged a prominent philanthropist not to fund a climate media plan I had proposed. She backed out. Gore's strange competitiveness was hard to fathom.

One day, I watched Gore review the organizational chart for the group he planned to found, the Alliance for Climate Protection (now the Climate Reality Project). He zeroed in on the person who would be in charge of all press releases. "I'd have to see every one of those," Gore said. As gently as possible, I pointed out that he traveled so much, the task would have to be delegated. He wouldn't agree.

As I've mentioned, people learn only when messages—and compelling stories—get repeated. But they must be repeated by several different people to break through. One lone person is insufficient, no matter how famous, which was why I urged Gore to use some of the money he was raising to increase the visibility of other climate activists, scientists, and spokespeople. Alas, he never quite understood the importance of this. (The only exception is the president of the United States, who can command daily media attention with every utterance and tweet. No one else has this repeated access to the public mind).

At one point, he kicked me out of his orbit completely, cutting off all communication, without any explanation. It was probably due to complaints that I was too radical, or just in it for the money or something. Or perhaps it was because the Alliance of Automobile Manufacturers (which included Ford, GM, and Chrysler) planted stories in the *Detroit News* and *USA Today* that attacked Gore for working with Fenton. Our crime? Running the "What would Jesus drive?" evangelical Christian campaign against planet-heating, polluting SUVs and working on Arianna Huffington's TV ad campaign, which showed that filling up gas-guzzlers helped finance terrorist groups.

In response to being frozen out, I knocked on his New York hotel room door unannounced, asking for an explanation. Graciously inviting me inside, Gore spent the next two hours delivering a brilliant, if grandiose, monologue, attempting to connect many disparate dots to form a road map of political change. It was heady and fascinating.

Yet he still cut all ties to Fenton and me. Shortly thereafter, Gore raised a whopping $150 million for a climate ad campaign. Unfortunately, the smart, longtime Gore loyalists he put in charge had little or no experience at such efforts (nor did he). Some of the ads were effective, like one that showed strange bedfellows Nancy Pelosi and Newt Gingrich agreeing climate change was important. Another ad attacked the notion of "clean coal."

But the ad campaign had a big flaw. It put the cart before the horse. It failed *first* to create simple, sticky, memorable images of the threats posed by

tried that, and it didn't work, so we won't do it again." As if we should only try to save the planet once. Finally, as I write in 2022, an important new climate advertising effort, The Potential Energy Coalition, is underway.

Don't get me wrong. Al Gore deserves enormous credit. He's a climate hero and should have been president. He has done more than anyone to increase awareness of the climate crisis and point the way to clean energy solutions. He remains the best-known public figure associated with this survival issue—although, sadly, that

ONLY THE PRESIDENT HAS REPEATED ACCESS TO THE PUBLIC MIND.

climate change to human health and prosperity. His effort assumed people already knew that, but most don't—even now. None of the ads clearly explained *how* humans are heating the planet and the consequences. Why should people care that Nancy Pelosi and Newt Gingrich agree on climate change if they don't understand how urgent the threat really is? Why should they care about false claims of clean coal if they don't first understand that burning coal will melt the glaciers and flood the world's coastal cities?

Without a clear strategy, the expensive campaign didn't have lasting impact. At one point, one of the ad agencies got Gore to feature a frankly silly attempt to turn the word "Me" upside down to "We," as in we all need to act together. Many derided this as trite and ineffective.

For years afterward, when we urged greater commitment to advertising campaigns on climate, philanthropists would say, "Well, Al Gore

hasn't helped with Republicans. *An Inconvenient Truth* greatly increased public concern about climate change—polling clearly showed that the movie caused a big bump in public concern.

RICHARD BRANSON SAYS "NO"

However, it didn't last. Soon after, and clearly in response to the documentary, the fossil fuel industry mounted a giant counterattack, especially with so-called Climategate, when horribly distorted emails from scientists at the Climatic Research Unit in the United Kingdom were leaked to the media. Some suspect the culprit was Russia, whose small economy, smaller than Italy's, is dependent on fossil fuel extraction. The spin doctors who released the pilfered emails claimed they showed that scientists were engaged in a conspiracy to manipulate data and suppress critics. That was hogwash, as eight independent investigations later showed. But

Visiting Richard Branson on his private island, 2009.

the sliming worked. The leak was timed just before the 2009 Copenhagen Summit, an international climate conference—it contributed to the gathering's failure to reach a real agreement.

No matter who masterminded the email distortions, the climate movement was ill-prepared for the pushback. Public opinion numbers on climate stopped climbing—public concern fell from its peak in 2007 after *An Inconvenient Truth* because of the counterattack and the 2008 financial crisis. Climate change became what is now the most polarized issue in the United States, even more than abortion. Most Republicans don't

believe humans are changing the climate. They are egged on by disinformation from Rupert Murdoch's Fox News, his *Wall Street Journal* editorial page, right-wing talk radio, and mountains of climate denial on Facebook. We lost more than a decade as the climate community failed to invest in truly educating the public to rebut this nonsense at a scale that had any chance to work.

Stubbornly, a group of us kept trying to finance a big public education campaign. In February of 2009, before the Copenhagen Climate Summit, I was invited to meet with billionaire Richard Branson at his private Necker Island in the

Caribbean. Surely Branson, the ultimate marketer, would understand the need for a huge public education campaign on climate.

I urged Branson and some of his billionaire friends to fund an ambitious marketing and education campaign. I was shocked when Branson declined, saying "No, we don't need that kind of expensive campaign."

"But, Richard, why not?"

"Because Obama is now in the White House. The Democrats control both houses of Congress. We are going to get a great climate bill, and an international climate agreement in Copenhagen," he explained.

"But," I said, "don't you think the fossil fuel industry sees just what you see? Do you think they are just going to let it happen without a fight? Don't you think they are going to spend a fortune to stop climate legislation?"

This failed to sway him. A few months later, the Waxman-Markey climate bill went down to defeat, never even being brought to the Senate floor for a vote, where it would certainly have lost. And no real agreement was reached at Copenhagen. Heat-trapping emissions have been climbing ever since.

While public understanding of climate has improved recently, it is still far from the levels needed to mobilize to save humanity in the little time we have left to keep the planet's temperature from rising out of control. The climate movement has never mounted a campaign at the scale necessary to reach the public effectively.

At least Al Gore tried. He made a big difference with *An Inconvenient Truth*. He's still at it. We should all thank him.

Al Gore and Richard Branson at the People's Climate March in D.C., April, 2017.

Heirs to an Oil Fortune Join the Divestment Drive

Rockefeller Charity To Drop Fossil Fuels

By JOHN SCHWARTZ

John D. Rockefeller built a vast fortune on oil. Now his heirs are abandoning fossil fuels.

The family whose legendary wealth flowed from Standard Oil is planning to announce on Monday that its $860 million philanthropic organization, the Rockefeller Brothers Fund, is joining the divestment movement that began a couple years ago on college campuses.

The announcement, timed to precede Tuesday's opening of the United Nations climate change summit meeting in New York City, is part of a broader and accelerating initiative.

In recent years, 180 institutions — including philanthropies, religious organizations, pension funds and local governments — as well as hundreds of wealthy individual investors have pledged to sell assets tied to fossil fuel companies from their portfolios and to invest in cleaner alternatives. In all, the groups have pledged to divest assets worth more than $50 billion from portfolios, and the individuals more than $1 billion, according to Arabella Advisors, a firm that consults with philanthropists and investors to use their resources to achieve social goals.

The people who are selling shares of energy stocks are well aware that their actions are unlikely to have an immediate impact on the companies, given their enormous market capitalizations and cash flow.

Even so, some say they are taking action to align their assets with their environmental principles. Others want to shame companies that they believe are recklessly contributing to a warming planet. Still others say that the fight to limit climate change will lead to new regulations and disruptive new technologies that will make these companies an increasingly risky investment.

Ultimately, the activist investors say, their actions, like those of the anti-apartheid divestment fights of the 1980s, could help

HIROKO MASUIKE/THE NEW YORK TIMES

Stephen Heintz, left, with Valerie Rockefeller Wayne and Steven Rockefeller on Tuesday.

has a disproportionate impact on the poor, it is "the human rights challenge of our time."

Just how transparent the various funds and institutions will be about the progress of their asset sales is uncertain.

At the Rockefeller Brothers Fund, there is no equivocation but there is caution, said Stephen Heintz, its president. The fund has already eliminated investments involved in coal and tar sands entirely while increasing its investment in alternate energy sources.

Unwinding other investments in a complex portfolio from the broader realm of fossil fuels will take longer. "We're moving soberly, but with real commitment," he said.

Steven Rockefeller, a son of Nelson A. Rockefeller and a trustee of the fund, said that he foresees financial problems ahead for companies that have stockpiled more reserves than they can burn without contributing significantly to climate damage. "We see this as having both a moral and economic dimension," he

take sensible "steps to reduce greenhouse gas emissions." The announcement did not satisfy students pressing for divestment.

Pitzer College, however, is one of a number of schools that have promised more extensive efforts to remove fossil fuels from their endowments. Donald P. Gould, a trustee and chair of the Pitzer investment committee and president of Gould Asset Management, said that everyone involved in the decision knew that the direct and immediate effect on the companies would be minimal.

"I don't think that anyone who favors divestment is arguing that the institutions' sale of the fossil fuel company stock is going to

A move timed to coincide with a week of climate change dialogue in New York.

to raise that percentage over time. "Divestment will itself not contribute to solving the challenges of global climate change, and we believe it is not a very wise way to try and solve the issue," the company said.

Torben Moger Pedersen, the fund's chief executive, added that if the returns from a traditional carbon-based power plant and a wind farm were equal, the fund would invest in the wind farm. But, he added, "We are not missionaries."

In an interview last week at the Rockefeller family's longtime New York offices at 30 Rockefeller Center, Mr. Heintz, Mr. Rockefeller and Valerie Rockefeller Wayne, the chairwoman of the fund, spoke of the family's longstanding commitment to use the fund to advance environmental issues.

The family has also engaged in shareholder activism with Exxon Mobil, the largest successor to Standard Oil. Members have met privately with the company over the years in efforts to get it to moderate its stance on issues

CHAPTER 16

RECENT CAMPAIGNS

IN WHICH I LEARN...

· USE SYMBOLISM:
THE ROCKEFELLERS
ARE SYNONYMOUS
WITH BIG OIL. THEIR
DIVESTMENT FROM OIL
WAS BIG NEWS.

· FACTS ALONE
DON'T WORK: SCIENCE
MOMS TALK ABOUT
THEIR CHILDREN'S
THREATENED FUTURE.

· ADVERTISE SIMPLE
SLOGANS: "CHANGE
THE CODE, NOT
THE CLIMATE."

· IT'S IMPORTANT TO
HELP CONSERVATIVES
TEACH OTHER
CONSERVATIVES HOW
CLIMATE CHANGE
THREATENS THEIR
VALUES.

In this chapter, I want to look at some of my recent media campaigns, noting how they make use of the eleven communications principles outlined in the introduction. We'll start with the Rockefellers.

THE ROCKEFELLERS DIVEST FROM OIL

Communications principle three is "your stories need good and bad characters," and principle six is "use symbolism." In 2014, the Rockefeller Brothers Fund announced it would divest its $860 million investment from polluting fossil-fuels. It made headlines around the globe. It helped launch the potent fossil fuel divestment movement, which has focused the world on the folly of continuing to invest billions in climate suicide. The movement has now grown close to a trillion dollars of investment capital pledged to avoid oil, coal, and gas.

The Rockefellers were the perfect, symbolic characters to catapult this story. John D. Rockefeller created the family fortune in 1870 by founding the Standard Oil Company. That monopoly was broken up while Teddy Roosevelt was president, its parts becoming Exxon, Chevron, and what is now part of British Petroleum (BP). The very name Rockefeller means oil—and great wealth.

Planning the announcement that a group of foundations and endowments would divest from fossil fuels, we knew the Rockefeller name would become the lede, the opening of the story. Without their participation, the story would have attracted far less attention. That's how the news works.

The Rockefellers divest from fossil fuels. The New York Times, September 22, 2014.

This story also illustrates the power of principle two—facts embedded in a moral narrative touch both the heart and mind. Steven Rockefeller told *The New York Times*, which broke the story, that "he foresees financial problems ahead for companies that have stockpiled more reserves than they can burn without contributing significantly to climate damage. 'We see this as having both a moral and economic dimension.'"

To emphasize the moral aspect of the story, Bishop Desmond Tutu spoke remotely from South Africa at the news conference, calling climate change "the human rights challenge of our time." To add some celebrity pizzazz, actor and activist Mark Ruffalo spoke as well.

Several people share credit for launching the fossil fuel divestment initiative, among them Ellen Dorsey, executive director of the Wallace Global Fund and writer Bill McKibben. Dorsey's inspiration? Her PhD thesis, which documented the 1980s movement to force companies to divest from South Africa and apartheid.

While the divestment movement has helped focus the world on the folly of continued investment in our own destruction, there is still a long way to go. Many big banks continue to invest in planetary destruction, notably JPMorgan Chase. What are they thinking? We can't burn all currently known reserves of fossil fuels and maintain a livable climate—and banks are investing in even more exploration and drilling. Investments in further oil exploration are likely to become stranded assets—and very bad for business. Hello, Jamie Dimon? Is anybody home?

ADVERTISING CLIMATE IN THE DENIALIST *WALL STREET JOURNAL*

Rupert Murdoch's *Wall Street Journal* is the nation's most influential and largest paper. After years of watching its editorial page deny climate change, I became so incensed that I raised money to buy a series of print ads on the paper's editorial pages. These marked the first time the scientific facts about climate change ever appeared on those pages, which are to the right of Attila the Hun. The *Journal's* official position is still, even now, that climate change isn't a problem!

When I asked a billionaire climate funder to help pay for the ads, he said he would "only if my name can be on them." I kid you not. I explained that I couldn't put his name on them. They were aimed at conservatives who read the *Journal's* editorials, people who didn't think well of this progressive funder. So, I had to go elsewhere.

We had great fun with the first ad in the series. Our headline: "Exxon's CEO Says Fossil Fuels Are Raising Temperatures and Sea Levels. Why Won't the *Wall Street Journal*?" At first, the super-right-wing editor of the editorial page, Paul Gigot, refused to take the ad. The head of revenue for the paper overruled him, but charged us $10,000 extra because it criticized the *Journal*. So, I called the media editor of the *Washington Post*, who broke the story of the criticism surcharge, which embarrassed the *Journal*.

The ad series, written by noted advertising veteran Josh Gold, explained the basics, with such headlines as "Carbon Dioxide Traps Heat on Earth. If We Can Agree on That, We Can Have Conversation." Others said, "The Earth Has Warmed. And We Did It," "What Goes Up Doesn't Come Down: CO2 Emissions Stay in the

Fossil Fuel Divestment press conference, New York, December 2016. From left: Wallace Global Fund head Ellen Dorsey, former Mobil Oil Executive Vice President Lou Allstadt, Islamic Society Imam Saffet Catovic, 350.org Executive Director May Boeve, actors Adrian Grenier and Mark Ruffalo.

Atmosphere for Centuries," "Your Assets Are at Risk. Beware the Carbon Bubble," and my favorite "If You're 97% Certain. You're Certain."

These ads illustrate communications principle eight, "ensure you are reaching people by advertising," and principle ten, "fight falsehood and disinformation immediately."

If humanity survives into the next century, ads like these might be featured in museums as people wonder why we let Greenland's ice melt, raising the seas twenty-five feet or more. A big part

of the answer? We just didn't do enough to warn the public. And vested interests intentionally spread lies to slow climate action.

THE DENTISTS CLIMATE TV AD

Most of the TV ads you see about climate change come from the polluting companies causing it. Some years ago, we produced TV ads about climate and placed them in on cable news in Washington, D.C.. What's really crazy is that, until 2021, we were just about the only agency who had done

EXXON'S CEO SAYS FOSSIL FUELS ARE RAISING TEMPERATURES AND SEA LEVELS.

WHY WON'T THE WALL STREET JOURNAL?

Exxon's CEO Rex Tillerson agrees that carbon dioxide emissions from fossil fuels are raising global temperatures and sea levels.

"I'm not disputing that increasing CO2 emissions in the atmosphere is going to have an impact. It'll have a warming impact." he told the Council on Foreign Relations in June of 2012.

Tillerson said that sea levels would rise as a result of human-induced climate change, and that changes in weather patterns could move crop production areas. And to help control emissions, Exxon Mobil has called for a carbon price.

If the CEO of the world's largest oil company accepts the basic physics that humans are heating the climate with excess CO2, why won't the editorial board of this newspaper? Isn't it about time?

Climate change threatens our liberty, prosperity and national security. Its mechanism is well understood and widely accepted by almost every climate scientist in the world. The uncertainty of the exact timing of its inevitable impacts is no excuse for inaction. That's poor risk management.

Rex Tillerson isn't the only head of a major oil company who acknowledges that humans are changing the climate. The CEOs of BP, Shell, Total, Statoil, BG Group and ENI call climate change "a critical challenge for our world," and have also called for a price on carbon.

Historically, when faced with a national security threat like climate change, Americans have set aside ideology, faced facts, and taken action. It is time for the WSJ to become part of the solution on climate change. Watch this space for how.

PARTNERSHIP FOR RESPONSIBLE GROWTH
www.pricecarbon.org | For a Free Market Solution to Climate Change

this—certainly not the big environmental groups whose budgets top $200 million a year.

One of our ads—made by Josh Gold again—showed a man in a dentist's chair, surrounded by fifteen dentists looking in his mouth. The script went like this: "If 97 percent of dentists told you your tooth needed to come out, you'd do it … well 97 percent of climate scientists say our Earth is warming dangerously … so we need to listen to them. If 97 percent of pilots told you not to get on a plane, you wouldn't." The Yale Program on Climate Change Communication tested this ad, finding it very effective for increasing support for climate action.

Another ad showed a father and son fishing—as the camera pulls back you see people stranded on rooftops by flooding. Another showed a fetus in the womb slapping mosquitoes as the announcer explains that there will be many more mosquitoes with climate change, increasing cases of Zika virus, which affects the unborn. Perhaps my favorite, entitled Art Class, showed a child painting a family stick-figure scene, then brushing blue lines over the family to signify flooding. The ad ended with the warning "By 2050, much of Miami Beach will be under water."

To make fun of Fox News—which like all of evil Rupert Murdoch's media properties still calls climate change a hoax—we made a TV ad featuring the typical blonde Fox News anchor. While she reports on extreme weather events, she is slowly inundated by rising waters in the studio. As the water rises to her mouth, she gurgles "have a wonderful day."

These ads followed principle two—speaking to the heart first, the mind second—but we could only raise enough money to run them for two weeks, violating principle four: "Repeat, repeat, repeat your messages." There wasn't enough repetition for our message to stick in people's brains.

HOW TO MOVE REPUBLICANS ON CLIMATE CHANGE

Pretty much what all Republicans see online about climate change is that it's a liberal hoax. How are we supposed to get conservative support for action if that continues? As an experiment, Fenton produced a series of videos featuring conservatives speaking about how climate change threatens conservative values, such as freedom, prosperity, property, security, and health.

Some of the videos starred the highly articulate, plainspoken climate scientist Dr. Katharine Hayhoe. Dr. Hayhoe is one of the most articulate spokespeople for saving our climate future. She's a Christian evangelical climate scientist based in Texas, whose husband, a former climate denier, is an evangelical preacher. She's perfect for Americans. Now that she has been named the chief scientist at the Nature Conservancy, hopefully more people will see her. (Don't miss her book, *Saving Us*.) Who ever heard of a movement without a household name, an appealing spokesperson? Remember principle three? "Your stories need good and bad characters."

Hayhoe's videos test marvelously with all audiences. In focus groups, even conservatives would say, "Well, I don't agree with this woman, but she's clearly sincere." And no wonder. She speaks in simple metaphors and down-home language and is eminently

First in a series of a dozen ads on the climate-denying editorial page of The Wall Street Journal, *June 2016.*

FOX NEWS LIVE

HOTTEST TEMPS ON RECORD

-BORNE DISEASES CAN ALSO BE EXPECTED TO INCRE   FOX H

Our satirical climate ad by Josh Gold shows a Fox News anchor being slowly submerged by rising waters. Fox wouldn't show it. Summer 2016. Ad written and produced by Josh Gold.

likable. An advertising executive told me, "She makes me feel so good about the end of the world."

Hayhoe also popularized the best-testing simple metaphor for explaining climate change: the pollution blanket. She explains that the gases from fossil fuels wrap the Earth in a blanket of pollution, which traps heat that used to radiate back to outer space. This is melting the polar ice, raising temperatures, and making storms stronger.

"It's like when you were a kid," Hayhoe explains, "and your mom would come in your room in the middle of the night and put an extra blanket on you, and you'd wake up *sweating*. That's what

we are doing to the Earth, so the Earth is now running a fever. And the good news is we know how to remove that extra pollution blanket—by switching to clean energy."

The other videos featured retired Air Force General Ronald Keys on how climate change threatens national security, former Republican Congressman Bob Inglis on how his kids convinced him climate change is real, and former Cato Institute climate skeptic Jerry Taylor on how the science changed his mind.

The Yale Program on Climate Change Communications tested these videos and found they significantly moved conservatives who saw them.

SCIENCE MOMS

Which segment of the population is most persuadable about the dangers of climate change? Good research shows it's suburban moms of both parties. They also happen to be the nation's most important voters.

Science Moms (ScienceMoms.com) was formed to speak to this audience. It was started by a group of climate scientists who are moms. They speak plainly—and with great emotion—about how they do their work for their kids, and all of ours.

Science Moms illustrate principle two, "speak to the heart first, the mind second." They hold the moral high ground. Science Moms videos make you tear up—they intersperse interviews with scientists with home videos of their kids growing up, playing outside, sledding, and participating in other normal kid activities that are now threatened by climate change and extreme weather. Their messages are simple (principle one) and accurate (principle seven). They buy a great deal of advertising (principle eight) to ensure they reach specific target audiences repetitively (principle four). The women of Science Moms have crafted some of the finest communications work ever produced on this issue. I hope more people will step up to support their important work.

Science Moms is strictly nonpartisan. (One of its leaders is Dr. Katharine Hayhoe.) It is the brainchild of the Potential Energy Coalition, a group of top creative people focused on climate change. It was founded by former corporate branding executive John Marshall. His kids learned about climate change, then started harassing their father to do something about it. Potential Energy's

it forms an extra heat-trapping blanket around the Earth

Dr. Katharine Hayhoe explains the "pollution blanket" in this 2019 climate video aimed at conservatives.

brilliant creative director, Casey Rand, was formerly with the top ad agency Droga5. I am honored to be one of Science Moms' advisors, while Fenton Communications has done a brilliant job publicizing the group.

FAMILIES FOR A FUTURE: BECAUSE OUR KIDS DESERVE ONE

As I write in early 2022, Yale researchers have shown that 35 percent of Americans are "alarmed" about climate change. That's about ninety million people, but that huge, potentially potent political force is neither visible nor activated.

If you want to go online and take action on climate change, where would you go? Most of the climate alarmed can't answer that question. In the early 2000s, MoveOn became a huge digital mobilization platform for democracy. Why not have an equivalent or similar campaign platform with mass appeal focused on climate survival, especially one that embraces principle one, "craft simple messages everyone can understand"?

Families for a Future (FFF) was formed in 2021 to fill the gap. It is a campaign platform (afurture.org) for parents and grandparents who want to save their kids from the fossil-fuel pollution that causes climate change—plus asthma and other health problems. FFF talks about *pollution*, not "emissions." It describes *clean energy that powers our lives better, at lower cost*, not "net zero." It talks about pollution as a moral issue—principle two—caused by *polluters*, adhering to principle three, "your stories need good and bad characters." Public opinion research consistently shows that the message "Make polluters pay" to clean up their mess has broad appeal. FFF avoids lefty-sounding rhetoric most people just don't get.

Turning the climate alarmed into an active, visible force is a huge imperative. If FFF succeeds, it could help change the politics of the issue. Remember the Tea Party? It represented far fewer people than the ninety million alarmed about climate change. Researchers estimate the Tea Party was supported by fewer than ten million. Yet it was *organized and visible*, becoming a force in 2019 simply by turning out about fifty people at each of about fifty Congressional town hall meetings on health care. Yale researchers have found that almost 50 percent of those alarmed about climate change want to be politically active—but only 4 percent of them are. When asked why they aren't yet active, most answer "because nobody has asked me."

Families for a Future came about when the daughters of Ellen Dorsey, head of the Wallace Global Fund, and Annie Leonard, the coexecutive director of Greenpeace USA, both separately told their moms they didn't want to have kids, fearing for the climate future. Many people, sadly, but understandably, feel this way. Ellen and Annie, longtime friends, decided to act. They enlisted me to help, then hired a veteran organizer to manage the campaign. Principle twelve is "organize to win." Communication campaigns work best when combined with organizing, the hard work of signing up real people to take action. This combines the media "air war" with the organizing "ground war."

Stay tuned to afuture.org, which has just begun. If our families employ people power to insist our politicians listen to us instead of the polluting oil, coal, and gas companies, we can save the climate future for the next generations. We must.

The Families for a Future website, afuture.org.

IT'S THEIR FUTURE.
LET'S PROTECT IT.

We are parents and families coming together to protect our kids from pollution and global warming.

I WANT TO HELP

As parents, we all want the best for our kids!

Today, pollution is casting a cloud of darkness over them — overheating the world, making them sick, and costing our families.

A better future is possible.

We have the tools to stop the pollution by replacing oil, gas, and coal with energy that makes our lives better, cheaper, and safer.

The only thing missing is the willingness of elected leaders to act.

But 70% of Americans are worried about global warming and support moving entirely to clean energy. We are the majority.

CLEAN UP BITCOIN POLLUTION

Mining Bitcoin requires vast arrays of computers that use enormous amounts of energy. As a result, Bitcoin is rapidly becoming a major source of pollution and an escalating climate threat. Dormant coal plants are being reopened just to mine Bitcoin. This is nuts and should clearly be illegal.

It is also completely unnecessary. With a simple change to its underlying software code, Bitcoin could use 99.9 percent less energy. Most of the other cryptocurrencies have already made the switch. Fewer than fifty people have the collective power to change the Bitcoin code. But they are resisting this common-sense change because of their huge investments in the existing Bitcoin infrastructure, and a kind of "religion" among miners that the sacred code is handed down by God, or something.

A campaign to "Change the code, not the climate" began in 2022, lead by Greenpeace and the Environmental Working Group (EWG), inspired and partially funded by successful crypto entrepreneur and climate activist Chris Larsen. The campaign aims to pressure the people with the power to change the code to hurry up and do so. I helped conceive and design parts of the campaign.

The stakes are high. As the price of Bitcoin rises, it consumes continually more energy. Already, as I write, the Bitcoin global infrastructure uses as much energy as entire nations. As one of our social media ads asks, "Does Bitcoin Use More Energy Than All of Sweden? Hell Ja."

If we don't make Bitcoin change its code, it could keep petrostates like Saudi Arabia in business. As nations restrict fossil fuels to save our climate, Bitcoin miners could move there and use cheap Saudi oil to keep producing Bitcoin. This would thwart global climate progress. It is no joke.

So how does this campaign adhere to the principles in this book?

It uses simple messages everyone can understand (principle one). The slogans "Change the Code, Not the Climate" and "Clean Up Bitcoin" are easy to remember. And it attacks pollution, a moral issue that speaks to the heart (principle two). "Pollution" is also effective framing (principle five), instead of nebulous words like "emissions" or "hurts our net zero goals."

The campaign is insuring it reaches people with a significant advertising budget (principle eight). This creates relentless message repetition (principle four). Some of the advertising appeals directly to well-known Bitcoin influencers, such as Elon Musk and Jack Dorsey, and financial institutions with household names, such as Fidelity, all of whom are funding the polluting Bitcoin infrastructure. This follows principle three, "your stories need good and bad characters. Additionally, the CleanUpBitcoin.com website has been rigorously researched and fact-checked, adhering to principle seven, tell the truth. The campaign personally briefed journalists before launching (principle eleven).

The "Change the Code, Not the Climate" campaign is prepared to rebut inevitably vicious attacks, following principle ten, fight falsehood and disinformation immediately. This includes massive greenwashing coming from some Bitcoin mining companies, who claim to use clean energy. Sorry, methane gas heats the planet; it is not "clean." Others promise to switch to renewable energy. This sounds good, right? But we need our still insufficient supplies of solar and wind energy to power homes and industrial processes, not mine digital coins. The clean energy option here is to change the code to use 99.9 percent *less* energy. Please join us at CleanUpBitcoin.com.

For the 2022 campaign to end bitcoin's climate pollution. Ad by Josh Gold.

THE BITCOIN CAMPAIGN

This series of digital ads for the 2022 campaign to urge Bitcoin to put a stop to its part in polluting our climate (www.cleanupbitcoin. com) ran in online versions of The Wall Street Journal and The New York Times, as well as on Politico, Facebook, and other media. The campaign is led by Greenpeace and the Environmental Working Group.

THE CALIFORNIA OIL CAMPAIGN

BIG OIL: RIPPING OFF CALIFORNIA WHILE BURNING IT DOWN.

GREENPEACE

BIG OIL: RIPPING OFF CALIFORNIA WHILE DRYING IT OUT.

GREENPEACE

These May 2022 digital ads for Greenpeace were a response to oil companies demanding more drilling permits from the Governor of California. They ran on the websites of California newspapers. Ads by Josh Gold and Matt Stein.

BIG OIL:
RIPPING OFF
CALIFORNIA
WHILE
POLLUTING
OUR LUNGS.
GREENPEACE

BIG OIL:
RIPPING OFF
CALIFORNIA
WHILE
HEATING
IT UP.
GREENPEACE

BIG OIL:
RIPPING OFF
CALIFORNIA
WHILE
PROFITING
OFF WAR.
GREENPEACE

CHAPTER 17

CLIMATE CHANGE: A COMMUNICATION FAILURE

IN WHICH I LEARN...

- THE LANGUAGE OF THE CLIMATE MOVEMENT DOESN'T WORK FOR MOST PEOPLE.

- NGOS FOCUS TOO MUCH ON POLICY, NOT GETTING THE PUBLIC ON BOARD.

- IN THIS PROPAGANDA WAR, WE AREN'T EVEN ON THE BATTLEFIELD.

- TV ADS ARE CHEAPER THAN YOU THINK.

In the next few decades, if we keep heating the planet, civilization risks collapse. Scientists are ringing alarm bells. Yet polls consistently show that most of the public still doesn't recognize the urgency of the climate crisis. Among progressive communications mistakes, this is the biggest and most important failure ever. How has this happened? In part because activists and scientists have ignored the communication principles outlined in this book's introduction. For our civilization's survival, the world must mount a World War II–type mobilization. We must totally and quickly transform the entire energy, built, transportation, and industrial infrastructures to stop polluting the planet with oil, coal, and gas. But how can the public be mobilized for war if they don't even know they are under attack? Unfortunately, only a minority of the global public knows that fossil fuel pollution threatens human life on Earth. We haven't gotten through to them.

It's as if Paul Revere had never made his ride to Lexington. Most people don't know that a disaster is coming quickly. Few can even explain simply what climate change is or what causes it. Forty percent of Americans think climate change is caused by the ozone hole. How can people support the massive changes we need when they don't even know what they're fighting?

If we don't get the public much more informed and engaged, quickly, we are unlikely to save humanity's future on a livable planet.

This is not an exaggeration.

In front of the Trump Hotel in Washington , D.C., at the People's Climate March, April 2017.

How can civilization survive the coming refugee crisis as many of the world's coastal cities are literally swamped and need to be abandoned? This will happen during my adult children's lifetime if we don't change course to 100 percent clean energy in a hurry. All the people of South Florida, Bangladesh, Mumbai, Tokyo, New Orleans, Karachi, Shanghai, New York, Manila, and Boston—where will they go?

How can civilization survive the coming food scarcity crisis from extreme weather in many parts of the world, which will cause price shocks? Or people who are unable to farm outside, like in most of South Asia, due to extreme heat and humidity? Or the looming collapse of the world's fisheries as we acidify the ocean? When carbon dioxide from burning fossil fuels hits the water, it turns into carbonic acid. In acid oceans, shellfish can't make shells and that, combined with increased temperatures, kills the great marine nurseries, the coral reefs.

How can the economy survive when fires, flooding, and storms make it impossible to get property insurance? Or when we have to divert limited resources to build sea walls, raise highways and airports? How can China and India cope with famine affecting billions when the Himalayan glaciers no longer provide reliable irrigation water and coastal rice fields are swamped by the sea? What happens in Nevada, Arizona, and California when the water runs out? It's starting to now, and the drying out will only get worse if we don't change course fast.

Climate change is COVID-19 in slow motion, only much more severe in its impact on health and the economy. Mosquito- and tick-borne illnesses are currently increasing with the temperatures, along with insect range. New viruses will likely emerge from habitat destruction and melting permafrost. Even allergies will worsen with increased carbon dioxide levels, as there will be more pollen.

Unfortunately, most of the public does not appreciate the urgency of the climate emergency. If we hope to avoid the worst consequences, time is rapidly running out. And few people understand that solving it will create greater, lasting prosperity and health for all.

As I write, only 45 percent of Americans think climate change will affect their lives. Only 35 percent believe the climate issue is extremely urgent. Only 54 percent accept that humans are the cause. And only 24 percent know that literally all the climate scientists agree we are heating the Earth catastrophically. (These findings are from the authoritative Yale Project on Climate Change Communication). Asked to rank twenty issues in order of importance, most Americans put climate well behind other issues. Although these figures are better than a few years ago, they are not nearly enough to win.

A group I advise, the Potential Energy Coalition, recently surveyed the owners of middle-class coastal homes in Florida. Their homes now flood regularly, but only 20 percent identified sea level rise from climate change as the cause—most blamed "bad sewage systems" or "overdevelopment." This, in the most climate-threatened state in the nation. In California, in the counties most ravaged by wildfire, the majority of the public still doesn't think climate change will affect their lives. Clearly, climate activists are not reaching the public.

Climate postcard series by Josh Gold.

**FOR CALIFORNIA PINOT,
THE FUTURE
COULD BE NOIR.**

Higher global temperatures mean fewer places to cultivate grapes, especially weather dependent varieties, like pinot noir. Food affects the world and everything in it. #FoodIsClimate **FoodIsClimate.org**

Among Republicans, the figures are even worse. A small minority believes climate change is caused by humans and threatens our way of life. According to Gallup, this number has actually declined in the past few years. We can't solve this without some conservatives, yet climate activists have mounted no serious effort to convince them.

Although there is scientific consensus on climate change, why do most people think there is enormous disagreement among climate scientists about whether humans are warming the planet? The fossil fuel industry did this. It intentionally and falsely spread doubt about the science, as outlined in the great book and documentary by sociologist Naomi Oreskes, *Merchants of Doubt*.

But it's not enough for progressives to blame the fossil fuel industry's disinformation campaign. Of course, that's a big part of the problem. So is the television news media's failure to cover the issue prominently. And it's not enough to blame the corruption of politicians by the biggest, most corrupting and dirtiest industry on Earth.

We also have to blame ourselves. So far, our climate movement has not reached the public successfully. We have failed to move them on the most important issue we face.

We have never had a campaign large enough to reach the public with the truth. So, they don't know. Dr. Anthony Leiserowitz, head of the Yale Project on Climate Communications, has shown repeatedly that when you inform almost any group that all the climate scientists agree, many more people conclude that we must address the issue.

So, what is the problem? Dr. Leiserowitz says, "We are in a propaganda war with the fossil fuel industry, but we aren't even on the battlefield."

THE ENLIGHTENMENT FALLACY

Linguist George Lakoff explains that progressives look down on selling ideas. They view selling as a dirty, slimy business, something beneath them.

As I mentioned in the introduction, people who study the humanities, arts, law, and sciences are trained to believe that the facts by themselves are persuasive. Lakoff calls it "the enlightenment fallacy." They honestly believe if they make one good presentation to someone in power, the world changes. But the world doesn't work that way.

We fact-obsessed progressives are up against people who went to business school, who advance their careers by mastering marketing, communications, and cognitive science to sell products and services. They learn the essential communications principle that the only way to change public opinion is to repeat simple messages, ideally those embedded in moral stories that tug at emotion. They also learn they have to *guarantee* that their messages reach audiences and do so *repeatedly*.

In my fifty years of experience, I've observed over and over again that progressives—NGOs, scientists, the college educated—love complexity and hate to simplify things or repeat themselves. This means they recoil from the very approach that's been proven to work. As I keep saying, we may understandably hate simplifications like the incessant "Make America Great Again." But, sorry folks, that *worked*. All too often, what progressives practice is the "telepathic theory of communications." Somehow, magically, when we know something, everybody finds out about it!

In the United States, the major environmental NGOs spend over $2 billion a year. Yet, the percentage of their budgets devoted to preaching beyond the choir is less than 1 percent of that. This guarantees failure. Almost none follow the rule that now, with media fragmentation, you have to buy advertising to reach the public effectively. These groups use social media mostly to raise money, not to win hearts and minds.

Plus, the climate messages they promote often miss the point. They focus too much on polar bears, not how climate change affects human beings. That doesn't work. They tend to preach sacrifice, which doesn't sell. In fact, we can have cars, planes, vacations, and well-heated homes—they just need to be powered differently and can be. Economically. With existing technology.

Unfortunately, many environmental groups have fallen prey to bureaucracy. They practice paralyzingly slow consensual decision-making, which produces an inbred subculture out of touch with the public. Of course, I'm simplifying and there are exceptions. I can't tell you how many meetings I have attended that go all day yet make no decisions. Too often, the result of progressive meetings is to schedule more meetings. Now, there are many wonderful, committed people in these organizations, but I'm afraid something is broken in the nonprofit model.

In the 1970s, the major environmental groups—then newly formed—were quick moving, entrepreneurial, bold, and willing to take risks. In 1970, after the first Earth Day, when a car was buried as a symbolic act seen round the world, their creative activism forced President Nixon to create the US Environmental Protection Agency (EPA). The groups successfully lobbied Congress to pass landmark legislation, including the Clean Air Act, Clean Water Act, Endangered Species Act, National Environmental Policy Act, and many others. The groups were in touch with the public and mobilized. That's much less true now.

Hardly any new environmental laws have been passed since then, even as the constituency for action has grown enormously. And under recent Republican administrations, enforcement of the existing laws has waned, without sufficient organized public outcry. The Trump administration literally was moving to poison people's air, water, and even food—but the public rarely heard much about it.

Maybe NGO leaders and board members should face term limits. Some have stayed in their positions far too long, as if granted tenure. Sadly, this does not foster creativity and innovation.

On the Right, and in business, if people fail repeatedly, they're fired. On the Left and in the Democratic Party, repeated failure is often no obstacle to retention and promotion. Once a member of the tribe, always a member. I know this sounds harsh, but it is frequently the case.

Lakoff also explains why liberal foundations and philanthropists spend so little money on transforming public opinion. "At conservative foundations," Lakoff once explained to me "the mission is to 'preserve the system at all costs because we benefit from it.' But at progressive foundations, the dominant view is 'engage in as many individually meritorious acts of charity as possible.'" No wonder the other side is winning. Our funders often fail to concentrate resources on the most important strategic goal—power. Their funding is often scattered about in mostly small grants. And they barely fund communications at all.

The climate foundations devote the bulk of their funding—a lot of money—to what I call the "supply of policy" commissioning studies, think tanks, reports, conferences, meetings, offices abroad, etc.

Today, we have no shortage of great policy ideas. We largely know what to do. We need a slowly rising price on carbon, so fossil fuels pay their true cost to society. We need to require utilities to switch to clean energy, and we need laws increasing appliance, building, and mileage efficiency. All new cars sold need to be electric starting in 2030. Homes need to be built with solar panels and with electric heating, not oil and gas. Low-cost loans need to be available to renovate and insulate all existing buildings, with new super windows to save energy. We need regenerative agriculture and the end of tax-subsidized meat production. And we need to pull enormous amounts of carbon out of the air through both natural and probably mechanical systems.

We lack *demand* for these policies, otherwise known as *political will*. There isn't enough public pressure on elected officials, so they ignore us, capitulating to polluting industries instead. We also need to elect new leaders who will change laws and transform the marketplace for clean energy products and services.

Alas, the climate funders hardly fund demand for change. Where is the massive public education at the scale needed? Where is widespread climate advertising to persuade the public? There isn't even a mass digital climate organizing platform, a MoveOn for climate, an obvious gap that could become self-supporting as well. (The recent launch of Families for A Future aims to fill the gap.)

TV ADS ARE CHEAPER THAN YOU THINK

The issue isn't mostly money. It's how the progressive community thinks, compared to our dirty-energy-promoting opponents.

Here's an example.

If you live in Washington, D.C., pretty much all you see on television are ads touting how wonderful fossil fuels are. Oil, coal, and gas will bring us prosperity, jobs, and energy independence, all of it explained by beautiful people.

But you almost *never* see TV ads explaining that if we keep using those fossil fuels, the National Mall, National Airport, and the Lincoln Memorial will be underwater, with the Potomac River flooding a big part of town. Why the paucity of progressive—*and true!*—messages? Because the climate and environmental groups don't buy much advertising. So, in one of the most important cities in the world for this issue, the consequences of climate change are largely *invisible*.

When I give presentations, I ask the audience how much they think it costs to buy a thirty-second television ad on Fox, CNN, or MSNBC in the Washington, D.C., metropolitan area. Most people answer $100,000. The real answer is $2,000. That's right, only about $2,000, a bit more for prime time.

So, the reason we don't counter the fossil fuel propaganda in our nation's capital isn't that we can't afford it. It's that *we don't think that way*. Our enemies do. They know from their business backgrounds that perception is reality, and perception can be manufactured and manipulated. They do it for evil, using falsehood. When are we going to do enough of it for good, with the truth?

This is a debate I have had several times with philanthropist George Soros. He hates advertising and marketing. It reminds him of his childhood growing up under the propaganda of Hitler and Stalin. "You're manipulating people," George often says. I reply, "No, we are *undoing* the manipulation the forces of evil have already accomplished. We need to do this, or falsehood will reign." George's main philosophy is that we are all imperfect, and none of us can see reality by ourselves. So, at this point, he'll accuse me of being too sure of myself.

Fortunately, it's not too late. As noted earlier, there's a hopeful new climate marketing effort called the Potential Energy Collation. It's run by John Marshall, who left a top corporate branding job to work on climate full-time. He is attracting significant foundation funding—finally! In the past, environmental groups were much better at using advertising and other PR techniques to define the terms of debate, thrust issues into the news agenda, or force polluters to play defense. Environmental legend David Brower, who ran the Sierra Club from 1952 to 1969, used advertising frequently. Fighting a plan that would have flooded portions of the Grand Canyon, he bought ads in the *New York Times* and *Washington Post* asking, "Should we also flood the Sistine Chapel so tourists can get nearer the ceiling?" I hope the leading environmental groups will return to their roots and do more of this once again. (David Brower broke with the Sierra Club when the board voted to support nuclear power, later founding Friends of the Earth, another leading environmental group.)

Which brings me to nuclear power. Many people alarmed about climate change wonder if we should build more nuclear plants, saying they don't release carbon dioxide. I respect their climate concern. But ever since I produced the 1979 No Nukes concerts at Madison Square Garden, nothing has changed my mind about the dangers of nuclear power. As I explained in the chapter about the concerts, it's simply too dangerous. And poisonous. A millionth of a gram of plutonium waste in your lungs and you're dead. And now it's the most expensive form of power. Increasingly, its economic clock is being cleaned by the rapidly falling prices of solar, wind, batteries, and energy efficiency. And those price reductions will only accelerate as we build more of them. As energy expert Amory Lovins has shown, every dollar invested in increasingly expensive nuclear is worse for the climate, as it snatches funding from far cheaper energy that's actually clean. Plus, nuclear plants take at least ten years to permit and build—we can build many gigawatts of solar and wind far faster and cheaper.

I'm confident we are unlikely to see a nuclear resurgence. Accidents could threaten millions, a risk we don't need to take. The plants produce poisonous wastes that need to be guarded for literally hundreds of thousands of years—talk about expensive! The plants themselves are terrorist targets. So are their adjacent waste pools.

When journalists call nuclear power "clean," I get an Orwellian cringe. Yes, nuclear power is low-carbon. But the waste products it creates are the most toxic substances ever created. There is no such thing as "clean cesium" or "clean strontium" or "clean plutonium." Any more than there is "clean coal."

Meanwhile, numerous studies have shown we really can become 100 percent renewably powered in time to ensure our survival. Studies also upend the claim that because solar and wind are variable, we need nuclear for "baseload" power. With an extended smart grid, various forms of storage, and demand-side management, truly clean energy can do the job.

Promoting "Fee and Dividend" in Washington, D.C., April 2017.

TAX POLLUTERS AND GIVE THE MONEY TO YOU

If civilization has a future, no doubt Dr. James Hansen will be one of its biggest heroes, for sounding the climate change alarm since the 1980s. He has been arrested several times, including at the White House, to raise attention to the dangers. (Of course, he's been attacked by the Right saying "scientists shouldn't be activists.") Like most economists, Hansen favors placing a price on carbon to solve climate change. The social costs of pollution from fossil fuels needs to be reflected in its price to influence consumer and investment decisions in our complex economy. It can't all be accomplished with top-down rules.

The form of carbon pricing Hansen supports looks to me like the only kind of carbon tax

Americans will ever support. It's a fee and dividend proposal and offers giant rebates to the American public. The idea was invented by Peter Barnes in his seminal book *Who Owns the Sky?* It involves charging a fee (you could call it a fine) on oil, coal, and gas, and then paying 100 percent of the combined fees equally divided to every legal US resident. Eventually rising to $100 a ton of carbon, the fee would add $1.00 a gallon to the price of gasoline. But it would also pay out almost $4,000 a year to a family of four, more than offsetting the higher gas costs for most people. The fee and dividend proposal is highly progressive, taking money from big polluters and corporations (who get no dividend) and giving it entirely to the public.

The fee and dividend proposal adheres to the principles of communications I listed in the introduction. It is simple to explain. We're going to tax polluters and give the money to you. It lends itself to simple terminology we can repeat—cash back, cash back to you. It occupies the moral high ground, as it makes polluters pay for their pollution. Properly and simply explained, it should have wide appeal.

Meanwhile, some prominent Republicans have endorsed the carbon fee and dividend idea. This has made some people on the Left of the climate movement recoil from it. What a shame. We won't solve climate change without some conservative support. This approach could be very powerful.

In recent years, I've worked with a number of Republicans to combat climate change. Some, like Jerry Taylor of the Niskanen Center and former Republican Congressman Bob Inglis, used to be massive climate deniers, but the evidence changed their minds. We need to welcome people like this to the cause. I'm shocked more funding isn't going to help raise their visibility. If they were better known, it would create safe political space for more Republicans to come forward on this most important issue.

One prominent Republican I have tried hard to convert, who made this very point to me, has so far refused to come forward himself. His name is Grover Norquist, the effective but notorious conservative organizer who got every Republican member of Congress to swear never to raise any taxes, ever (sadly, starving the nation of badly needed investments in its future). I brought Dr. James Hansen to spend half a day with him. Norquist clearly became convinced of the science. Grover knows the truth, but won't come forward.

LIKE EXPLODING 600,000 ATOM BOMBS A DAY

People learn from metaphors, and climate scientist James Hansen has created a very effective one. It happened while I was helping him write a 2012 TED Talk in Vancouver with clean tech investor Dan Miller. Hansen wanted to explain how very out of energy balance the Earth had become. "So much more energy is now coming into the Earth's atmosphere in the form of heat from the sun than is able to go back out to space, like it used to," he said.

I asked "How much extra energy is it?"

"It's an enormous amount," he answered. "It's a quarter of a watt per square meter."

"Jim, that doesn't sound like very much."

"What do you mean?" he said, a bit irritated. "There's a lot of square meters on the Earth!"

"Can you come up with a simpler figure that people can understand to show it's a lot of energy?" I asked. At that point Dan Miller whipped out his calculator and announced, "It's the same amount of energy as exploding 450,000 Hiroshima-size atomic bombs in the Earth's atmosphere *every day*."

"Bingo," I said. "People can understand that." You gotta love scientists and their sometimes nerdy ways of explaining things.

So, under the pollution blanket we have put around the Earth, there are 450,000 atomic bombs going off daily, whose energy remains on Earth, fueling stronger storms, more severe droughts, melting polar and glacial ice, increasing rainstorms, and flooding. Pretty simple, right? Actually, it's now 600,000 atom bombs a day, as even more energy is being trapped on Earth now than when we wrote the TED Talk in 2012.

I submit that if the entire climate movement used this kind of language, in a unified way, people would understand the danger far better. Instead, the language is complex and difficult to understand, and we have the Tower of Babel, with everyone explaining it differently.

Consider President Biden. This clearly well-meaning, good person cares about climate change. Yet he talks about it as "an existential threat," a term few Americans understand. He mostly discusses climate in terms of all the good jobs solving it will create—and that is certainly true. However, that's just one side of the message equation. People have to understand *why* we need to create those jobs—and they largely do not. Biden almost never talks about the threat from extreme weather. He never uses the term "pollution," nor does he ever mention the cause of climate change—burning oil, coal, and gas. I so wish the president should make better use of what Teddy Roosevelt called his bully pulpit, his unique daily access to the public mind, to *teach* people the truth about climate change.

Biden and Democrats have made many language mistakes. First, they allowed their big social policy and climate bill to be known as "reconciliation." Nobody knows what that means. Then they allowed it to be characterized as the "$3.5 trillion plan," which sounds too costly. Actually, that amount was $350 billion a year for ten years, half the military budget. Meanwhile, it would have been far better to use language about what was *in* the bill, which people widely support—child care, paid family leave, climate protection, etc. Perhaps it should have been called the Protect American Children and Families Act.

HOW TO HELP VULNERABLE COMMUNITIES

The climate movement is making another language error, and this is a delicate subject.

I have been involved in the fight for civil rights and racial justice for decades, working with criminal justice reform activists Bryan Stevenson, Nelson Mandela, Rev. Jesse Jackson, and many others. But I think the climate movement has made a big mistake in *overfocusing* on the disproportionate impact climate change has on racial minorities and low-income "frontline communities."

The racial element of climate justice is really important. But hardly anybody knows what the slogan "climate justice" means, so it will never be a mass rallying cry. Plus, we need everyone—rich, poor, Black, white, Latinx, Asian, Indigenous, everyone—to see that *everyone* is going to be hurt by climate change. Until the vast majority of people understand that, we won't have enough public support to solve the problem. Yes, minority and low-income communities are being disproportionately affected, but our rallying cry should be that everyone is on the frontlines of climate change.

Is this the best message? Climate March, April 2017.

Jane Fonda arrested for climate civil disobedience at the U.S. Capitol, October 11, 2019.

We can only help frontline communities if we get the majority of people to demand policies that stop climate change fast. This takes broad, mainstream majority appeal. When President Franklin D. Roosevelt introduced the concept of Social Security in the early 1930s, imagine what would have happened if he had proposed that a disproportionate amount of the benefits should go to elders who were poor and Black. It would have been a just proposal, but *it never would have passed*. The reason Social Security made it through Congress was that it benefited everyone. And nothing has done more to alleviate poverty in elderly Black Americans than Social Security. We have to be smarter about selling the changes needed to prevent climate catastrophe.

Of course, focusing only on the destructive impact of climate change can be a real downer. I've ruined dinner parties that way. People's nervous systems shut down if you don't mostly stress that *we can solve the crisis* and create a much greener and more prosperous world for all.

The leading proponent of that view is Amory Lovins, a truly inspirational climate and energy visionary going back to the 1970s. He founded the Rocky Mountain Institute, the preeminent clean energy think tank whose reports have consistently shown how solar, wind, batteries, electrified transportation, and energy-efficiency investments can largely mitigate the climate problem, while saving everyone loads of money.

But Lovins does more than write reports. In the 1980s, he built a house in Snowmass, Colorado, elevation seven thousand feet, that has never used one drop of fossil fuels in that cold, gray, snowy climate. Not one drop. And he did it using the technology of that time, which has advanced considerably since then. Amory calls his house "the banana farm." In his greenhouse, he grows two banana crops a year using only renewable energy and efficient design. Amory is truly an inspiration.

We really can have a clean, prosperous, green future in harmony with nature. But only if we communicate effectively *and hurry up*.

THE
EPILOGUE

During the 1960s, Timothy Leary, the LSD evangelist, told a generation to "turn on, tune in, and drop out." I did all three.

That tumultuous decade turned me into a lifelong activist. Now almost seventy, I am still at it and will remain so to my last. It's not like there's any lack of injustice to fight. Racism and excessive income inequality aren't about to disappear. Climate change will remain the fight of our lives for a long time. Count me in. And now US democracy itself is under threat, fueled by disinformation. So, if you're interested in what an older white guy has to say, here's what I've learned that might be useful, especially for younger activists.

First and foremost, *beware of either/or, black-and-white thinking*. It's the curse of Western civilization and sometimes leads activists to inflexible dogmatism. Western dualism—that is, black-and-white thinking—views everything as divided, as composed of separate, disconnected parts. Its opposite is dialectics, or the view espoused by Asian traditions, Hegel, and later Marx, that everything is composed of fluid contradictions within a whole. In the East, this concept is called yin and yang. China is becoming dominant, in part, because their cultural history emphasizes a dialectical worldview. In the Eastern method of seeing the world, nothing is a choice between black and white, because everything—really, everything—is composed of both. Philosophers called this the "universality of contradiction."

Yin and yang: the unity of opposites, always in flux.

Yin and yang exist simultaneously in all of nature and all human endeavors. But they are not static, which one might presume looking at the yin-yang symbol. Those two black-and-white "halves" are actually always in motion—their proportions constantly changing. Sometimes the yin dominates, sometimes the yang, and then back again. Often things turn into their opposites—love to hate, hate to love, good into evil, evil into good, and sometimes back again.

Matter and antimatter exist together. Electricity consists of both positive and negative charges. Over geologic time, even the north and south poles reverse their polarity. You can read more examples in Friedrich Engels's *The Dialectics of Nature*. Day turns into night. Life turns into death. And through actions like composting, death can nurture new life. It's all *one* thing. I'm sure you've noticed that life comes in waves—this is another form of yin and yang. So do your cortisol levels—down at night, up during the day. Ever notice how fevers are usually worse at night? Take a look at a stock market graph: waves upon waves, never a straight line. Scientists are proving that

Me at Big Sur, California, 2016.

interval training—making heart waves—may be the best form of exercise.

You can see the flow of contradictions in the pendulums of history. Periods of wealth hoarding by kings and barons have been followed by revolutions, or other enforced means of sharing wealth and power—like the creation of Parliament or the Magna Carta. Such post-rebellion forms of government have often been followed by a return to domination by elites and overlords. It isn't easy to know when the trend is reversing, but it will.

During the US progressive era of the late nineteenth and early twentieth centuries, several monopolies, such as Standard Oil, were broken up. Workers organized and established unions and won better wages and working conditions, which reduced the power of elites. But the elites bounced back during the Roaring Twenties, causing the Great Depression, at which point President Roosevelt used the government to redistribute wealth and return some power to the people. This, in turn, led to the greatest period of wealth redistribution in human history: FDR's New Deal (and World War II government deficit spending) gave birth to the American middle class. Then Ronald Reagan came along, greatly reduced taxes, stopped most public investment (except for the military), and returned corporate overlords to their former prominence, where they remain to this day.

Contradiction, paradox, ebb and flow, waves—this is what nature, personalities, the human body, and social systems are made of. Learn to recognize and ride the swinging pendulum, and you will be far more effective.

For example, we don't face a choice between a "free" market and regulation. It's not one or the other—it's *both*! The issue is the *right balance* between market freedom and needed rules that keep capitalism from turning into total thievery. Get the balance right, as we did after World War II, and you can set off great waves of prosperity. Get it wrong, with too much regulation, and you get a stifling Communist state like the Soviet Union. Have too few rules and here come the robber barons, controlling and robbing the country as they do now.

Are politicians or individuals good or bad? Usually, they are combinations of both. You have to judge *which is predominant* at any given time. If they are mostly a positive force, support them, and work over time to push on their shortcomings. Sure, Hillary Clinton is not Snow White, but overall, had she been elected, this country would be in a much different place.

Among Western philosophers, Hegel came closest to getting this right with his postulation of thesis, antithesis, synthesis. Dialectics is not only a method for argument, as Plato and Socrates taught. It's really how nature and human society *works*. I urge you to study dialectics.

The job of activists is to push the pendulums of history in the right direction. As Martin Luther King said, "The arc of the moral universe is long, but it bends towards justice." In the moral fight between good and evil, our job is to bend it faster and farther, while recognizing we will never get all the way there. There will always be new contradictions to sort through, always, always.

Since I'm just a high school dropout, maybe you don't want to listen to my reflections on applied philosophy. I never learned any of this at school. You can learn it on your own, too. Let's see how it might apply to some of what I have seen and learned.

WHAT I HAVE SEEN AND LEARNED

ONE. As I've recounted—and lamented—the cutting-edge environmental activist organizations that changed the world dramatically in the 1970s have too often devolved into overly cautious bureaucracies. They have turned into their opposite. As a result, they have become much less effective. Some bureaucracy will emerge, but as much as possible beware bureaucracy. If you don't watch out, the stultifying kind becomes inevitable. Conservatives are right to detest it in government, business, and NGOs. We should, too. It reduces the effectiveness of the people and organizations who make the world better. How to combat bureaucracy? If you run an NGO, consider periodically shuffling people among different jobs. Insist on term limits for leaders and board members. Create clear evaluation and reward systems, and, yes, if someone isn't working out, help them kindly to move on. To foster innovation and excellence, NGOs should create bonus systems. Too few do, and many are opposed to this in principle. But hey, we aren't a utopia yet, and people respond to incentives, whether we like it or not.

TWO. Organizations that used to be in touch with the public are often much less so now. Activists and nonprofit organizations need to prioritize effective communication with the general public, and with key target audiences. If I were to create a new organization, it would spend 40 percent of its budget ensuring it reached the public effectively. In today's fragmented media world, with a few exceptions, if you don't buy attention, you probably won't get enough of it.

You certainly won't be able to control your own message. Conservatives make a priority of communications in simple, straightforward language. In the '60s and early '70s, we did, too. We need to return to that model. Facts do not sell themselves. Sorry.

The Left needs to build new, more contemporary institutions, as the Right has done for decades. We need our own media, better funded and more prominent think tanks, institutions to teach organizing and communications effectively, and a more robust equivalent to the Right's Federalist Society which has taken over the courts with crazy right-wing judges. Our funders need to stick to building these on a long-term basis, and not insist on "measurable results" in just the first few years. Most of what they fund fails anyway! And they should fund the leaders of these institutions sufficiently so they don't have to spend most of their time fundraising, as they do now. The Koch brothers don't do that to the heads of their institutions—and it's not just because they have more money than we have. Plus, we need to pay people more, so they can be activists their entire lives, while raising families.

The Koch brothers and other right-wing funders maintain laser focus on communications and changing the public's mind. We don't. Yet, as Abraham Lincoln said, "public sentiment is everything." To get it behind your cause, create simple messages and tell compelling stories that touch people's hearts, not just their minds. Embed your messages in moral narratives. Then ensure they reach your audiences with so much repetition that you become sick to death of hearing them. Only then does your argument reach anyone. The Right knows this. We used to.

THREE. Beware the Left's classic error of dualism, most prominently, sectarianism, in which you think your group owns the truth and is superior to everyone else. This is the political equivalent of cult worship. Remember, no person or group has a monopoly on the truth—they will be victims of their own contradictions. No party line is right all the time, and everyone makes mistakes. Nobody can see reality clearly all by themselves.

FOUR. Also, watch out for rigid ideology—dogmatism. Beware narcissism and big egos masquerading as leadership. Beware ultra-leftist intimidation, the claim that you have to listen to one "vanguard" group above everyone else. Remember, anyone who urges violence is most likely a government agent or nutcase. In the twenty-first century, we aren't going to defeat the heavily armed state through violence. Violence usually turns the public against progressives and helps our enemies. In the debate about violence between proviolence Malcolm X and nonviolent Martin Luther King, MLK was clearly proven right. Disciplined nonviolence went a long way toward ending segregation. And beware anarchists, whose absolute dogmatic rejection of leadership has ruined so many social movements. For example, consider Occupy Wall Street. It showed such great promise before bogging down in absurd, extreme, collective decision-making, egged on by anarchists. Nobody wins a war without generals. Anything else is wishful thinking.

FIVE. While the word "identity politics" has been poisoned by our opponents, there is some truth **that in *excess* it's a problem**. It can be another form of sectarianism, where the issues of one group take precedence over anything or anyone else. Remember, successful social movements create broad, unified appeal to very large mass audiences, seizing and keeping the moral high ground. No matter how oppressed any one group might be, no matter how understandable its members' needs, rarely does focusing on identity attract the mass support required to change the power structure—and thereby help that group. These days, what some have called "identitarianism" is paralyzing too many organizations.

I urge progressives of all identities to appeal to what 1960s Black Panther leader Fred Hampton, and later Rev. Jesse Jackson, called the Rainbow Coalition. We must unite people who are White, Black, Asian, Hispanic, and other ethnicities, as well as people of all genders. You might read Bobby Kennedy's speeches when he was running for president. He appealed equally to everyone for the cause of justice. This truly threatened the power structure, which divides to conquer. Their approach may be part of why RFK and Hampton were assassinated. I agree with African American Professor Adolph Reed of the University of Pennsylvania—racism is largely an outgrowth of a system that oppresses all poor and working people. We are only going to solve it by reaching all of them together with a clear, simple, unifying narrative repeated endlessly, and a nonviolent creative course of action. I'm convinced we can.

Choose *unifying* slogans that most people can support. Consider the horribly mistaken slogan "Defund the police." These words activate mental circuitry that makes people think "you don't want any police." As I write, only 16 percent of the public support "defund the police," while 70 percent express strong support for ending police brutality and improving racial justice. That slogan has also been a gift to the Right. It may well have lost the Democrats several House seats in 2020, narrowing their majority. It is certainly understandable that some people victimized by the police would want to use this slogan, as activist groups in the '60s used "Off the Pigs." But it won't help win power or help the oppressed. It will narrow, instead of broaden, your support. Other slogans would work better: "Reimagine policing" or "Change police priorities."

Our current culture wars can be conceptualized in many ways. But in my opinion, they involve the great divide between people who correctly *feel* and understand that they are connected to nature and each other, versus those who suffer the illusion of being separate from both. *Nothing is separate*—everything is connected; that's reality and physics. People who know everything is connected want to save the planet, not trash it—or each other.

During the '60s, our culture war began with the civil rights and anti–Vietnam War movements. At that time, a large number of young people took psychedelic drugs and *experienced* that they were one with nature. I don't advocate using psychedelics as party drugs. That can be dangerous, and won't give you a deep experience. But in controlled settings, in relaxed natural places, with trained guides, and people you trust, psychedelics can be helpful tools to raise consciousness and advance humanity. (Hint: If you take them, lie down under a blanket and close your eyes. The universe is inside you.) After many decades, I've recently explored both mushrooms and LSD again, and found them deeply enriching. The latest clinical research shows that psychedelics hold great promise for treating anxiety, depression, alcoholism, and PTSD. In people with terminal conditions, they even reduce the fear of dying. You can also use other tools to experience the unity of all things, yoga and meditation, for example, which also improve your health.

SIX. Speaking of emotion, part of my emotional enrichment has always come from great Black American music. How remarkable that such inspirational beauty was created from so much pain and suffering. If you haven't yet, immerse yourself in John Coltrane, Thelonious Monk, Duke Ellington, Ella Fitzgerald, Billie Holiday, Charles Mingus, Sonny Rollins, Sun Ra, Charlie Parker, Lester Young, Count Basie, Ben Webster, Chuck Berry, Little Richard, Bob Marley, Howlin' Wolf, Muddy Waters, Aretha Franklin, Otis Redding, James Brown, Elmore James, and so many other geniuses who improved the human condition with their music. I like Beethoven, Chopin, and Mozart, too, but to me, at least, Duke Ellington will **touch *both* your mind and** body even more.

Imagine the United States without Black culture, music, dance, literature, and art. It would be a far less feeling and soulful place. Racist oppression is what drove so many great Black jazz players to heroin to kill their pain, especially in the '40s, '50s, and '60s, when Jim Crow segregation ruled. White Americans owe a huge debt to Black Americans for all they have done for our nation. They literally built our country during slavery and deserve reparations to narrow the harrowing wealth gap that holds America back, denies justice, and perpetuates a form of modern slavery. Our country continues to suffer from its original sin, racism. We see it every day in the brutality Black Americans have suffered at the hands of the police and our other institutions—education, employment, banking, and health care. The apartheid of today's mass incarceration is among the most shameful and heinous aspect of our country's history.

Slavery haunts us still, through the undemocratic electoral college and the filibuster in the Senate. These must be done away with for the survival of our democracy—and our planet.

As I write, a historic wave of new activism is emerging, making me hopeful for the future. After George Floyd's 2020 murder, opinion polls showed a 25 percent surge in public understanding—and condemnation—of police brutality. Amazing! And in the wake of the COVID-19 pandemic, support for science has grown. Let's hope this carries over to climate change—before it's too late. I'm particularly optimistic about young people, my children's generation. They are far less racist than previous generations, and they know we must save the atmosphere for their future.

We have the knowledge and tools to create a lasting, better world. Let's let people know! As Black Panther Party cofounder Huey P. Newton said: "People can only act on the information made available to them." To win, we must use effective messages that touch people's hearts and *reach them*. Over and over. Our enemies do this. So what are we waiting for?

—David Fenton,
Berkeley, California, March 2022

ACKNOWLEDGMENTS

Thanks to the hundreds of people who worked at Fenton Communications over the past four decades, including Lisa Witter, Parker Blackman, Jeremy BenAmi, Ira Arlook, Kristin Grimm, Suzanne Turner, Kalee Kreider, Gil Duran, Chris DeCardy, Javier Caballero, Myrna Miguel, Valarie de la Garza, and hundreds of others. Also to creative advertising collaborators Pacy Markman, Bill Zimmerman, and Josh Gold. Special thanks to my editor, Michael Castleman, and editorial consultant, Layla Forrest-White. And to my longtime photography agent, Lely Constantinople. Thanks to those at Insight Editions, including senior editor Karyn Gerhard, publisher Roger Shaw, and CEO Raoul Goff. And to those who gave important early feedback on the manuscript, including Christine Doudna, Gil Duran, Sarah Lazin, Bill Adler, Naomi Wolf, David Talbot, Diana Edelman, Mark Hertsgaard, Arthur Sulzberger, Ira Arlook, and Howard Kohn.

A salute to my children, Cole, Theo, Alexander, and Adrian. And to my angel wife, the amazing osteopath Sylvie Erb.

I post frequent commentary on progressive communications and climate change on Twitter at @dfenton. Find me there or at my website, www.DavidFentonActivist.com.

PHOTO CREDITS

All images are courtesy of the David Fenton archive, except those noted below:

Ann Arbor District Library (www.aadl.org): 98, 101; **CBS News Archives:** 155; **Sylvie Erb:** 234; **Equal Justice Initiative:** 171; *High Times magazine:* 105; **Johanna Lawrenson:** 116, 118 (both), 121; © **Ken Light:** 70, 240; **Muse/Kobal/ Shutterstock:** 109; **NYP Holdings:** 114; **Charles Mohr, Marilynn K. Yee,** © **1984 The New York Times Company:** 123; **Paramount Classics/ Photofest:** 194, 199; **Stephen Shames:** 46; **Leni Sinclair:** 82, 88; **John Schwartz, Hiroko Masuike,** © **2014, The New York Times Company:** 204; **United Archives GmbH / Alamy Stock Photo:** 131; **Henry Wilhelm:** 16; **Roy Yuval/AP/ Shutterstock:** 134.

Photographing an Ann Arbor policeman as cops raid the commune, during my photojournalist years, 1971.

RESOURCES

BOOKS FOR ACTIVISTS

Don't Even Think About It: Why Our Brains Are Wired to Ignore Climate Change by George Marshall

Don't Think of an Elephant: Know Your Values and Frame the Debate by George Lakoff

Moral Politics: How Liberals and Conservatives Think by George Lakoff

The Political Mind: Why You Can't Understand 21st Century American Politics with an 18th Century Brain by George Lakoff

Saving Us: A Climate Scientist's Case for Hope and Healing in a Divided World by Katharine Hayhoe

The New Climate War: The Fight to Take Back Our Planet by Michael E. Mann

Manufacturing Consent: The Political Economy of the Mass Media by Edward Herman and Noam Chomsky

Earth in the Balance by Al Gore

The End of Nature by Bill McKibben

Propaganda by Edward Bernays

Confessions of an Advertising Man by David Ogilvy

RECOMMENDED ACTIVIST WEBSITES

Fenton Communications   www.fenton.com

CLIMATE AND ENVIRONMENT:

Families for a Future	www.afuture.org
Science Moms	www.sciencemoms.com
Skeptical Science	www.skepticalscience.com
Climate Nexus	www.climatenexus.org
350.org	www.350.org
Third Act	www.thirdact.org
Environmental Working Group	www.Ewg.org
Mom's Clean Air Force	www.momscleanairforce.org
Mothers Out Front	www.mothersoutfront.org
Sunrise Movement	www.sunrisemovement.org
CERES	www.ceres.org
Potential Energy Coalition	www.potentialenergycoalition.org
Carbon Tracker Initiative	www.carbontracker.org
The Solutions Project	www.thesolutionsproject.org
Yale Project on Climate	
Change Communications	www.climatecommunication.Yale.edu
Greenpeace USA	www.greenpeace.org
Climate Justice Alliance	www.climatejusticealliance.org
Fossil Free Media	www.fossilfree.media
Covering Climate Now	www.coveringclimatenow.org
Earth Justice	www.Earthjustice.org

Inside the Movement	www.itm.earth
Resource Media	www.resource-media.org
Rocky Mountain Institute	www.RMI.org
The Cool Down	www.thecooldown.com
Extinction Rebellion	www.extinctionrebellion.us
Sierra Club	www.Sierraclub.org
Climate Reality Project	www.climaterealityproject.org
Divest/Invest	www.divestinvest.org
Climate Power	www.ClimatePower.us
Protect Our Winters	www.protectourwinters.org
NRDC	www.NRDC.org
Environmental Defense	www.EDF.org
League of Conservation Voters	www.lcv.org
New Climate Voices for Conservatives	www.newclimatevoices.org

JUSTICE:

Death Penalty Info Center	www.deathpenaltyinfo.org
Equal Justice Initiative	www.Eji.org
ACLU	www.aclu.org
Color of Change	www.colorofchange.org
Human Rights Watch	www.HRW.org
Amnesty International	www.amnesty.org
Oxfam	www.oxfam.org
MoveOn	www.MoveOn.org
Avaaz	www.Avaaz.org
Black Voters Matter	www.blackvotersmatterfund.org
NAACP Legal Defense Fund	www.naacpldf.org
Leadership Conference on Civil Rights	www.civilrights.org
Democracy for All	www.democracyforall2021.org
Planned Parenthood	www.plannedparenthood.org
Human Rights Campaign	www.hrc.org
GLAAD	www.glaad.org
Unidos US	www.unidosus.org
Labor Network for Sustainability	www.labor4sustainability.org
Fight for $15	www.fightfor15.org
Working America	www.workingamerica.org
Worker Rights Consortium	www.workersrights.org

To access videos and podcasts with David Fenton, to learn more, or to contact the author, please visit www.DavidFentonActivist.com

Follow David Fenton on Twitter @dfenton or on Instagram @dfenton1

Also by David Fenton:
SHOTS: An American Photographer's Journal 1968 to 1972

INDEX

Italic page numbers indicate images.

EARTH AWARE

PO Box 3088
San Rafael, CA 94912
www.MandalaEarth.com

Find us on Facebook: www.facebook.com/MandalaEarth
Follow us on Twitter: @mandalaearth

Library of Congress Cataloging-in-Publication Data available.

ISBN: 978-1-64722-866-8

PUBLISHER: Raoul Goff
VICE PRESIDENT, PUBLISHER: Robert Shaw
VP CREATIVE: Chrissy Kwasnik
ART DIRECTOR: Allister Fein
SENIOR EDITOR: Karyn Gerhard
PRODUCTION MANAGER: Joshua Smith
PRODUCTION ASSOCIATE: Tiffani Patterson

ROOTS of PEACE   REPLANTED PAPER

Insight Editions, in association with Roots of Peace, will plant two trees for each tree used in the manufacturing of this book. Roots of Peace is an internationally renowned humanitarian organization dedicated to eradicating land mines worldwide and converting war-torn lands into productive farms and wildlife habitats. Roots of Peace will plant two million fruit and nut trees in Afghanistan and provide farmers there with the skills and support necessary for sustainable land use.

Manufactured in Turkey by Insight Editions

10 9 8 7 6 5 4 3 2 1